Foreign Direct Investment

Foreign Direct investment is a critical tool for any local economic growth and development. Most FDI books maintain a general context and focus. Therefore, this book, offering individual case studies on selected economies and sectors is essentially novel. It is an invaluable resource for researchers and scholars in the field of International Business, Finance, Economics and Management. It is equally an invaluable resource for local economic policy makers for driving local economic growth and development.

— ***Dr Inalegwu Ode-Ichakpa*, Associate Professor of Accounting,**
Lynn Pippenger School of Accountancy,
Muma College of Business, University of South Florida, USA

I have long admired Dr. Chibuzo Amadi's ability to see beyond statistics and systems, to the people whose lives are shaped by them. In this book, he presents a comprehensive account of Foreign Direct Investment as a global capital with local impacts, that directly shapes human welfare and economic trajectories. This book is not only intelligent and timely, it is born of a genuine concern for the world and economies we are building together.

— ***Kingsley O Omeihe* PhD CMBE FRSA. President,**
Academy for African Studies

INTERNATIONAL STUDIES IN SMALL BUSINESS AND ENTREPRENEURSHIP RESEARCH

Series Editors: Kingsley Obi Omeihe and Ibiyemi Omeihe – University of the West of Scotland, UK

The *International Studies in Small Business and Entrepreneurship Research* series opens a new chapter, as it seeks to advance discussions that consolidate conventional knowledge. The purpose of this initiative is to invite new reflections on the nature of entrepreneurship and small business across contexts. The collections in this series aim to improve the theoretical rigor and practical relevance of the field. The emphasis is to advance contemporary contributions that matter for small business and entrepreneurship, directing us to underexplored and undertheorized contexts.

Forthcoming Volumes

The Emerald Handbook of Digital Transformation, Environmental Sustainability and Wellbeing in the Global South
Edited by Bridget Nneka Irene, Julius Irene, Kingsley Obi Omeihe and Joan Lockyer

Leadership in Entrepreneurial Contexts
Edited by Kingsley Obi Omeihe, Ibiyemi Omeihe, Oladipupo Folorunsho and Caroline Kom

Foreign Direct Investment: Global Capital, Local Impact

BY

CHIBUZO AMADI

University of South Wales, UK

emerald PUBLISHING

United Kingdom – North America – Japan – India – Malaysia – China

Emerald Publishing Limited
Emerald Publishing, Floor 5, Northspring, 21–23 Wellington Street, Leeds LS1 4DL

First edition 2026

British Library Cataloguing in Publication Data
A catalogue record for this book is available from the British Library

ISBN: 978-1-83662-901-6 (Print)
ISBN: 978-1-83662-900-9 (Online)
ISBN: 978-1-83662-902-3 (Epub)

Printed and bound by CPI Group (UK) Ltd, Croydon, CR0 4YY

INVESTOR IN PEOPLE

To GOD Almighty for Wisdom and Knowledge
To the good people of AMADI AMADI Family Dynasty
To the good people of OZUZU Community
To the good people of ETCHE Ethnic Nationality
To the good people of RIVERS STATE, NIGERIA

Contents

About the Author

Dr Chibuzo Amadi is a distinguished academic with over 10 years higher education practice experience in UK universities (Manchester Metropolitan University, Cardiff University, University of South Wales). Dr. Amadi obtained a B.Sc. in Administration (Accounting major) from the University of Ghana Business School in 2008. He further obtained an M.Sc. in Financial Forecasting and Investment from the University of Glasgow in 2010; as well as a PhD in the broad field of Business, Finance, and Economics from Manchester Metropolitan University in 2019. His teaching, learning, and scholarship activities in higher education have been acknowledged by the award of senior fellow (SFHEA) by AdvanceHE UK. Senior fellowship is awarded to higher education academics who have achieved the D3.7 criteria of the UK Professional standards framework for teaching and supporting learning in higher education. The D3.7 criteria is summarized as "successful co-ordination, support, supervision, management and/or mentoring of others (whether individuals and/or teams) in relation to teaching and learning." His mentorship of doctoral candidates through doctoral research supervision and contributions to graduate education in the United Kingdom, in general, has been acknowledged by the award of recognized research supervisor (RRS) by the UK Council for Graduate Education (UKCGE). The RRS by UKCGE is awarded to research supervisors who have demonstrated satisfactory peer-reviewed evidence of their supervision practice to the standard of the Good Supervisory Practice Framework. Dr Amadi has published in reputable peer-reviewed academic journals including *Africa Journal of Management*, *Cogent Business & Management*, *Cogent Economics & Finance*, *Journal of Banking Regulation*, among others. He has presented at, and co-organized international academic conferences such as the 24th Academy of African Business and Development (AABD) Annual Conference in the United States of America (Washburn University, Topeka, Kansas, USA, from May 14 to 18, 2024), where he also chaired the session on Sustainability, Business Ethics and Social Responsibility. His research interests are broadly in business management (sustainability/ESG/CSR, sustainable business & society, foreign direct investment, accounting & finance, corporate governance & performance) and economic growth and development.

Preface

In an era defined by rapid globalization and dynamic economic transformation, *Foreign Direct Investment: Global Capital, Local Impact* emerges as a timely and essential contribution to the study and understanding of foreign direct investment (FDI). This book delves into the complex mechanisms through which global capital interacts with local economies, influencing patterns of growth, industrial transformation, and sociopolitical change. As nations continue to integrate into an increasingly interconnected global system, the movement of capital across borders has become both a driver of opportunity and a source of profound challenge.

The central premise of this book is that FDI serves as a vital conduit between global capital and local development. It is a powerful force that transcends national boundaries, reshaping economic landscapes, advancing technological innovation, and creating pathways for sustainable growth. Yet, the dynamics of FDI are evolving rapidly in response to the shifting global context—marked by trade tensions, geopolitical realignments, the rise of digital economies, and the growing imperative for environmental and social sustainability. Understanding these evolving patterns is no longer optional; it is an essential requirement for policymakers, scholars, and business leaders navigating the complexities of the global economy.

Foreign Direct Investment: Global Capital, Local Impact seeks to fill the urgent need for a comprehensive and contemporary resource on FDI. It explores the multifaceted role of FDI in national economic development through country-specific case studies. These case studies illuminate how national policies, institutional frameworks, and market dynamics interact to shape FDI strategies and outcomes. The insights offered here aim to inform both theoretical understanding and practical policymaking, providing readers with a holistic perspective on the drivers, challenges, and implications of foreign investment in today's world.

The book also underscores the intrinsic connection between FDI and the global development agenda, aligning closely with key United Nations Sustainable Development Goals (SDGs). Specifically, it highlights the following:

- **SDG 4: Quality Education**, by promoting awareness and understanding of FDI theories and concepts among learners, policymakers, and development practitioners.

- **SDG 8: Decent Work and Economic Growth**, by examining how appropriately deployed FDI contributes to job creation, entrepreneurship, and inclusive growth.
- **SDG 9: Industry, Innovation, and Infrastructure**, by demonstrating how FDI serves as a catalyst for industrial development, technological innovation, and infrastructural advancement in host economies.

Ultimately, this book invites readers to engage critically with the ongoing evolution of FDI and its profound impact on both global and local scales. It challenges conventional perspectives by showing that while FDI can be a vehicle for growth and innovation, its benefits are neither automatic nor evenly distributed—they depend on the policies, institutions, and strategic choices that guide its implementation.

In bridging theory and practice, *Foreign Direct Investment: Global Capital, Local Impact* aspires to be more than a scholarly reference. It aims to be a tool for informed decision-making, a resource for capacity-building, and a guide for those seeking to harness global capital for sustainable and inclusive local development.

Dr Chibuzo Amadi
Author

Acknowledgment

My research and teaching in the field of FDI sparks curiosity among my postgraduate students, some of whom subsequently find it a field of interest for their research projects under my supervision. Special recognition of the contribution of some of my supervisees, whose supervised projects provide context and background to some chapters in this book.

Special recognition and acknowledgement of the support and contributions of University of South Wales and its research leadership, for promoting strong institutional research culture and environment that enables achievements like this.

Chapter 1

Foreign Direct Investment: General Overview

Abstract

This chapter will set the foundation and tone of the discussion on the interaction of foreign direct investment (FDI) and host economies. Literature is awash with research studies that echo the benefits of FDI on the domestic economy, namely that foreign companies introduce new processes and products to the domestic market, leading to productivity gains. Foreign firms also accelerate the diffusion of new technology and the transfer of managerial skills and technical know-how. In recognition of these benefits, the evolving literature on FDI suggests that the positive impact of FDI on economic growth is dependent on absorptive capacities.

Keywords: FDI; economic growth; developing countries; absorptive capacity; inflows and outflows

1.1 Introduction

Foreign direct investment (FDI) has become a key component of economic growth and development, especially in emerging countries (e.g. Comes et al., 2018). FDI comprises of external resources such as technology, capital, marketing and management expertise, and other externalities, which create a significant influence on a host country's productive capacities (Caves, 1996). Given the huge resource base of the Nigerian economy, the country's foreign policy on investment has moved toward the attraction and encouragement of more foreign capital inflow. The desire for FDI is borne out of the level of development of the domestic economy (manifesting in fundamental problems like inflation, unemployment, and exchange rate instability), which has essentially stalled the pace of the country's development. One of the most convincing economic justifications for allowing special inducements for attracting FDI is built on the notion that

Foreign Direct Investment, 1–15

Published under exclusive licence by Emerald Publishing Limited
doi:10.1108/978-1-83662-900-920261001

FDI bridges the "idea gaps" between the rich and the poor nations as well as its ability to generate technological spillovers and transfers (Danja, 2012).

FDI has been found by numerous studies to exert a positive impact on economic growth and development by boosting employment, productivity, technological development and reducing the difference seen between the desired gross domestic investment and gross domestic savings (Ehimare, 2011). However, there is also a general notion that the impact FDI has on economic growth is quite ambiguous, i.e. sometimes positive and sometimes detrimental (e.g. Gorg & Greenaway, 2004). A likely explanation for these sundry findings may be the failure to model the effects of eventuality in the relationship between FDI and growth. Several economic models propose that the association between FDI and growth may be reliant on other dominant factors. For example, models by Alfaro et al. (2010) and Hermes and Lensink (2003) predict that the effect of FDI on economic growth is reliant on the development of the local financial markets and institutions of the host country. These studies opine that well-functioning financial markets enable FDI to promote economic growth through the backward linkages, where economic agents in the host country can take advantage of knowledge spillovers from FDI. This leads to an improvement in the absorptive capacity of the country with respect to FDI flows. For example, credit-constrained entrepreneurs will find it easier to set up their own businesses as the local financial markets develop and improve (Alfaro et al., 2010). In essence, well-functioning financial institutions augment capital accumulation, innovation in technology, and foster entrepreneurial activity, which then leads to economic growth and development.

1.2 History and Overview of World FDI

FDI, by definition, is the net inflow of investments in order to gain a lasting management interest (10% voting stocks or more) in a company operating in an economy different from that of the investor. To further explain this, it comprises the investment of foreign assets, which are not essentially monetary, in a domestic economy other than that of the investors. Thus, FDI is the process in which residents of one country (known as the source/home nation) gain ownership of resources to control the production, distribution, and other activities of a company in another country known as the host nation/country (Moosa, 2002). FDI is a parameter for international exchange, which has gained reception over the years due to the desire for global interaction and competition, foreign ownerships, as well as the prospect of channeling resources to developing and emerging economies. Ever since its inception, FDI has led to the transfer of such assets as technology, knowledge, capital inflows, and management skills, to mention just a few.

The earlier accounts of FDI transactions were predominantly in the form of money lending by Great Britain to other host countries to enable the host countries' economic development and growth in the global scene. Nevertheless, foreign investment decayed after a while (especially post Second World War), which then saw Great Britain's position as the only provider of funds for direct investment in host countries overturned by the United States (USA), which became the highest single provider of FDI. In the aftermath of the Second World War, there was an increase in FDI transfers to host countries. This was because of the arrival of new technologies that were to be sold or globally spread, the need to help in rebuilding most countries and economies devastated by the war (for example, Japan), as well as the desire of most US corporations to spread their corporate activities across national boundaries. The United States, among the top countries that participated in this regard, has always engaged FDI as a vital macro-economic variable to help fast-track economic growth and development, as well as global inter-dependence among participating countries, as reported in Luke and Caiden (1989) and McIntyre (1983). Over the last two decades, the positive impact of FDI has been felt in so many countries, beginning with the developed countries, which made up both the home and host countries. It later gained acceptance among the developing ones (e.g. China, India, Russia, Brazil, etc.). They have also, in recent times, presented themselves as the big hosts for FDI inflows across the world. There are available statistics to support the increased volume of inflows and outflows of FDI from the United States and other developed countries to other regions of the world in the last decades (see UNCTAD Statistics database).

1.3 Economic Rationale for FDI in Developing Countries

Foreign investment is often seen as a complementing driver of economic performance amid the inadequate investment base of emerging and transitional economies. This section brings to the fore more specific issues usually discussed concerning the impact FDI has on growth in emerging and transitional economies. First, we examine inward FDI as a policy response to strategic development. Second, we examine the ways through which FDI may be growth constraining or growth inducing. These two aspects are intertwined and may reflect intuitively inter-dependent opinions. However, they exhibit some distinctiveness for which their understanding will provide the reader with some detailed outlook into the mechanisms of FDI and growth. Therefore, the question to ask is not whether FDI is good for growth, since there is almost a consensus agreement to this. Rather, the question is, how can it be galvanized effectively in developing and transition countries and in what fraction should it be applied so that it can produce preferred results especially for economic growth?

1.3.1 FDI as a Strategic Host Economic Development Policy Response

This perspective is underscored by a publication, UNCTAD (2003), which illustrates the need for coordinating and integrating FDI with regards to the "corporate strategies and the competitive advantage of the host-countries." According to this view, FDI should be used as a global response to economic development and should be tailored in accordance with the circumstances of the recipient country. Within this viewpoint, one school of thought is predicated in the neo-liberal development rational, which comprises the biggest international financial organizations (IFOs) like the World Bank, the IMF, and the United Nations Organization (UNO). They believe that the weak growth dilemma of most developing countries is because of central issues like lack of globally open economies and extreme state involvement (Rodrik, 2006). The idea is that the openness of a domestic economy would stimulate FDI inflows and then bring about growth by boosting domestic savings. Some IFO country's specifics and general reports are published frequently to buttress their claims on the effectiveness of inward FDI in developing countries and transitional economies (e.g. Utz, 2008). This school of thought therefore suggests that the policy instruments of openness, liberalization, and the relegation of the state to regulatory responsibilities are a very effective undisputable channel to the development of the economies lagging in growth. Hence, FDI can generally promote growth with such measures in the environment.

However, another school of thought believes and suggests that an unregulated liberalized economy may be more detrimental than beneficial to growth (UNCTAD, 2003). For instance, to attract FDI, host economies may have to provide some incentives such as implementing subsidy regimes, tax incentives, and other forms of incentives to encourage foreign investment, which may not be sustainable in the long run. Another argument was that the promotion of FDI should be done in a way that reflects the intrinsic competitiveness of the host countries (ESCAP[1]-UN, 2003). This publication emphasized that it is misleading to think that FDI determines a host country's competitiveness, instead of the host country's competitiveness dictating the volume and type of FDI that should be attracted (p. 2). Certainly, this opinion is reinforced by the strategic location and outsourcing of manufacturing by major multinational corporations (MNCs) in the Asian economies to benefit from the relatively cheap labor within these countries. This publication further outlined the determining factors of such a competitive advantage-oriented FDI. These are broadly categorized into two: first is firm specific and second is host country specific (p. 12). This approach has become popular, as many governments all over the world are beginning to adopt it rather than the approach that just opens the economy to FDI without any policy plan.

Kumar (2009) suggests that if developing countries want to catch up with their developed counterparts, the interests of both the host and home states in relation to FDI flows need to be aligned through carefully formulated host nation policies. Another side of the argument in favor of FDI that is focused on domestic policy suggests that it may even be more beneficial because of the belief that different sectors and different types of FDI have opposing influences on the host economies. Another area of worry for which policing or monitoring has become a main FDI initiative is about risk mitigation and aversion. FDI as a

[1]ESCAP: Economic and Social Commission For Asia And The Pacific.

flow of capital exposes both the investors and the recipient economies to the risk of political and economic shocks typical of emerging and developing economies. And if these economies are to attract, secure, and promote FDI inflow, hedging their economies is unavoidable and necessary. An IMF report on FDI in emerging economies offers some theoretical explanations as to why expectations of such confidence are important—to avoid the risk of volatility of capital flows arising from a possible risk of capital repatriation (IMF, 2003, pp. 25–29).

1.3.2 Avenues Through Which FDI May Be Growth Inducing or Constraining

Several research in the FDI body of literature attempt to offer explanations as to the circumstances in which FDI can be growth persuading and when it can be harmful or detrimental to growth in host countries. As already mentioned in the previous sub-section, the nature or manner in which FDI inflows enter and leave the economy matters to a very large extent. It has often been suggested that FDI affects growth positively through externalities such as by augmenting domestic investment, large capital mobilization, and technological transfers (Chakraborty & Nunnenkamp, 2008; OECD, 2002; UNCTAD, 2003). Nevertheless, factors such as corruption, economic and political instability, and other general domestic bottlenecks also impede FDI benefits or discourage FDI entirely in host economies (World Bank, 2010).

An avenue that has been extensively recognized for growth-promoting FDI is through multinational enterprises (MNEs) and their activities. Lall and Narula (2004) argue that due to their access to production and knowledge economies, MNEs can encourage productivity in host countries resulting in externalities or spillovers from their activities. However, for MNEs to successfully and effectively contribute to the performance of the domestic economy, the host institution must have an "'internalisation' strategy to interact effectively with the country's capabilities and resources" (p. 450). Lall and Narula (2004) conclude on their claim that FDI does not and will not necessarily guarantee growth unless a domestic industrial sector, which has the appropriate technological capabilities to gain from the MNEs' activities, exists. Another major MNEs-FDI activity, which provides the possibilities of economic development and growth in most emerging countries, is with the privatization of state-owned enterprises (SOEs) and their acquisitions by MNEs. Within this area, Portelli and Narula (2006) show that the gains from MNEs' acquisitions in Tanzania produced positive gains in the economy for specific industries, particularly through enhanced backward linkages. Their research, which was country specific, is in harmony with that of Lall and Narula (2004) already reviewed above. These gains were seen in the sectors that had a domestic comparative advantage, and the sectors with "wider technology gaps" between domestic- and foreign-owned sectors may result in "fewer backward linkages" (p. 789).

As already clearly highlighted above, MNEs are central to bringing pro-growth FDI through backward linkages and technological externalities and spillovers. However, what and how much do we know about the mechanisms behind this assertion? Alfaro et al. (2010) offers some empirics, which suggests that a crucial factor that would guarantee the backward FDI linkages and spillovers provided by MNEs activities is local financial markets development. They also found considerable growth effects emanating from FDI when goods that are produced by domestic firms and those produced by foreign MNEs are substitutes to each other. Human capital stock is also recognized to be an important resource for host economies, if they are to effectively benefit from the positive spillovers and linkages from MNEs-driven FDI.

Several other works have emphasized the importance of the availability of resources (either natural or reproductive resources), or geographical elements, as factors that could particularly promote and attract FDI inflows. In this regard, Wei (2005) found an evidence-based difference in FDI inflows between China and India as mainly due to the differences in "international trade ties" and "size of domestic market." This was regardless of the comparatively better position India had with regards to her comparatively "cheaper labor cost," "lower country risk," and "geographical closeness to OECD countries." However, even these noninduced factors, though essential, are not conditions sufficient for promoting and attracting FDI inflows. The importance of this argument in this section, which is different from the previous argument, is summarized in the following question: how could FDI be an adequate incentive for the maximization of its growth-yielding influence on economic growth?

One maximization approach which has been well discussed is the strategic use of state collaborations, particularly for transitional/emerging economies. It is because such collaborations will see through a relationship whereby the lead country in the relationship through project-specific frontiers can encourage spillovers through, for example, MNEs' activities in the countries in which they have interest. Pereira (2003) gives an example in which this kind of solution has thrived, where he gives a detailed exposition on the China-Singapore Suzhou National Park MNEs relationship from 1992 to 2002. In this paper, he explored the benefits that could be derived from collaboration instead of competition, especially in a global economy that is rapidly globalizing. From a wider viewpoint, both source categories of inward FDI as previously reviewed above can adequately be grouped into "host-country specific" determinants as well as "industry/sector specific" determinants (ESCAP-UN, 2003, p. 3). As explained earlier, both of them are evidently mutually inclusive and reinforce each other.

1.4 Does FDI Promote Economic Growth?

Over the past two decades, many country-specific and cross-country studies have examined the role of FDI in stimulating economic growth in less developed countries (LDCs). But the direction of causality remains an unresolved issue. There have been findings that support the notion that FDI has the tendency to promote economic growth. According to this view, FDI provides important ingredients that are necessities for economic growth. By providing managerial skills, new production processes and techniques, as well as new varieties of capital goods, FDI invariably promotes economic growth of LDCs (Samad, 2009). Borensztein et al. (1998) found that FDI is a vital channel for the transfer of new technologies, contributing to growth in much more measures than domestic investment could possibly do. However, their result suggests that FDI contributes to growth when the host country attains a minimum threshold level of human capital. Blomstrom et al. (1992) found evidence to suggest that FDI Granger causes economic growth. However, FDI's positive contribution is based on the condition that the host country attains a sufficiently high per capita income. De Mello (1997) also found that FDI had significantly positive effect on economic growth in the countries with high-income level. Caves (1996) encapsulates the positive effects of FDI as introduction of new processes, productivity gains, technology transfers, managerial skills and technical know-how in the domestic market, access to markets, employee training, and international production networks. Jyun-Yi and Chih-Chiang (2008) used a GMM method, which specifies FDI to be endogenous and found an insignificantly negative relationship between FDI and growth. However, when they used threshold models, their results indicated that FDI can have a significantly positive impact on growth in countries which have attained relatively better levels of human capital and initial output. Adams (2009) analyses the impact of FDI and domestic investment on economic growth in Sub-Saharan Africa for the period of 1990–2003 employing OLS and fixed effects estimation. Their results showed that both domestic investment and FDI are positive and significantly correlated with economic growth but found evidence of a net crowding out effect of FDI on domestic investment.

On another hand, some studies found that economic growth precedes FDI. According to this view, economic growth first provides the necessary and favorable economic factors upon which FDI will play a positive role for economic growth and development. For instance, the spillover effects of technological transfers through FDI can only be effective when the absorptive capacity of host countries is developed. In his argument, Zhang (2000) suggested that economic growth leads to FDI growth. Speedy economic growth in the host country increases total demand, which in turn stimulates higher demand for investments and by extension FDI. Other authors found a bidirectional link between FDI and growth, implying that FDI and economic growth are positively interdependent. Among the authors that found a bidirectional causal relationship are Caves (1996) and Chowdhry and Mavrotas (2006). Caves (1996) found that robust economic growth provides high profit opportunities that attract higher domestic and foreign direct investments. Again, FDI through its spillover effects has direct positive impact on economic growth of the host countries. Chowdhry and Mavrotas (2006) found that in Chile, GDP causes FDI (and not vice versa) but found strong evidence of bidirectional causality between FDI and GDP in Malaysia and China. Within the context of Southeast Asia and Latin American countries, Samad (2009) also found evidence of both unidirectional causality flowing from GDP to FDI in some countries and bidirectional causality from GDP to FDI. Turkan and Yetkiner (2008) adopted a two-equation simultaneous GMM estimation method on several OECD countries, treating economic growth and FDI variables as endogenous. They found FDI growth and economic growth to significantly define each other. This means that they have a reinforcing relationship, which is endogenous in nature.

In a similar vein to the above authors, they found that export growth and human capital were statistically significant determinants of both FDI and economic growth. Jayachandran and Sellan (2010) explored the relationship that exists between trade, FDI, and growth for India over a period of 38 years from 1970. Their findings were unambiguously contradictory to those of both authors reviewed above, which suggested that the direction of causality is unidirectional from exports to growth, as well as unidirectional from FDI to growth. Therefore, for India, over the period, exports and FDI clearly caused economic growth. In the same vein, Asiedu (2002) suggested through her findings that FDI had different impact on different regions, particularly comparing Sub-Sahara Africa (SSA) countries and non-Sub-Sahara African (non-SSA) countries. She compared impacts based on access to relative distinctive features of high returns on investment and levels of infrastructural. She found that the impact of FDI was not reactive to such criteria in SSA countries when compared to more reaction to these thresholds for non-SSA countries. She then concludes that the marginal gains to openness are less successful to SSA countries in relative terms.

In the literature, we discovered another area that has gained attention and has been theoretically reviewed above. This is with regards to accounting for specific industrial or sectoral impacts when evaluating the impact of FDI. This approach evaluates FDI with specific impacts focus rather than generally with a superficial "neo-liberal" notion that FDI is prevalently beneficial. Fillat and Woerz (2011), considering country and industry heterogeneity among 35 OECD countries, Eastern Europe, and Asia over the period 1987–2002, conducted an examination of sectoral FDI on productivity growth, while they controlled for the effect of developmental stages. They found that FDI has a much-pronounced impact on economic growth for emerging economies, which includes Eastern Europe and Eastern Asian emerging economies. Additionally, these FDI impacts also differed across industries, supporting claims that FDI policies should reflect various industrial abilities across countries. Again, Chakraborty and Nunnenkamp (2008) conducted a study on postreform India and controlled for the impacts of sectoral FDI and causality in a framework of cointegration model. They found that the impacts of FDI were different across the different sectors and that the relationships that exists between FDI and growth varied across the different sectors. For example, they found no evidence of a causal relationship between FDI stock and productivity in the primary sector, and an endogenous relationship in the manufacturing sector. Evidence was also found of inter-industry spillovers, one of which flows from the services sector to the industry sector. With regards to financial market development, Alfaro et al. (2010), in their paper connecting FDI, financial markets, and economic growth, found that countries that have comparatively more developed financial markets generally exhibited positive gains from FDI. They also suggested that analyzing FDI impacts in isolation yields results with ambiguity.

Another area of attention is the increasing flow of additional financial resources besides FDI, such as immigrant remittances, from developed countries to developing countries, and its potential impact on capital accumulation and economic development in receiving countries. Since remittances from immigrants represent a substantial inflow of financial resources, the role of this financial inflow in economic development is another important issue for research and policy-making, albeit not for this study. A more recent study by Comes et al. (2018) examines the impact of FDI and remittances on economic growth using a panel of seven countries from Central Europe and Eastern Europe with a GDP per capita under $25,000. Their study found a positive impact of both FDI and remittances on GDP, but FDI had a higher influence in all analyzed countries.

According to Samad (2009), an investigation of the causal link between FDI and economic growth has both policy and strategic implications for LDCs. FDI and economic growth may have a link in three possible ways: (1) Causal link may flow from economic growth to FDI (unidirectional). If the causal link flows from economic growth to FDI, it implies that economic growth is a precondition for attracting, absorbing, and sustaining FDI. In such instance, the policy implication is that LDCs must strive to develop and grow their economies, rather than chasing after FDI in futility. (2) Causal link may flow from FDI to economic growth. Where there exists a unidirectional causality from FDI to economic growth, it lends credence to the view that FDI does not only lead to employment generation and capital formation but also economic growth of host countries. The policy implication in such scenario will mean that corporate rules and regulations of host countries must be addressed and enforced to attract FDI. (3) Causal relation may flow in both ways (bi-directional). If the causal link is bidirectional, it therefore means that economic growth and FDI have reinforcing effects on each other.

In conclusion, the evaluations on the empirical evidence for the impact of FDI on growth, which though appears to be prevalently questionable, have in recent times been supportive to the claim that the FDI-Growth nexus and its impacts are better understood haven controlled (or thresholding) for other important predeterminants of growth and when analyzed across different sectors of the economy. This idea is better understood in the following section.

1.5 Problems of FDI

1.5.1 Crowding-Out

A host country's economy may be impacted both favorably and unfavorably by FDI. The main negative impact of the crowding-out effect is the monopolistic control that MNEs acquire over the market. In this field, empirical results are inconsistent. Nasritdinova (2018) conducted econometric research of 39 countries between 1970 and 1996 and discovered the impact of crowding out in 10 economies. In contrast, 19 economies showed the impact of crowding in. The crowding-out effect, however, could be clearly seen throughout Latin America.

This diversity may be explained by the fact that various economies are drawn to various types of FDI. Due to the growth of overseas subsidiaries, there will be crowding out in nations that get primarily domestic market-seeking investments. On the other end, investment focused on exports might not be as profitable. An MNE with lower marginal costs increases production in comparison to its local counterpart when imperfectly competitive companies in the host nation are faced with fixed production expenses. Due to the increased demand from foreign companies who produce goods for the domestic market, local businesses are thus forced to reduce their output. Because their fixed costs are dispersed over a smaller area, local companies are less efficient in smaller markets. When the productivity loss brought on by this demand impact is significant enough, total domestic productivity may be diminished even if the MNE provides technology or a firm-specific asset to local businesses (Farrell, 2000).

1.5.2 Balance of Payment

Studies have demonstrated a bidirectional relationship between foreign investment and imports. The number of imports into the host country from the home country also rises as FDI from the home country does. The MNE purchasing supplies from its traditional suppliers, or the increased entrance of foreign capital may be the source of an increase in the inflation rate in the home country. As investment rises, the economy of the host nation relies more and more on the MNE's native manufacturing technologies. Since extra resources and semi-finished products must be imported from the nation where the MNE is situated, this may restrict the expansion of the local sector in the host country. The host country may experience trade imbalances in the absence of investments focused on exports (Ohno & Le, 2014).

1.5.3 Unfavorable Pay

The pay spillovers of FDI are thought to be mostly favorable since it boosts the competitiveness of local enterprises when employees of multinationals quit their employment to launch their own businesses. However, this could have serious consequences if MNEs hire the best people due to their high salaries and leave lower-quality employees at domestic businesses (Ziying, 2014). To prevent their top talent from departing for foreign companies, local businesses may artificially raise or mimic MNEs' salaries in response. The issue is that MNEs outperform local businesses in terms of productivity. Therefore, this might reduce their ability to compete. However, in some developing countries, it could be challenging for one party to influence the other due to the great distance between MNEs and local businesses. The labor markets in some developing countries are sufficiently fragmented for wages in one sector to affect wages in the other (Lipsey & Sjöholm, 2004).

1.5.4 Environmental Impact

FDI is an important source of funding for the natural resource industry in emerging and underdeveloped countries. Most of these countries have laxer or nonexistent regulatory frameworks. Some governments go to great pains to exclude or scale back its regulatory requirements to promote FDI. FDI can have positive effects on the economy and environments of host countries, but it can also have negative effects that are detrimental (Gray, 2002). The solution to these problems is to increase the host nation's capacity to control and create global environmental standards. Nongovernmental organizations (NGOs) and other members of the society can have a significant impact on government regulations and MNE environment protection, both in the home nation and the host country.

1.5.5 Dual-Economy Effect

Emerging nations may have a dual economy because of FDI, with a developed sector under the control of multinational firms and an underdeveloped sector under the control of homegrown businesses. Due to the host nation's reliance on the developed sector, its economic structure changes. The host's nation industry tends to be capital-intensive, while other sectors are labor-intensive. Since most of the population lives in the labor-intensive sector of the economy, the dual economy effect has a detrimental influence on the economic growth of nations. In many oil-rich nations, the agricultural and industrial sectors have not flourished because of the resource boom brought on by foreign investment in the oil and gas business. The Dutch disease effect could result from this unfavorable effect of FDI on countries with abundant natural resources.

According to the Dutch Disease model, a resource surge pulls resources away from long-term prosperity-enhancing activities, especially when significant investments have been made in the area. Industrial exports started to decrease because of a rise in the country's currency rate brought on by the resource boom (Bulte et al., 2005). Due to growing competition from the resource business, manufacturing costs have grown. If the competitiveness of the nation's non-tradable commodities grows and that of the nation's produced tradable goods drops, export-led manufacturing expansion is less likely. Decreased activity in the manufacturing sector, which is the nation's main "growth engine," contributes to long-term economic stagnation (Ohno & Le, 2014). One approach to the issue is to diversify the economy by making investments in other sectors.

1.5.6 Profits Reimportation

The major objective of MNCs' foreign investments is to increase profits. MNCs can profit from these countries' advantages, including their low labor costs, rich natural resources, and top-notch expertise. Big firms can transfer their investment profits back to their parent companies in a few methods, such as through dividend and royalty payments to shareholders and the straightforward transfer of accumulated earnings. They can minimize paying additional taxes than they otherwise would by using transfer pricing. However, when profits are returned to a host country, there are significant capital outflows to the home country that hurt the host country's current account. As a result, host countries frequently place limitations on the amount of revenues that multinational firms can repatriate to prevent a shortfall in their balance of payments or a decrease in their foreign exchange reserves. This strategy may encourage large multinational firms to invest their earnings in a variety of projects in the host countries (Farrell, 2000). However, there is a chance that MNEs will forego investing in these countries and instead direct FDI to nations with less onerous profit repatriation regulations. Most industries in India are a major receiver of FDI, allowing foreign businesses' profits to be reinvested in their home nations.

1.6 Definition of Key Terms

1.6.1 Foreign Direct Investment

FDI is seen as an investment made by an entity or a company based in one country into an entity or a company located in a different country. FDI is substantially different from other forms of indirect investments such as portfolio inflows, where foreign-based institutions invest in listed equities on a country's stock exchange. Companies making direct investments will typically acquire a lasting interest in the company into which the investment is made and have a significant degree of control and influence over it.

1.6.2 FDI Inflows and Outflows

Net FDI inflows are seen as the value of inward direct investment made by foreign investors in a host economy. Net FDI outflows are considered as the value of outward flowing direct investments by the residents of a reporting economy to foreign economies.

1.6.3 FDI Spillovers

FDI spillovers are generally seen as the impact the presence of foreign firms have on domestic firms regarding their economic performance. The standard analytical approach in the empirical literature is to analyze spillovers as additional inputs that explain total factor productivity (TFP) in the framework of a production function.

1.6.4 Economic Growth

Economic growth is defined as an upward rise in the capacity of an economy in the production of goods and services, when compared from one economic period to another. Economic growth is measured in either nominal terms (i.e. nominal

GDP), or in real terms, after adjusting for inflation (i.e. real GDP). To account for the average output of the economy per person, the real GDP per capita is often used as a more appropriate measure of economic growth because it helps in international comparison. This latter measure will be used in this study.

1.6.5 Financial Development

The development of financial sector in emerging markets and in developing countries is part of the strategy for private sector development to stimulate growth in the economy and reduce poverty. The financial sector is a set of markets, instruments, and institutions. It comprises the regulatory and legal framework that permit transactions to be conducted through the extension credit. Financial development is the process of making improvements in quantity, quality, effectiveness, and efficiency of financial services and its intermediaries (Amadi, 2019).

1.6.6 Absorptive Capacity

Absorptive capacity is defined as an economy's capacity to absorb the benefits spilled over by FDI. It can also be related to a host institution's ability to value, assimilate, and apply new knowledge (Cohen & Levinthal, 1989).

1.7 Conclusion

FDI has continued to gain increasing acceptance over the years as an important strategy for economic growth particularly in developing countries. Statistics show that the United States and other major economies of the world (e.g. Germany, Japan, France, Canada, the Netherlands, Spain, the United Kingdom, and Italy) are the top providers of FDI, while Developing Asia (particularly China and India), Europe, Latin America and the Caribbean, and North America are major FDI hosts.

References

Adams, S. (2009). Foreign direct investment, domestic investment, and economic growth in Sub-Saharan Africa. *Journal of Policy Modeling, 31*, 939–949.

Alfaro, L., Chanda, A., Kalemli-Ozcan, S., & Sayek, S. (2010). Does foreign direct investment promote growth? Exploring the role of financial markets on linkages. *Journal of Development Economics, 91*, 242–256.

Amadi, C. (2019). *FDI and economic growth in Nigeria: An analysis of the role of financial development on linkages* Doctoral dissertation. Manchester Metropolitan University.

Asiedu, E. (2002). On the development of foreign direct investment to developing countries: Is Africa different? *World Development, 30*(1), 107–119.

Blomstrom, M., Lipsey, R. E., & Zejan, M. (1992). *What explains developing country growth.* NBER Working Paper No. 4132. NBER.

Borensztein, E., Gregorio, J. D., & Lee, J. W. (1998). How does foreign direct investment affect economic growth? *Journal of International Economics*, *45*, 115–135.

Bulte, E. H., Damania, R., & Deacon, R. T. (2005). Resource intensity, institutions, and development. *World Development*, *33*(7), 1029–1044.

Caves, R. E. (1996). *Multinational enterprise and economic analysis* (2nd ed.). Cambridge University Press.

Chakraborty, C., & Nunnenkamp, P. (2008). Economic reforms, FDI and economic growth in India: A sector level analysis. *World Development*, *36*(7), 1192–1212.

Chowdhry, A., & Mavrotas, G. (2006). FDI and growth: What causes what? *The World Economy*, *29*(1), 42–58.

Cohen, W., & Levinthal, D. (1989). Innovation and learning: Two faces of R&D. *Economic Journal*, *99*, 569–596.

Comes, C., Bunduchi, E., & Vasile, V. (2018). The impact of foreign direct investments and remittances on economic growth: A case study in Central and Eastern Europe. *Sustainability*, *10*(238), 1–16.

Danja, K. H. (2012). Foreign direct investment and the Nigerian economy. *American Journal of Economics*, *2*(3), 33–40.

De Mello, L. R. (1997). Foreign direct investment in developing countries and growth: A selective survey. *Journal of Development Studies*, *34*(1), 1–34.

Ehimare, O. A. (2011). Foreign direct investment and its effect on the Nigerian economy. *Business Intelligence Journal*, *4*(2), 253–261.

ESCAP-UN. (2003). *Investment promotion and enterprise development, Bulletin for Asia and The Pacific No. 2*. Economic and Social Commission for Asia and The Pacific/United Nations.

Farrell, R. (2000). Research issues in Japanese foreign direct investment. *SSRN Electronic Journal*. https://doi.org/10.2139/ssrn.231118

Fillat, C., & Woerz, J. (2011). Good or bad? The influence of FDI on productivity growth: An industry-level analysis. *Journal of International Trade & Economic Development*, *20*(3), 293–328.

Gorg, H., & Greenaway, D. (2004). Much ado about nothing? Do domestic firms really benefit from foreign direct investment? *The World Bank Research Observer*, *19*, 171–197.

Gray, C. (2002). Entrepreneurship, resistance to change and growth in small firms. *Journal of Small Business and Enterprise Development*. https://doi.org/10.1108/14626000210419491

Hermes, N., & Lensink, R. (2003). Foreign direct investment, financial development and economic growth. *Journal of Development Studies*, *40*, 142–163.

IMF (International Monetary Fund). (2003). *Foreign direct investment in emerging market countries*. Report of the working group of the Capital Markets Consultative Group (CMCG). http://www.imf.org/external/np/cmcg/2003/eng/091803.pdf. Accessed on June 25, 2016.

Jayachandran, G., & Sellan, A. (2010). A causal relationship between trade, foreign direct investment and economic growth in India. *International Research Journal of Finance and Economics*, *42*, 74–88.

Jyun-Yi, W., & Chih-Chiang, H. (2008). Does foreign direct investment promote economic growth? Evidence from a threshold regression analysis. *Economics Bulletin*, *15*(12), 1–10.

Kumar, S. (2009). Rethinking the linkages between foreign direct investment and development: A third world perspective. *NALSAR Student Law Review*, 85–104.

Lall, S., & Narula, R. (2004). Foreign direct investment and its role in economic development: Do we need a new agenda? *European Journal of Development Research*, *16*(3), 447–464.

Lipsey, R., & Sjöholm, F. (2004). *Host country impacts of inward FDI: Why such different answers?* European Institute of Japanese Studies.

Luke, J. S., & Caiden, G. E. (1989). Coping with global interdependence. In J. L. Perry (Ed.), *Handbook of public administration* (pp. 83–93). Jossey-Bass Publishers.

McIntyre, J. R. (1983). The role of State Governments as international economic actors. *Southern Review of Public Administration*, (Winter), 465–488.

Moosa, I. A. (2002). *Foreign direct investment: Theory, evidence & practice*. Palgrave.

Nasritdinova, G. (2018). FDI scenario in Uzbekistan: Current reforms and future prospects. *International Journal of Management Science and Business Administration*, *4*, 38–42.

OECD. (2002). *Foreign direct investment for development: Maximizing benefits, minimizing costs*. Organization for Economic Cooperation and Development.

Ohno, K., & Le, H. T. (2014). Key issues for FDI policy re-formulation in Vietnam. *Journal of Economics and Development*, *16*(3), 5–31.

Pereira, A. A. (2003). *State collaboration and development strategies in China: The case of the China-Singapore Suzhou Industrial Park (1992-2002)*. RoutledgeCurzon.

Portelli, B., & Narula, R. (2006). Foreign direct investment through acquisitions and implications for technological upgrading: Case evidence from Tanzania. *European Journal of Development Research*, *18*(1), 59–85.

Rodrik, D. (2006). Goodbye Washington consensus, Hello Washington confusion? A review of the World Bank's "Economic growth in the 1990s: Learning from a decade of reform". *Journal of Economic Literature*, *44*, 973–987.

Samad, A. (2009). *Does FDI cause economic growth? Evidence from South-East Asia and Latin America*. Woodbury School of Business Working Paper 1-09. Utah Valley University.

Turkan, B., & Yetkiner, H. (2008). *Endogenous determination of FDI growth and economic growth: The OECD case*. Working Papers in Economics No. 09/07. Izmir University of Economics.

UNCTAD. (2003). *Foreign direct investment and performance requirements: New evidence from selected countries*. United Nations.

Utz, R. J. (2008). *Sustaining and sharing economic growth in Tanzania*. The World Bank.

Wei, W. (2005). China and India: Any difference in their FDI performance? *Journal of Asian Economics*, *16*(4), 719–736.

World Bank. (2010). *Investing across borders 2010*. The World Bank Group. http://iab.worldbank.org/~/media/FPDKM/IAB/Documents/IAB-report.pdf. Accessed on June 25, 2016.

Zhang, K. H. (2000). Human capital, country size and north-south manufacturing multinational enterprises. *International Economics*, *52*(2), 237–260.

Ziying, M. (2014). Inward foreign direct investment, entrepreneurial behavior, and outward foreign direct investment: Evidence from China. *International Journal of Business and Management*, *9*(9). https://doi.org/10.5539/ijbm.v9n9p108

Chapter 2

Factors Affecting FDI Spillover Effects: A Host Economy Case Study

Abstract

Several economic models suggest that the spillover effects of foreign direct investment (FDI) on economic growth may be contingent on some intervening factors in the host economy which determine the host country's absorptive capacity. These factors include financial development, human capital development, economic freedom, institutional quality, trade openness, infrastructure, and so on. This chapter briefly explains the meaning and implications of these factors for the relationship between FDI and economic growth.

Keywords: FDI spillover; host economy; financial development; human capital; economic freedom; trade openness; institutional quality; infrastructure development; inflation; foreign exchange

2.1 Introduction

Literature is awash with research studies that echo the benefits of foreign direct investment (FDI) on the domestic economy, namely that foreign companies introduce new processes and products to the domestic market, leading to productivity gains. Foreign firms also accelerate the diffusion of new technology and the transfer of managerial skills and technical know-how. In recognition of these benefits, the evolving literature on FDI suggests that the positive impact of FDI on economic growth is dependent on absorptive capacities (World Bank, 2001).

Foreign Direct Investment, 17–26

Published under exclusive licence by Emerald Publishing Limited
doi:10.1108/978-1-83662-900-920261002

2.2 Financial Sector Development

It is claimed that the benefits of FDI in the domestic economy can be enhanced and amplified with well-functioning financial markets. From examination of key studies, this argument is based on three key premises. First, functional financial institutions can offer access to external finance for entrepreneurs wishing to establish or expand their businesses in line with new technological developments. Second, financial institutions will ensure that capital is efficiently allocated to deserving businesses and will monitor these funds. Third, well-developed financial markets reduce the cost of external finance by lowering the cost of conducting transactions (Alfaro et al., 2004). The overall effect of these is that well-developed and functional financial markets will consolidate productivity gains from FDI and lead to capital accumulation and in-turn promotes economic growth (Amadi, 2019).

Models by Hermes and Lensink (2003), as well as Alfaro et al. (2010), predict that the impact of FDI on economic growth is dependent on the development of the local financial markets (namely credit markets and stock markets) of the host country. According to these studies, well-functioning financial markets enable FDI to promote economic growth through backward linkages, where economic agents in the host country can take advantage of knowledge spillovers from FDI, thereby improving the absorptive capacity of the country with respect to FDI flows. For example, a more developed the local financial market will make it easier for credit-constrained entrepreneurs to start their own firms (Alfaro et al., 2010). In other words, well-functioning financial institutions augment capital accumulation and technological innovation, promoting entrepreneurial activities and hence economic development.

Recent studies also show that financial development is a robust predictor of FDI inflows in developing countries (e.g. Shah, 2016). Baharumshah et al. (2017) also found evidence on the effects of differential growth for three types of foreign capital inflows (FDI, debt inflows, and portfolio equity). Their study revealed, among other results, that the positive gains of the three types of capital inflows are only found in countries that already have a level of financial market development beyond a threshold level. Thus, a robust and more active financial sector is crucial for economic progress as hypothesized by earlier studies.

2.3 Human Capital

Human capital and FDI are generally classed among the key drivers of economic growth in both developing and developed countries. While human capital and FDI separately affect growth, they also reinforce each other though complementary effects. Generally, enhanced human resource development increases FDI inflow by making the investment environment attractive to foreign investors. This is done through a direct effect of upgraded skill level of the country's workforce, as well as through indirect effects such as improved sociopolitical stability and health (Majeed & Ahmad, 2008). On another hand, FDI contributes to human capital development since multinational enterprises (MNEs) by themselves can be active providers of training and education for skill development, as well as information and technology to host developing countries.

Ultimately, therefore, these complementary effects lead to a robust circle of FDI as well as human capital development where host countries experience continuous inflow of FDI over time (long run) by progressively attracting higher value-added MNEs and at the same time, upgrading the skill contents of pre-existing MNEs and local enterprises.

Many studies have researched the relationship and impact of FDI and human capital on growth. For example, Borensztein et al. (1998) found that there is a strong "complementarity between FDI and the stock of human capital" in terms of the impact on economic growth. They used secondary school enrollment as a proportion of the total population as a measure of human capital development or the importance of education. They show from their study that a higher level of secondary school enrollment and attainment is largely related with greater spillover effects. Therefore, the importance of school enrollment as a precondition for the absorption of the gains of FDI was evident. In fact, they went as far as calculating a threshold for secondary school attainment of 0.52, as the level beyond which the host country would begin to benefit from the spillover effects of FDI. Blonigen and Wang (2005) repeated the process undertaken by Borensztein et al. (1998) using the same sample but distinguished between developing and developed countries. Their results are in line with those of Borensztein et al. (1998) but only for the developing countries. Therefore, Blonigen and Wang (2005) found schooling a significantly important factor in terms of absorptive capacity in the case of developing countries.

However, schooling was found not to be a significant factor of absorptive capacity in the case of developed countries. Li and Liu (2005) also found evidence supporting the importance of schooling for absorptive capacity. On another hand, some researchers did not find schooling to be a significant absorptive capacity factor. For instance, the findings of Carkovic and Levine (2005) are not in support of the claim that more schooling allows better absorption of FDI gains and benefits. Similar results are observed in several other studies, such as Darrat et al. (2005), and Kinoshita and Lu (2006).

Education as a factor of absorptive capacity as portrayed in literature does not explore the issue of quality of education. It will be unreasonable to believe that one year of education in one country will be equivalent to one year of education in another country. The significance of education does not lie in the number of years of education but essentially in the quality of the education provided or attained. Failure to take quality of education into consideration could produce results, which are misleading. The problem of researching the effects of quality of education lies in the difficulty of its measurement in the first instance. Some researchers have been studying schooling inputs, such as the ratio student-to-teacher as well as expenditure on schooling, as possible proxies for measuring the quality of education.

Some other studies use a combination of secondary and tertiary institution enrollment as a proportion of total population (e.g. Ayanwale, 2007). Hanushek and Kimko (2000) in their study proposed using international examination scores as proxies for cognitive ability, reflecting the quality of education. They used their constructed variable to study its influence on economic growth and found that the labor-force quality has a steady, stable, and strong relationship with economic growth. Hanushek and Woesmann (2008) confirmed this finding through a more robust study. In addition, human capital has been observed to contribute to growth through different channels, which could be seen as different measures of educational quality. For example, using a Chinese panel data study, Li and Wang (2016a) find that basic human capital (i.e. human capital obtained from literacy programs and primary and secondary school education) contributes to growth via the "capital accumulation channel". While advanced human capital (i.e. human capital obtained from tertiary education, such as vocational college and postgraduate programs) contributes to growth via the "productivity channel". According to Li and Wang (2016a), while basic human capital augments production like any other normal factor input, advanced human capital is mostly productive in innovation and technological adaptation. The role of education quality as a factor for absorptive capacity will however not the focus of this study.

2.4 Economic Freedom

The economic freedom index is also controlled for by some studies when examining the impact of FDI on economic growth. The economic freedom index is an annual index and ranking by the Wall Street Journal and heritage foundation in 1995 as to measure the degree of economic freedom in the nations of the world. It takes scores countries across many measures such the rule of law (i. e. the degree of a country's legal protection for the rights of private property, non-prevalence of political corruption), government size and spending, fiscal freedom, regulatory efficiency (including labor freedom, monetary freedom and business freedom), openness of markets (i.e. financial freedom, trade freedom and investment freedom). Ajide and Eregha (2014) examined the relationship between the inflow of FDI and economic freedom in 12 ECOWAS member countries selected based on data availability over a period of 1995–2010. While they found a significant positive impact of financial freedom on FDI inflow, business and property rights freedom created some set back on the ability to attract FDI among those countries. In a similar study for the Middle East and North Africa (MENA) region in comparison with the European Union (EU), Caetano and Caleiro (2009) found that the extent of FDI inflows depend on the level of economic freedom, especially measures of transparency and corruption. Therefore, it will be beneficial for counties to improve the situation with corruption and level of transparency. In fact, many low-income developing countries suffer from restricted business freedom, flagrant abuses of copyrights, patent and franchise rights, political instability and risks as well as limited regulatory and financial architecture, and as such their ability to attract and sustain FDI is severely constrained as would any growth benefits that are attributable to FDI.

2.5 Trade Openness

Trade openness is another factor that can also play a significant role in the facilitation of the spillover of FDI gains to the host nation. There is the hypothesis that trade openness and FDI can be balancing for economic growth and that economies that promotes more open trade policies, particularly policies on export promotion, stand a better chance to benefit from the gains of FDI and its spillovers. Balasubramanyam et al. (1996) investigated the effect of inward FDI on economic growth but focused on the role of the trade regime. The results showed that the impact of FDI on economic growth is much stronger during an export-promotion trade regime rather than an import-substitution trade regime. Makki and Somwaru (2004) found that trade openness enables the spillover of FDI benefits to occur. On another hand, Carkovic and Levine (2005) failed to find a robust significant role for trade openness as a factor of absorptive capacity. Similarly, in a recent study, Mohamad and Bani (2017) investigate the impact of high FDI inflows and absorptive capacity on technological innovations in 39 developing economies using panel data from 1997 to 2014. Their observation was that while FDI inflows induce technological innovation in the country with an adequate level of absorptive capacity, trade openness is not significant in determining the level of technological innovations for the sample countries. With respect to causal linkages, Seyoum et al. (2014) used a balanced panel data for 25 sub-Saharan African countries over the period of 1977–2009 to examine the causal relationship between FDI and trade openness for the region and found a bidirectional causal relationship between FDI and trade openness among the sub-Saharan countries. Their result suggests that the promotion and attraction of FDI in SSA countries could expand their productive and export capacity and hence address supply-side constraints. This means that FDI could have positive multiplier effects on trade.

2.6 Institutional Quality

Institutional quality is the fifth factor, which has recently emerged in the literature as one of the factors of absorptive capacity. It has increasingly become an important variable in growth regression functions; therefore, it is hypothesized by some researchers as having the capability to act as a facilitating factor for FDI spillovers. A strong institutional set (such as the efficient legal systems, political stability, democratic accountability, and reduced bureaucracy) in the host nation/country would permit stronger linkages and connections between local firms and the foreign capital; hence, it would possibly increase the prospect of a spillover effect. Institutional quality has been examined as a factor of absorptive capacity in studies that generally examined the impact of financial openness such as Kose et al. (2009), Bekaert et al. (2010), and others that examined the impact of foreign R&D on the economy, such as Seck (2009) and Coe et al. (2009). All these studies, with the exception of Kose et al. (2009), found that institutional quality is a facilitating factor. Kose et al. (2009) found that a higher level of institutional quality is linked with a lower FDI impact. They interpreted their findings by arguing that with high institutional quality, even FDI is not very significant to Total Factor Productivity (TFP). With respect to developing countries, Cleeve (2012) found that institutional factors are important for attracting FDI to sub-Saharan Africa (SSA) countries, arguing that since FDI flows to Africa is highly sensitive to economic and political risks, policies to improve the institutional environment could significantly improve a country's ability to attract more FDI.

2.7 Infrastructure Development

Good infrastructure will reduce operating costs, facilitates production, and thereby stimulate FDI (Wheeler & Mody, 1992). Infrastructure leads to an increase in the productivity of investments and thereby lead to economic growth (Asiedu, 2002). In the literature, infrastructure development has often been measured by the number of telephones per 1,000 population (e.g. Asiedu, 2002). However, with the rising use of mobile phones, the amount of mobile phone subscriptions relative to the population is now an acceptable measure. Other measures that have been used in the literature include electric power transmission or consumption (e.g. Ayanwale, 2007), transport infrastructure (e.g. Pradhan et al., 2013), and gross fixed capital formation (e.g. Adi et al., 2015).

Some studies have examined the mediating role of infrastructure development on the relationship between FDI and growth while others examine the linkages between infrastructure, FDI and growth. Nourzad et al. (2014) examined the possible interaction between FDI and the host country's infrastructure base using a panel comprising 46 countries and 5-year averages over the period of 1980–2000. They base their empirical assessment on the hypothesis that the effect of FDI on real per capita income is dependent at least in part, on the size of infrastructure in the host country, using three types of infrastructure capital: power generation, telecommunication, and network of roads and highways. Their results showed that the size of the host country's infrastructure base helps in improving the marginal effect of FDI on real income. Asiedu (2002) also analyzed the determinants of FDI in developing countries and examined why countries in SSA have been relatively unsuccessful in the attraction of FDI despite policy reforms. Among other factors, her study showed that infrastructure (as measured by number of telephone lines per 1,000 population) promotes FDI to non-SSA countries but has no effect on FDI to SSA. This finding confirms those of Cleeve (2012) admitting that FDI flows to Africa is highly constrained by political and institutional impediments, of which poor infrastructure is one.

By contrast, FDI flows to some Southeast Asian countries and its impact on growth seem to be driven by the rapid rate of infrastructural development. For example, Pradhan et al. (2013) examined the long-run relationship between transport infrastructure, FDI, and economic growth in India and found evidence of a bidirectional causality between all three variables. Their study thus concluded that to generate additional FDI and economic growth, transport infrastructure development is a condition necessary to foster a faster economic growth while attracting more FDI can also foster transport infrastructure development and higher economic growth. In a similar vein, maintaining high economic growth can fast-track both FDI inflows and rapid transport infrastructural development in India. Bakar et al. (2012) also found that infrastructure has a positive and significant effect on FDI inflows to Malaysia as do other variables such as human capital, market size and trade openness.

2.8 Inflation

Increases in the consumer price index (CPI) are signs of inflation. Inflation can range from very high to very low. However, high inflation is mostly common in most developing countries. Inflation of 5%–8% is considered to be mild, and it appears to be beneficial to growth, but higher levels of inflation would be harmful to the economy in question (Thirlwall, 1974). Inflation can make domestic and foreign investors uncertain about the future profitability of investment projects, causing them to adopt more conservative investment strategies. This would result in lower levels of investment and thus slower economic growth. In addition, high inflation has the potential to harm a country's international competitiveness. The balance of payments suffers when a country's exports become more expensive relative to goods from other countries. Inflation can also have an effect on the tax system, causing lending and borrowing decisions to be distorted.

2.9 Market Size

The size of a country's market demand, as measured by GDP per capita, has a significant impact on foreign direct investment. FDI into developing economies with high buying power is primarily because companies can earn higher returns on their capital and thus generate more profit in such markets (Chege, 2015). This leads to a positive relationship between FDI inflows and GDP per capita because the increased market demand enables companies to raise their prices of goods and services, thereby increasing their profits. Inflows of FDI into economies with low GDP per capita are primarily because companies can operate more effectively in such markets because the cost of producing goods and services is lower. This ultimately leads to a negative relationship between FDI and GDP per capita because companies are less profitable and may even go out of business (Chege, 2015).

FDI into a country's economy is primarily aimed at making importable goods rather than exportable goods to capitalize on the low exchange rate (Shamsuddin, 1994). The size of the domestic market has a significant impact on FDI, which tries to make importable goods rather than exportable goods to capitalize on the low exchange rate (Shamsuddin, 1994). As one's native country's population grows, so does the demand for high-quality goods and services.

This creates a significant opportunity for multinational corporations to enter the market and fill the void by providing essential goods and services.

2.10 Foreign Exchange

The foreign exchange rate can be used to gauge international commerce. The main argument for increased exchange rate volatility resulting in lesser foreign trade is that there are risks, uncertainties, and transaction costs associated with exchange rate volatility, which limit the incentives to trade. Rather than short-term causality, the link between foreign exchange and economic growth is most likely driven by promoting long-term policy credibility (Tsangarides & Qureshi, 2010). Furthermore, any relationship between variability and international commerce could be driven by reverse causation, in which trade movements aid in the stabilization of actual foreign exchange rate swings, hence decreasing volatility (Broda & Romalis, 2011).

2.11 Conclusion

Most studies admit that FDI is a great source of growth capital, knowledge, and technology transfers to the host economy. However, many studies found that for the gains of FDI to be appropriated, the host country needs to develop absorptive capacities, which include improved financial markets, better human capital, greater economic freedom, more trade openness, increased transparency, institutional quality, and better infrastructure amongst other enabling factors.

References

Adi, A. A., Wobilor, A. K., & Adimani, W. E. (2015). Determinants of foreign direct investment and its effect on economic growth: Evidence from Nigeria. *Journal of Economics and Sustainable Development*, *6*(20), 17–25.

Ajide, K. B., & Eregha, P. B. (2014). Economic freedom and foreign direct investment in ECOWAS countries: A panel data analysis. *Applied Econometrics and International Development*, *14*(2), 163–174.

Alfaro, L., Chanda, A., Kalemli-Ozcan, S., & Sayek, S. (2004). FDI and economic growth: The role of local financial markets. *Journal of International Economics*, *64*, 89–112.

Alfaro, L., Chanda, A., Kalemli-Ozcan, S., & Sayek, S. (2010). Does foreign direct investment promote growth? Exploring the role of financial markets on linkages. *Journal of Development Economics*, *91*, 242–256.

Amadi, C. (2019). *FDI and economic growth in Nigeria: An analysis of the role of financial development on linkages* Doctoral dissertation. Manchester Metropolitan University.

Asiedu, E. (2002). On the development of foreign direct investment to developing countries: Is Africa different? *World Development*, *30*(1), 107–119.

Ayanwale, A. B. (2007). *FDI and economic growth: Evidence from Nigeria*, Africa Economic Research Consortium Research Paper No 165, AERC. https://publication.aercafricalibrary.org/handle/123456789/22

Baharumshah, A. Z., Slesman, L. Y., & Devadason, E. S. (2017). Types of foreign capital inflows and economic growth: New evidence on role of financial markets. *Journal of International Development*, *29*, 768–789.

Bakar, N. A. A., Mat, S. H. C., & Harun, M. (2012). The impact of infrastructure on foreign direct investment: The case of Malaysia. *Procedia - Social and Behavioral Sciences*, *65*, 205–211.

Balasubramanyam, V. N., Salisu, M., & Sapsford, D. (1996). Foreign direct investment and growth in EP and IS countries. *Economic Journal*, *106*, 92–105.

Bekaert, G., Harvey, C. R., & Lundblad, C. (2010). *Financial openness and productivity*. National Bureau of Economic Research Working Paper 14843.

Blonigen, B., & Wang, M. (2005). *Inappropriate pooling of wealthy and poor countries in empirical FDI studies*, In T. H. Moran, E. M. Graham, & M. Blomström (Eds.), In *Does foreign investment promote development*? (pp. 221–244). Institute for International Economics Center for Global Development.

Borensztein, E., Gregorio, J. D., & Lee, J. W. (1998). How does foreign direct investment affect economic growth? *Journal of International Economics*, *45*, 115–135.

Broda, C., & Romalis, J. (2011). Identifying the relationship between trade and exchange rate volatility. In *Commodity prices and markets* (pp. 79–110). University of Chicago Press.

Caetano, J., & Caleiro, A. (2009). Economic freedom and foreign direct investment: How different are the MENA countries from the EU? *iBusiness*, *1*, 65–74.

Carkovic, M., & Levine, R. (2005). *Does foreign direct investment accelerate economic growth*? In T. H. Moran, E. M. Graham, & M. Blomström (Eds.), In *Does foreign investment promote development*? (pp. 195–220). Institute for International Economics Center for Global Development.

Chege, I. (2015). Impact of foreign direct investments on economic growth in Kenya (1984-2013). *International Journal of Economics, Commerce and Management*, *3*(11).

Cleeve, E. (2012). Political and institutional impediments to foreign direct investment inflows to Sub-Saharan Africa. *Thunderbird International Business Review*, *54*(4), 469–477.

Coe, D. T., Helpman, E., & Hoffmaister, A. W. (2009). International R&D spillovers and institutions. *European Economic Review*, *53*(7), 723–741.

Darrat, A. F., Kherfi, S., & Soliman, M. (2005). FDI and economic growth in CEE and MENA countries: A tale of two regions In *Economic research forum, 12th annual conference*.

Hanushek, E. A., & Kimko, D. D. (2000). Schooling, labor-force quality, and the growth of nations. *The American Economic Review*, *90*(5), 1184–1208.

Hanushek, E. A., & Woessmann, L. (2008). The role of cognitive skills in economic development. *Journal of Economic Literature*, *46*(3), 607–668.

Hermes, N., & Lensink, R. (2003). Foreign direct investment, financial development and economic growth. *Journal of Development Studies*, *40*, 142–163.

Kinoshita, Y., & Lu, C. H. (2006). *On the role of absorptive capacity: FDI matters to growth* (p. 845). William Davidson Institute Working Paper.

Kose, A. M., Prasad, E. S., & Terrones, M. E. (2009). Does openness to international financial flows raise productivity growth? *Journal of International Money and Finance*, *28*(4), 554–580.

Li, X., & Liu, X. (2005). Foreign direct investment and economic growth: An increasingly endogenous relationship. *World Development*, *33*(3), 393–407.

Li, T. and Wang, Y. (2016) Growth channels of human capital: A Chinese panel data study. *China Economic Review* (in press). https://doi.org/10.1016/j.chieco.2016.11.002

Majeed, M. T., & Ahmad, E. (2008). Human capital development and FDI in developing countries. *Journal of Economic Cooperation*, *29*(3), 79–104.

Makki, S. S., & Somwaru, A. (2004). Impact of foreign direct investment and trade on economic growth: Evidence from developing countries. *American Journal of Agricultural Economics*, *86*(3), 795–801.

Mohamad, A., & Bani, Y. (2017). Foreign Direct Investment, absorptive capacity and technological innovation: Empirical evidence in developing economies, Governance and Sustainability on Global Business Economics. In *Proceedings of the Global Conference on Business and Economics Research (GCBER)*, 14-15 August 2017 (pp. 72–78). Universiti Putra Malaysia.

Nourzad, F., Greenwold, D. N., & Yang, R. (2014). The interaction between FDI and infrastructure capital in the development process. *International Advances in Economic Research*, *20*(2), 203–212.

Pradhan, R. P., Norman, N. R., Badir, Y., & Samadhan, B. (2013). Transport infrastructure, foreign direct investment and economic growth interactions in India: The ARDL bounds testing approach. *Procedia - Social and Behavioral Sciences*, *104*, 914–921.

Seck, A. (2009). International technology diffusion: Explaining the spillover benefits to African and other developing economiesIn *GLOBELICS, 7th international conference*.

Seyoum, M., Wu, R., & Lin, J. (2014). Foreign direct investment and trade openness in sub-saharan economies: A panel data granger causality analysis. *South African Journal of Economics*, *82*(3), 402–421.

Shah, M. H. (2016). *Financial development and foreign direct investment: The case of Middle East and North African (MENA) developing nations*. MPRA Paper No., 82013.

Shamsuddin, A. F. (1994). Economic determinants of foreign direct investment in less developed countries. *The Pakistan Development Review*, *33*(1), 41–51.

Thirlwall, A. P. (1974). *Inflation, saving and growth in developing economies*. Macmillan.

Tsangarides, C. G., & Qureshi, M. S. (2010). The empirics of exchange rate regimes and trade: Words vs. Deeds. *SSRN Electronic Journal*. https://doi.org/10.2139/ssrn.1562416

Wheeler, D., & Mody, A. (1992). International investment location decision: The case of US firms. *Journal of International Economics*, *33*, 57–70.

World Bank. (2001). *Global development finance report*. The World Bank.

Chapter 3

Foreign Direct Investment: The UK Case Study of Employment in the Technology Sector

Abstract

This chapter discusses the impact of foreign direct investment (FDI) on employment trends within the technology sector of the United Kingdom over a decade. The specific objectives include analyzing trends in FDI inflows, assessing correlations between FDI and employment levels, and identifying factors influencing this relationship. The chapter presents a correlation between FDI inflows and employment growth in the UK technology sector, with steady increases in both FDI investment and employment in the technology sector since 2012. Despite the positive impacts, challenges such as potential job displacement due to automation and the need for workforce upskilling were also identified.

Keywords: FDI; United Kingdom; employment; technology sector; technology transfer

3.1 Introduction

Globally, foreign direct investment (FDI) is one of the significant drivers of economic growth and development with countries actively competing to attract international capital. Among these countries, the United Kingdom stands out as one of the major destinations for FDI, with its technology sector being a key recipient. The United Kingdom's technology industry is known for its innovation, strength, and ambition and has consistently attracted investments from multinational corporations (MNCs) seeking to leverage its expertise and market potential (ONS, 2021). As FDI continues to flow into the United Kingdom's technology sector, it is important to understand its implications on the employment dynamics.

Foreign Direct Investment, 27–44

Published under exclusive licence by Emerald Publishing Limited
doi:10.1108/978-1-83662-900-920261003

Over the years, modern development of world economy often involves processes including transfer of new technologies, digitalization, internationalization of capital, and increase in the use of skilled labor (Popoola, 2020). To enhance and promote globalization, it is important for the field of communication among countries to improve and the global financial and stock market must develop (Nosova, 2022). FDI is an important tool that fosters globalization in these ways as it attracts foreign investors and capital into countries and contributes to increasing development in different sectors as well as the technological capabilities of the country. Several studies (Amadi, 2019; Dao et al., 2023; Saurav et al., 2020; Shittu et al., 2020) have shown efforts to understand the impact of FDI on economic growth, the investment motivations of its spillover effects, as well as the short- and long-term problems and possibilities.

Starting from the time of industrial revolution, the United Kingdom has a long history of attracting foreign investment. The country has positioned itself as a center for finance, commerce, and technological innovation as it attracts MNCs seeking access to its markets, human resources, and infrastructure. FDI inflows are further facilitated into the United Kingdom through government policies including tax incentives, streamlined regulations, and investment promotion agencies, which are aimed at promoting investment (HM Government, 2020). This contributes to the United Kingdom emerging as one of the key destinations for FDI in Europe and the world.

FDI can facilitate technology transfer, skill development, and collaboration between domestic and foreign firms (Comes et al., 2018). Technology transfer is one of the major benefits of FDI inflow through internationalization of research and development (R&D) and migration of skilled workers. According to Geng and Saggi (2019), FDI plays a crucial role in the dissemination of ideas and distribution of technologies across borders. The impact of international technology on growth greatly depends on the FDI policies in terms of level of compliance of new technologies with existing policies and how well the country received it (Hasna et al., 2023).

The United Kingdom is a high-level recipient country to FDI inflows as the government policies promote compliance with technologies. The technology sector in the United Kingdom experiences a rapid growth because of factors such as advancements in digital technology, increased venture capital investment, and government support for innovation and entrepreneurship (Nosova, 2022). Tech clusters in cities like London, Cambridge, and Manchester have flourished, attracting startups, established firms, and investors from around the globe (Tech Nation, 2020). The increase in the development of technology-driven businesses, ranging from fintech and biotech to artificial intelligence and cybersecurity, solidifies the United Kingdom as a leader in the global tech ecosystem.

FDI plays a crucial role in driving innovation, productivity, and competitiveness within the technology sector. Casella et al. (2023) in their study mentioned that it is important to measure the international presence in terms of FDI as the rate of employment in international affiliates compared to that of the total employment in the industry. Foreign corporations investing in the United Kingdom bring with them capital, technology, know-how, and access to international markets, which can stimulate growth and create employment opportunities.

3.2 Theoretical Perspectives on FDI and Employment

3.2.1 Neoclassical Theory

Neoclassical theory offers a fundamental perspective on the relationship between FDI and employment, emphasizing the role of market forces, investment, and productivity growth in driving economic development. According to this theory, FDI inflows result in increased investment, which in turn stimulates economic activity and job creation within the host country (Nguyen, 2022).

Neoclassical theory posits that FDI leads to job creation through increased investment and productivity. According to this perspective, MNCs invest in foreign countries to access new markets, resources, and labor at lower costs, thereby stimulating economic growth and employment (Sijabat, 2023). Rahman (2022) highlights that FDI inflows result in the expansion of existing firms or the establishment of new ventures, creating demand for labor and contributing to job creation within the host country. Additionally, he mentioned that FDI is believed to enhance efficiency and competitiveness in domestic industries, leading to further employment opportunities. Dimitrios (2023) added that one of the key mechanisms through which FDI contributes to employment is through capital accumulation. MNCs invest in physical capital, such as machinery, equipment, and infrastructure, to establish or expand their operations in foreign markets. This investment not only creates demand for construction and manufacturing workers but also enhances the productive capacity of the economy, leading to further job creation across various sectors (Sijabat, 2023).

Moreover, neoclassical theory posits that FDI promotes technological transfer and innovation, which drive productivity gains and competitiveness in domestic industries. MNCs often bring advanced technologies, managerial expertise, and best practices to host countries, facilitating knowledge spillovers and skill development among local firms and workers (Nguyen, 2022). As domestic firms adopt and adapt these technologies, they become more efficient and competitive, leading to increased output and employment opportunities. Neoclassical theory highlights the importance of market liberalization and deregulation in attracting FDI and promoting employment growth. By reducing barriers to entry, streamlining regulations, and promoting investment-friendly policies, host countries can create an enabling environment for MNCs to invest and operate, thereby fostering economic development and job creation (Rahman & Atiqur, 2022).

However, critics of neoclassical theory argue that it oversimplifies the complexities of the relationship between FDI and employment, overlooking potential negative externalities such as environmental degradation, labor market distortions, and income inequality (Rahman & Atiqur, 2022). Additionally, the theory may not fully account for the heterogeneity of FDI impacts across different industries, regions, and economic contexts.

3.2.2 Endogenous Growth Theory

Endogenous growth theory offers a nuanced perspective on the relationship between FDI and economic growth, emphasizing the role of innovation, technology adoption, and human capital accumulation in driving long-term prosperity (Chang et al., 2022). Chang et al. (2022) identifies that this theory provides valuable insights into the mechanisms through which FDI can contribute to sustained economic development while it also faces several limitations and challenges. According to this perspective, FDI inflows facilitate the transfer of knowledge, technology, and managerial practices from MNCs to domestic firms, leading to productivity gains and sustained economic growth (Nguyen, 2022). Through technology spillovers and knowledge diffusion, FDI stimulates innovation and enhances the human capital of the domestic workforce, thereby creating high-skilled employment opportunities in the host country's technology sector.

Moreover, endogenous growth theory highlights the importance of human capital accumulation in driving economic development. MNCs often invest in workforce training, skill development, and education programs in host countries, thereby enhancing the capabilities and productivity of the local workforce (Nguyen, 2022). As the level of human capital increases, countries are better equipped to absorb and adapt to new technologies, leading to sustained improvements in productivity and living standards.

However, endogenous growth theory also faces several criticisms and challenges. One of the main criticisms is the assumption of diminishing returns to capital, which implies that sustained economic growth requires continuous innovation and technological progress (Oughton et al., 2023). While FDI inflows may initially lead to productivity gains and employment creation, these effects may diminish over time as the economy reaches its technological frontier. Oughton et al. (2023) stated that endogenous growth theory may not fully account for the distributional effects of FDI on income inequality and poverty reduction. The study argued that while FDI inflows may contribute to overall economic growth, they may also exacerbate disparities in income distribution if the benefits of growth are not equitably distributed among different segments of the population. In the end, FDI-driven growth may lead to structural changes in the economy, resulting in job displacement and wage stagnation in certain sectors.

3.3 Conceptual Framework of FDI and Employment

FDI refers to the investment made by a company or individual from one country into business interests located in another country, with the intent of establishing lasting interest and control over the foreign business entity (Geng & Saggi, 2019). FDI entails a significant level of ownership and control, distinguishing it from portfolio investment where investors merely hold equity securities without actively managing the business operations. There are several types of FDI including horizontal and vertical FDI. In a study by Jinji et al. (2022), horizontal

FDI is described to involve MNCs establishing similar production facilities or conduct similar business activities in different countries. The primary motive behind horizontal FDI is to access new markets, exploit cost advantages, or mitigate risks such as trade barriers or currency fluctuations. Suryanta and Patunru (2023) discuss the FDI flow in Indonesia, emphasizing on the coexistence of horizontal and vertical FDI. The study described Vertical FDI as the integration of different stages of the production process across multiple countries. MNCs engage in vertical FDI to optimize production efficiencies, reduce costs, and enhance supply chain management. This type of investment often occurs when certain stages of production are more cost-effective or technologically advanced in foreign locations (Al-kasasbeh et al., 2022). Conglomerate FDI occurs when MNCs invest in businesses that are unrelated to their existing operations or industry focus. These investments are typically driven by opportunities for diversification, risk reduction, or strategic expansion into new markets or sectors (Jinji et al., 2022).

FDI can also be classified based on the mode of entry into foreign markets. Greenfield investment involves establishing new facilities or operations in a foreign country, while M&A involves acquiring existing businesses or assets. According to the study by Al-Kasasbeh et al. (2022), each mode of entry offers distinct advantages and challenges in terms of market access, risk management, and operational control. Understanding the different types of FDI is essential for analyzing its implications for economic development, employment generation, and industrial structure within host countries.

3.4 Impact of FDI on Employment Dynamics

3.4.1 FDI Inflows

FDI inflows play a crucial role in shaping employment dynamics within host countries, including the United Kingdom. While previous studies including Akinwalere and Chang (2023) have stated that FDI can have positive effects on employment through job creation, skill development, and technology transfer, Hakim et al. (2023) stated that its impact on employment dynamics is contingent upon various factors, including the level, composition, and nature of FDI inflows. The volume, composition, and characteristics of FDI inflows constitute the starting point of analysis. Factors such as the source country, sectoral distribution, and motives behind FDI play a crucial role in shaping its impact on employment dynamics (UNCTAD, 2022).

FDI inflows often lead to the establishment or expansion of MNCs and foreign-owned enterprises, creating direct employment opportunities for local workers (Dao et al., 2023). Dao et al. (2023) mention that MNCs may hire employees for various roles, including production, administration, R&D, and managerial position. For example, investments in manufacturing facilities, research centers, or service outlets can result in the recruitment of workers from the local labor market. It also states that MNCs bring advanced technologies, managerial expertise, and best practices to host countries through FDI inflows.

As local workers engage with these technologies and practices, they have the opportunity to acquire new skills, enhance their productivity, and improve their employability (Al-kasasbeh et al., 2022). For example, participation in training programs, knowledge-sharing initiatives, and technology transfer activities facilitated by MNCs can contribute to skill development among local employees.

However, the extent to which FDI inflows translate into job creation and skill development depends on the type and nature of FDI. Akinwalere and Chang (2023) highlighted that while greenfield investments involving the establishment of new ventures or facilities tend to create more jobs and opportunities for skill transfer, mergers and acquisitions may result in restructuring, downsizing, or relocation of operations, potentially leading to job losses. Therefore, the composition of FDI inflows is a critical determinant of their impact on employment dynamics. The impact of FDI inflows on employment varies across sectors and industries. FDI in high-tech sectors such as information technology, biotechnology, and pharmaceuticals may create high-skilled, knowledge-intensive jobs whereas FDI in traditional manufacturing sectors may generate low-skilled, labor-intensive employment (Hakim et al., 2023; UNCTAD, 2020). Therefore, the sectoral composition of FDI inflows influences the quality and distribution of employment opportunities within the economy.

In the United Kingdom, FDI inflows have contributed significantly to employment dynamics across various sectors. For instance, investments in the automotive industry by multinational automakers such as Nissan, Toyota, and Jaguar Land Rover have led to the creation of thousands of jobs in manufacturing, research, and engineering (HM Government, 2020). Similarly, FDI in the financial services sector has resulted in the establishment of new banking and investment firms, supporting employment growth in areas such as finance, accounting, and consultancy (Tech Nation, 2020). Unfortunately, challenges persist, particularly in sectors that are vulnerable to technological disruption and global competition. For instance, the retail sector has witnessed job losses and store closures due to changing consumer preferences and the rise of e-commerce platforms, leading to concerns about the impact of FDI on employment stability and job quality (ONS, 2020).

3.4.2 Investment Allocation

Investment allocation refers to the distribution and utilization of FDI inflows across different sectors and projects to significantly influence employment dynamics within host countries such as the United Kingdom. Nguyen (2023) emphasizes the need to analyze the distribution of FDI across industries, geographic regions, and types of investment to provide insights into their differential impact on employment. FDI allocation decisions often prioritize sectors with high growth potential, technological innovation, and comparative advantages. Investments in sectors such as technology, healthcare, and renewable energy can lead to the creation of high-quality, skilled employment opportunities (UNCTAD, 2022). For example, FDI allocations in R&D projects or innovation hubs can stimulate the creation of knowledge-intensive jobs, including researchers, engineers, and software developers. Investment allocations can also influence regional disparities in employment and economic development (Nguyen, 2023). Strategic FDI placements in regions with underutilized resources, infrastructure, or human capital can spur local job creation, infrastructure development, and industrial diversification (HM Government, 2020). For instance, investments in manufacturing plants or logistics centers in economically deprived regions can generate employment opportunities and stimulate economic growth.

However, despite the potential benefits of FDI allocations, there is a risk of sectoral imbalance and over-reliance on certain industries. Overemphasis on capital-intensive sectors or export-oriented industries may lead to job polarization, wage inequality, and vulnerability to external shocks (Bloom et al., 2019). An example is the excessive FDI allocations in finance or real estate sectors can inflate asset prices, exacerbate housing affordability issues, and distort labor markets. In addition, investment allocations may not always align with the skill needs and demands of the labor market. While FDI inflows in high-tech sectors can create opportunities for skilled workers, they may also exacerbate skills mismatches and labor market segmentation (Saucedo et al., 2020). Insufficient investments in education, vocational training, and lifelong learning initiatives may hinder the ability of the workforce to adapt to changing skill requirements, limiting their employability and productivity.

In the United Kingdom, investment allocations have played a significant role in shaping employment dynamics across different sectors and regions. For instance, government-led initiatives such as the Industrial Strategy Challenge Fund have allocated FDI to strategic sectors such as advanced manufacturing, artificial intelligence, and clean energy (ONS, 2020). Investments in projects such as the Offshore Wind Sector Deal have stimulated job creation in regions with strong offshore wind potential, such as the Northeast of England and Scotland, through the establishment of manufacturing facilities, research centers, and supply chain networks. However, challenges persist, particularly in sectors facing structural changes and technological disruptions such as investments in automation and digitalization leading to job displacement in traditional industries such as manufacturing, retail, and hospitality (ONS, 2020). Moreover, Saucedo et al. (2020) state that regional disparities in investment allocations may exacerbate inequalities in employment opportunities and economic outcomes across different regions of the United Kingdom.

3.4.3 Technology Transfer

Technology transfer refers to the process by which knowledge, skills, and technologies are disseminated from MNCs to domestic firms. It is a key mechanism through which FDI influences employment dynamics within host countries. The study by Newman et al. (2015) argued that despite technology transfer being able to enhance productivity, innovation, and competitiveness, its impact on employment is shaped by various factors and presents both opportunities and challenges that warrant critical examination. Assessing the extent and mechanisms of technology transfer is essential for understanding its implications for skill development, productivity, and employment creation (Geng & Saggi, 2019). Chan et al. (2024) state that FDI inflows often bring advanced technologies, R&D capabilities, and managerial expertise to host countries, facilitating productivity gains and efficiency improvements in domestic firms. The study further mentioned that through technology transfer initiatives, MNCs can share proprietary knowledge, best practices, and production techniques with local partners, leading to increased output per worker and higher value-added activities. The findings of Chan et al. (2024) identified technology transfer as a stimulant to innovation and skill development among local workers, contributing to long-term economic growth and employment generation. By engaging with cutting-edge technologies and research collaborations facilitated by MNCs, employees can acquire new skills, adapt to technological changes, and participate in knowledge-intensive activities (Casella et al., 2023). For example, investments in research centers, innovation hubs, and technology parks can foster collaboration between academia, industry, and government, leading to the creation of high-skilled, knowledge-intensive jobs.

Newman et al. (2015) added that the effectiveness of technology transfer depends on the absorptive capacity of domestic firms and institutions to assimilate, adapt, and leverage foreign technologies. The findings from the study stated that host countries with weak innovation ecosystems, inadequate infrastructure, and limited human capital may struggle to fully capitalize on FDI-induced technology transfer, leading to suboptimal outcomes in terms of productivity and employment generation. Concerns about intellectual property rights (IPR) protection and technology leakage may inhibit the transfer of proprietary technologies and know-how from MNCs to domestic firms (Dabnichi & Abderrahim, 2023). This may lead to MNCs hesitating to share sensitive technologies or invest in R&D activities in host countries with weak IPR enforcement mechanisms, fearing unauthorized imitation or appropriation of their intellectual assets.

In the United Kingdom, technology transfer facilitated by FDI has contributed to employment dynamics across various sectors. For instance, investments by multinational technology companies, such as Google, Microsoft, and Apple, have led to the establishment of research centers, innovation labs, and software development hubs in cities like London, Cambridge, and Edinburgh (Tech Nation, 2020). These investments have created high-skilled, knowledge-intensive jobs in areas such as software engineering, data analytics, and artificial intelligence. Moreover, collaborations between multinational pharmaceutical firms and UK-based research institutions have resulted in technology transfer agreements, joint ventures, and licensing agreements, leading to the development of new drugs, medical devices, and biotechnologies (HM Government, 2020). For example, investments in biotechnology clusters such as the Golden Triangle (Oxford, Cambridge, and London) have stimulated innovation, entrepreneurship, and job creation in the life sciences sector.

3.4.4 Labor Markets

FDI can impact labor markets through various channels, including direct employment by foreign affiliates, job creation in domestic supplier firms, and changes in wage levels and working conditions (Dao et al., 2023). FDI inflows are often attracted to countries with competitive labor costs relative to productivity levels. Lower wage levels or favorable wage-productivity ratios can incentivize MNCs to invest in labor-intensive industries, such as manufacturing, assembly, and customer service, leading to job creation and employment growth (Kharel, 2020). For example, investments in automotive manufacturing plants in regions like the West Midlands have capitalized on the availability of skilled and semi-skilled labor, contributing to job creation and industrial development (HM Government, 2020). Labor market dynamics influence the availability and quality of skills essential for attracting and retaining FDI. Saurav et al. (2020) identified regions with a well-educated workforce, strong vocational training programs, and specialized skill sets as preferred destinations for knowledge-intensive investments, such as R&D centers, software development hubs, and high-tech manufacturing facilities (Tech Nation, 2020). For instance, investments in technology clusters like Silicon Roundabout in London have benefited from the availability of skilled software engineers, data scientists, and technology entrepreneurs.

However, labor market regulations, including employment protection legislation, minimum wage laws, and collective bargaining agreements, can influence the flexibility and cost of hiring and firing workers (Hakim et al., 2023; Li et al., 2023). Li et al. (2023) posits that while stringent labor regulations may enhance worker protections and social welfare, they can also deter investment and job creation, particularly in industries with uncertain demand or fluctuating market conditions. For example, concerns about labor market rigidity and compliance costs may influence investment decisions in sectors such as manufacturing, logistics, and hospitality where flexibility and cost competitiveness are crucial for competitiveness.

In the United Kingdom, labor market dynamics have shaped FDI patterns and employment outcomes across different sectors and regions. For instance, investments in the financial services sector in cities like London and Edinburgh have benefited from the availability of skilled professionals in areas such as finance, accounting, and consultancy. Similarly, investments in creative industries such as film production, advertising, and design have capitalized on the availability of creative talent and cultural diversity in cities like Manchester, Bristol, and Glasgow (Creative Industries Federation, 2020).

However, challenges persist, particularly in sectors facing structural changes and technological disruptions. For example, investments in automation and digitalization may lead to job displacement in traditional industries such as manufacturing, retail, and hospitality (ONS, 2020).

3.5 Historical Overview of FDI in the United Kingdom

Following World War II, the United Kingdom pursued a policy of economic liberalization and openness to foreign investment, seeking to attract capital, technology, and expertise from abroad (Lim, 2001). The United Kingdom's accession to the European Economic Community (EEC) in 1973 further facilitated FDI inflows by providing access to a larger market and promoting trade and investment integration within Europe. During the 1980s under the Thatcher government, the United Kingdom embarked on a program of privatization and deregulation, aiming to reduce state intervention in the economy and promote private sector-led growth (Dunning, 1998). Privatization of state-owned enterprises and liberalization of key sectors such as telecommunications, utilities, and transportation attracted significant FDI inflows from MNCs seeking investment opportunities in newly privatized industries.

In recent years, the United Kingdom has adopted a more cautious approach toward FDI, particularly in sensitive sectors such as defense, telecommunications, and critical infrastructure. Growing concerns about foreign influence, espionage, and technology transfer have prompted policymakers to strengthen investment screening mechanisms and introduce stricter regulations to safeguard national security interests (HM Government, 2020). The UK Government has undertaken initiatives to modernize and streamline the FDI regulatory framework to enhance transparency, predictability, and efficiency for investors (Gurshev & Hamza, 2021). The establishment of the Investment Security Unit (ISU) within the Department for Business, Energy, and Industrial Strategy (BEIS) aims to provide guidance, assess national security risks, and review proposed investments in strategic sectors.

The evolving FDI policy landscape in the United Kingdom reflects a delicate balance between promoting openness to foreign investment and safeguarding national security interests. Striking the right balance requires policymakers to consider the potential benefits of FDI for economic growth, innovation, and job creation while also addressing legitimate concerns about foreign control, technology transfer, and industrial competitiveness. Ensuring coherence and consistency across different government departments and agencies involved in FDI regulation is essential for effective policymaking and implementation (Treisman, 2020). Clear guidelines, transparent decision-making processes, and stakeholder engagement are critical for maintaining investor confidence and minimizing regulatory uncertainty.

3.5.1 Trends and Patterns in FDI Inflows Into the United Kingdom Over the Decade

Over the past decade, FDI inflows into the United Kingdom have increasingly favored the services sector, particularly finance, information technology, and professional services. London, as a global financial hub, continues to attract significant investments from multinational banks, fintech firms, and insurance companies, bolstering its position as a leading financial center (Tech Nation,

2020). Despite uncertainties surrounding Brexit and geopolitical tensions, high-tech industries such as pharmaceuticals, biotechnology, and digital technology have remained attractive destinations for FDI (HM Government, 2020). Investments in R&D facilities, innovation hubs, and technology clusters have contributed to job creation, innovation, and economic resilience (ONS, 2020).

Historically, the majority of FDI inflows into the United Kingdom have originated from European countries, particularly from the European Union (EU) member states. However, Brexit-related uncertainties have led to some reorientation of investment flows, with investors from EU countries adopting a more cautious approach or exploring alternative markets within the EU single market (HM Treasury, 2021). In recent years, there has been growing interest from Asian investors, particularly from China, Japan, and South Korea, seeking opportunities in the UK market. Investments in infrastructure, real estate, and technology sectors by Asian sovereign wealth funds, conglomerates, and technology giants have diversified the sources of FDI inflows into the United Kingdom.

The United Kingdom's large consumer market, skilled workforce, and business-friendly environment continue to attract FDI inflows, particularly from companies seeking access to European markets post-Brexit (HM Government, 2020). London's status as a global financial center, cultural diversity, and vibrant startup ecosystem also contribute to its attractiveness for foreign investors (Tech Nation, 2020). Investments in technology-intensive industries, including digital technology, artificial intelligence, and biotechnology, reflect growing investor interest in innovation-driven sectors with high growth potential (HM Government, 2020). The UK Government's support for research and innovation, through initiatives such as the Industrial Strategy Challenge Fund and the Catapult Network, has further incentivized investments in R&D and technology transfer activities.

The United Kingdom's decision to leave the EU has introduced uncertainties and challenges for FDI inflows, particularly in sectors highly dependent on access to the EU single market, such as financial services, automotive, and aerospace (HM Treasury, 2021). Driffield and Karoglou (2019) argued that while some companies have relocated operations or adopted wait-and-see approaches, others have chosen to invest in the United Kingdom to maintain market presence and access talent pools. The United Kingdom's FDI inflows are also influenced by broader global economic trends, including shifts in trade patterns, geopolitical tensions, and macroeconomic stability. Economic recovery from the COVID-19 pandemic, changes in trade policies, and technological disruptions will shape investor perceptions and decisions regarding FDI inflows into the United Kingdom in the coming years (HM Treasury, 2021).

3.5.2 The Role of FDI in Shaping the United Kingdom's Economic Landscape With a Focus on Employment Over the Decade

FDI inflows have been instrumental in creating employment opportunities across a wide range of sectors in the United Kingdom. MNCs investing in the United Kingdom establish new businesses, expand existing operations, and invest in infrastructure, thereby generating jobs for both skilled and unskilled workers. FDI often brings advanced technologies, managerial expertise, and best practices to the United Kingdom, leading to skill development and capacity building among the workforces. According to ONS (2019), investments in R&D centers, innovation hubs, and technology clusters contribute to the upskilling of employees and the creation of high-value jobs in knowledge-intensive industries. FDI has played a crucial role in promoting regional economic development and reducing geographical disparities in employment opportunities across the United Kingdom (Khan, 2023).

Khan (2023) states that while FDI contributes to job creation, it can also lead to job displacement, particularly in sectors facing technological disruptions and structural changes. Investments in automation, digitalization, and artificial intelligence may result in the substitution of labor with capital-intensive technologies, leading to job losses and skills mismatches in traditional industries (ONS, 2020). Unfortunately, the distributional effects of FDI on wages and income inequality remain a concern. The FDI inflows create high-paying jobs in knowledge-intensive sectors, they may also exacerbate wage differentials between skilled and unskilled workers, contributing to widening income disparities and social inequalities (Driffield & Karoglou, 2019).

3.6 Empirical Evidence on FDI and Employment in the United Kingdom

A growing body of quantitative research has investigated the relationship between FDI inflows and employment levels in the United Kingdom, with mixed findings regarding the magnitude and direction of the impact. While some studies find evidence of a positive association between FDI and employment, others suggest more nuanced relationships influenced by sectoral characteristics, firm-level dynamics, and macroeconomic factors (Hakim et al., 2023). Studies focusing on the technology sector have highlighted the importance of FDI in driving job creation, innovation, and productivity growth. Research by Nosova (2022) suggests that FDI inflows into the United Kingdom's high-tech industries positively contribute to employment levels, particularly in research-intensive activities such as R&D, engineering, and software development. Quantitative studies employ various econometric techniques, including panel data analysis, difference-in-differences estimation, and instrumental variable regression, to assess the causal relationship between FDI inflows and employment outcomes (Jinji et al., 2022). By controlling for endogeneity, simultaneity, and omitted variable biases, researchers aim to identify the causal impact of FDI on employment levels in the United Kingdom. These studies rely on comprehensive datasets, including firm-level surveys, national employment statistics, and FDI databases, to analyze the relationship between FDI inflows and employment dynamics. By leveraging rich data sources, researchers can capture sectoral heterogeneity, regional variations, and temporal trends in FDI-induced job creation within the United Kingdom (Li et al., 2023). Studies provide evidence of a positive association between FDI inflows and employment levels in the United Kingdom, particularly in technology-intensive sectors such as information technology, biotechnology, and telecommunications. Khan (2023) highlights FDI-induced investments in R&D, innovation, and technology transfer stimulate job creation, skills upgrading, and knowledge spillovers, leading to overall employment growth. However, the relationship between FDI and employment outcomes varies across sectors and industries. Newman et al. (2015) argued that while high-tech industries may benefit from FDI-induced innovation and technology adoption, traditional sectors facing structural challenges may experience job displacement and skill mismatches. The sectoral composition, absorptive capacity, and regulatory environment play crucial roles in shaping the employment effects of FDI in the United Kingdom.

Qualitative case studies provide in-depth explorations of specific FDI projects or investment decisions, offering insights into the unique features of FDI projects, including investment size, sectoral focus, geographical location, and institutional context. By contextualizing FDI inflows within broader economic, social, and political frameworks, researchers can identify key drivers, barriers, and implications for employment dynamics in host countries (Buckley et al., 2018). Qualitative research methods, such as interviews, surveys, and focus groups, enable researchers to capture diverse stakeholder perspectives on the employment effects of FDI.

According to Nguyen (2023), engaging with policymakers, industry representatives, trade unions, and local communities helps to explore the distributional impacts, social consequences, and policy implications of FDI-induced employment changes. Studies like Gurshev and Hamza (2021) employ narrative analysis and storytelling techniques to unpack the lived experiences, narratives, and discourses surrounding FDI and employment dynamics. By examining individual stories, organizational narratives, and media discourses, researchers can uncover the sociocultural, psychological, and ideological dimensions of FDI-induced employment transformations.

Research like Dabnichi and Abderrahim (2023) has revealed the complex interactions between FDI inflows, firm strategies, and labor market dynamics, highlighting the heterogeneity of employment outcomes across sectors, regions, and firms. By capturing the lived experiences and perspectives of stakeholders, these qualitative research offers nuanced insights into the mechanisms through which FDI influences employment patterns, wage structures, and job quality.

3.7 Factors Affecting the Relationship Between FDI and Employment

3.7.1 Level of Innovation

The technology sector is characterized by high levels of innovation, R&D investment, driving productivity growth and employment creation. FDI inflows into the technology sector stimulate innovation diffusion, knowledge spillovers, and skill upgrading, leading to the creation of high-value jobs in research-intensive activities such as software development, biotechnology, and engineering. FDI fosters the formation of innovation networks, collaborative partnerships, and knowledge clusters within the technology sector, enabling firms to leverage external knowledge sources, share best practices, and access global markets (Akinwalere & Chang, 2023). By investing in innovation hubs, technology parks, and research institutions, FDI enhances the absorptive capacity of local firms and stimulates entrepreneurship, leading to job creation and economic diversification.

3.7.2 Competition Dynamics

The technology sector exhibits dynamic competition dynamics, characterized by rapid product cycles, disruptive innovation, and market entry barriers (Nosova, 2022). FDI inflows into the technology sector may lead to market consolidation, industry restructuring, and changes in firm ownership, influencing employment patterns through mergers, acquisitions, and strategic alliances. FDI enables MNCs to leverage their technological expertise, brand reputation, and global networks to gain a competitive advantage in the technology sector (Suryanta & Patunru, 2023). While FDI-induced investments in innovation and technology transfer may enhance the competitiveness of domestic firms, they may also pose challenges for small and medium-sized enterprises (SMEs) and startups, which face difficulties in accessing capital, talent, and markets (Newman et al., 2015).

3.8 Conclusion

There is a positive correlation between FDI inflows and employment levels in the United Kingdom's technology sector over the past decade. Evidence indicates that increased FDI has contributed to expansion of the technology industry, leading to the creation of new job opportunities and promoting the workforce. The growth in FDI has contributed to the workforce expansion, particularly in specialized areas such as software development, IT support, and telecommunications. Asides the number of new jobs and increase in employment by foreign companies, FDI also impacts other aspects of employment including wages and quality of skills. This can be linked to increase in competition between foreign and local firms and the overall increase in the GVA (Gross Value Added). The influx of foreign investment has enhanced the United Kingdom's technology landscape and attracted skilled talent and fostering innovation.

Despite the positive impacts, challenges have emerged. This includes potential job displacement due to automation and the introduction of new technologies by foreign investors. Research highlights the critical importance of upskilling and reskilling the workforce to adapt to evolving technological demands as well as to minimize the negative effects of automation on employment as well as proactive policy interventions to maximize the benefits of FDI. This should be done alongside mitigating its potential adverse impacts on employment. Policymakers must prioritize investments in education and training programs tailored to the needs of the technology sector. Moreso, policy frameworks should incentivize innovation and entrepreneurship to stimulate job creation and economic growth.

Despite the uncertainties in global economy, the United Kingdom remains an attractive destination for FDI in technology sector, particularly in areas such as software development, IT support, and telecommunications. It is important to maintain a conducive and favorable business environment, such as regulatory stability, access to skilled labor, and robust infrastructure, to sustain the momentum of FDI inflows and stimulate economic growth.

References

Akinwalere, S., & Chang, K. (2023). The determinants of foreign-direct-investment (FDI) inflows in Nigeria. *Journal of Developing Areas*, *57*(4), 91–105.

Al-kasasbeh, O., Alzghoul, A., & Alghraibeh, K. (2022). Global FDI inflows and outflows in emerging economies post-COVID-19 era. *Future Business Journal*, *8*, 53. https://doi.org/10.1186/s43093-022-00167-z

Amadi, C. (2019). *FDI and economic growth in Nigeria: An analysis of the role of financial development on linkages*. Doctoral dissertation. Manchester Metropolitan University.

Bloom, N., Van Reenen, J., & Heidi, W. (2019). A toolkit of policies to promote innovation. *The Journal of Economic Perspectives*, *33*(3), 163–184.

Buckley, P. J., Chen, L., Clegg, L. J., & Voss, H. (2018). Risk propensity in the foreign direct investment location decision of emerging multinationals. *Journal of International Business Studies*, *49*(2), 153–171.

Casella, B., Borga, M., & Wacker, K. (2023). *Measuring multinational production with foreign direct investment statistics*. IMF Working Papers, 2023(113), A001.

Chan, S. G., Har, W. M., Kanapathy, K., Celik, S., & Aktan, B. (2024). Country-of-origin effects on technology transfer in foreign direct investment. *The Journal of International Trade & Economic Development*, *33*(7), 1345–1370.

Chang, Q., Wu, M., & Zhang, L. (2022). Endogenous growth and human capital accumulation in a data economy. *Structural Change and Economic Dynamics, Forthcoming*. https://ssrn.com/abstract=4248918. https://doi.org/10.2139/ssrn.4248918.

Comes, C. A., Bunduchi, E., Vasile, V., & Stefan, D. (2018). The impact of foreign direct investments and remittances on economic growth: A case study in Central and Eastern Europe. *Sustainability*, *10*(1), 238.

Creative Industries Federation. (2020). *Creative Industries in the UK: Facts and Figures 2020*. https://www.creativeindustriesfederation.com/statistics-hub

Dabnichi, Y., & Abderrahim, F. (2023). FDI, technology transfer and economic growth, what's the connection? The case of Morocco. *American Journal of Applied Statistics and Economics*, *3*(1), 33–43. https://doi.org/10.54536/ajase.v3i1.2276

Dao, T., Khuc, V., Dong, M., & Cao, T. (2023). How does foreign direct investment drive employment growth in Vietnam's formal economy? *Economies*, *11*(11), 266.

Dimitrios, N. (2023). Revisiting cournot and neoclassical economics. *History of Economics Review*, *84*(1), 4–20. https://doi.org/10.1080/10370196.2022.2149130

Driffield, N., & Karoglou, M. (2019). Brexit and foreign investment in the UK. *Journal of the Royal Statistical Society Series A: Statistics in Society*, *182*(2), 559–582. https://doi.org/10.1111/rssa.12417

Dunning, J. H. (1998). Location and the multinational enterprise: A neglected factor? *Journal of International Business Studies*, *29*, 45–66. https://doi.org/10.1057/palgrave.jibs.8490024

Geng, D., & Saggi, K. (2019). *Foreign direct investment and international technology diffusion*. Oxford Research Encyclopedia of Economics and Finance.

Gurshev, O., & Hamza, S. (2021). BITs, colony ties, and offshore centers: The case of United Kingdom outward FDI. *Journal of Economic Integration*, *36*(2), 203–226. https://www.jstor.org/stable/27019033

Hakim, D. R., Ahman, E., & Kusnendi, K. (2023). The effect of FDI on the host countries' employment: A meta-regression analysis. *Russian Journal of Economics*, *9*(2), 158–182. https://doi.org/10.32609/j.ruje.9.98252

Hasna, M. Z., Jaumotte, M. F., Kim, J., Pienknagura, S., & Schwerhoff, G. (2023). *Green innovation and diffusion: Policies to accelerate them and expected impact on macroeconomic and firm-level performance*. International Monetary Fund.

HM Government. (2020). *UK investment support directory*. https://www.great.gov.uk/international/content/about/investment-support-directory/

HM Treasury. (2021). *UK economic and fiscal outlook: March 2021*. https://assets.publishing.service.gov.uk/government/uploads/system/uploads/attachment_data/file/969766/Economic_and_Fiscal_Outlook_March_2021_web.pdf

Jinji, N., Zhang, X., & Haruna, S. (2022). Vertical versus horizontal foreign direct investment and technology spillovers. In *Deep integration, global firms, and technology spillovers advances in Japanese business and economics* (Vol. 26). Springer. https://doi.org/10.1007/978-981-16-5210-3_6

Khan, E. U. (2023). The post-Brexit paradigm: Investigating the effects of foreign direct investment on economic growth in the United Kingdom. *Archives of the Social Sciences: A Journal of Collaborative Memory*, *2*(1), 94–110. https://doi.org/10.5281/zenodo.8151602

Kharel, K. R. (2020). Foreign direct investment in Nepal: A study on its impact on employment. *Interdisciplinary Journal of Management and Social Sciences*, *1*(1), 54–66. https://doi.org/10.3126/ijmss.v1i1.34511

Li, Y., Miao, Z., Wang, J., & Zhang, Y. (2023). *The FDI liberalization and skill structure of labor market in China: The predicament of migrants*. https://ideas.repec.org/p/pra/mprapa/117923.html

Lim, E. G. (2001). *Determinants of, and the relation between, foreign direct investment and growth a summary of the recent literature*. IMF Working Papers, 2001(175), A001. https://digitallibrary.un.org/record/458080

Newman, C., Rand, J., Talbot, T., & Tarp, F. (2015). Technology transfers, foreign investment and productivity spillovers. *European Economic Review*, *76*, 168–187. https://doi.org/10.1016/j.euroecorev.2015.02.005

Nguyen, M. (2022). *Foreign direct investment and economic growth: The role of financial development* (Vol. 9, p. 1). Cogent Business and Management. https://doi.org/10.1080/23311975.2022.2127193

Nguyen, V. C. (2023). Monetary policy and foreign direct investment – Empirical evidence. *Economies*, *11*(9), 234.

Nosova, O. (2022). The impact of foreign direct investment in the high-tech sector economy. *Applied Business: Issues and Solutions*, *1*, 3–9.

Office for National Statistics (ONS). (2020). *Labour market overview, UK: September 2020*. https://www.ons.gov.uk/employmentandlabourmarket/peopleinwork/employmentandemployeetypes/bulletins/uklabourmarket/september2020

ONS. (2021). *Foreign direct investment involving UK companies: 2021*. https://www.ons.gov.uk/economy/nationalaccounts/balanceofpayments/bulletins/foreigndirectinvestmentinvolvingukcompanies/2021

Oughton, C., Tobin, D., & Robinson, J. (2023). Early endogenous growth theorist. *Cambridge Journal of Economics*, *47*(5), 943–964. https://doi.org/10.1093/cje/bead032

Popoola, J. (2020). Globalization and Nigeria's economic development—A study of the interconnectedness. *Open Journal of Political Science*, *10*, 460–480.

Rahman, M. A. (2022). A critical review of neoclassical and behavioural theories of merger waves. *Financial Studies*, *26*(1), 6–22.

Rahman, M., & Atiqur, A. (2022). A critical review of neoclassical and behavioural theories of merger wave. *Financial Studies*, *26*(1), 6–22. https://ssrn.com/abstract=4127143

Saucedo, E., Ozuna, T., & Zamora, H. (2020). The effect of FDI on low and high-skilled employment and wages in Mexico: A study for the manufacture and service sectors. *Journal for Labour Market Research*, *54*, 9. https://doi.org/10.1186/s12651-020-00273-x

Saurav, A., Liu, Y., & Sinha, A. (2020). *Foreign direct investment and employment outcomes in developing countries*. World Bank.

Shittu, W. O., Yusuf, H. A., El Moctar El Houssein, A., & Hassan, S. (2020). The impacts of foreign direct investment and globalisation on economic growth in West Africa: Examining the role of political governance. *Journal of Economic Studies*, *47*(7), 1733–1755.

Sijabat, R. (2023). The association between foreign investment and gross domestic product in ten ASEAN countries. *Economies*, *11*, 188. https://doi.org/10.3390/economies11070188

Suryanta, B., & Patunru, A. A. (2023). Determinants of foreign direct investment in Indonesia. *Global Journal of Emerging Market Economies*, *15*(1), 109–131. https://doi.org/10.1177/09749101211067856

Tech Nation. (2020). *Tech Nation Report 2020* [Online]. https://technation.io/wp-content/uploads/2020/03/Tech-Nation-Report-2020-UK-Tech-For-A-Changing-World-v1_0.pdf

Treisman, D. (2020, May). Economic development and democracy: Predispositions and triggers. *Annual Review of Political Science*, *23*, 241–257. https://ssrn.com/abstract=3602493. https://doi.org/10.1146/annurev-polisci-050718-043546

UNCTAD. (2020). World investment report 2020. In *United Nations conference on trade and development*. https://unctad.org/system/files/official-document/wir2020_en.pdf

UNCTAD. (2022). *World Investment Report 2022*. United Nations Conference on Trade and Development. https://unctad.org/system/files/official-document/wir2022_en.pdf

Chapter 4

Foreign Direct Investment: South Africa Case Study on Climate Change

Abstract

The relationship between economic development and environmental sustainability has become a pivotal concern in the contemporary world, particularly in the context of global climate change. Foreign direct investment (FDI) has emerged as a crucial factor in this discourse, often posited as both a driver of economic growth and a potential contributor to environmental degradation. This chapter delves into the intricate relationship between economic growth and environmental sustainability, with a particular focus on how FDI impacts climate change in South Africa. The chapter aims to provide a comprehensive understanding of the patterns connecting FDI and climate change in South Africa.

Keywords: FDI; economic growth; climate change; South Africa; environmental sustainability

4.1 Introduction

Foreign direct investment (FDI) is considered one of the engines of economic growth in developing countries because it can provide additional capital, technology, and management skills that can increase productivity and create jobs (Amadi, 2019). However, the impact of FDI on South Africa's economic growth is not clear-cut and depends on several factors, such as the quality of institutions, the level of human capital, and the quality of infrastructure. For example, Ndou and Mokoena (2019) found that the impact of FDI on economic growth in South Africa is greater in provinces with better infrastructure and higher levels of human capital. The study also found that the impact of FDI on economic growth is lower in provinces with higher levels of corruption. Empirical evidence shows that FDI has a positive effect on economic growth in South Africa, but this effect depends on several factors. Policymakers should focus on creating an enabling

Foreign Direct Investment, 45–63

doi:10.1108/978-1-83662-900-920261004

environment for FDI by improving institutions, investing in human capital, and improving infrastructure.

4.2 Foreign Direct Investment

FDI entails making investments to get a significant managerial stake and at least 10% of the stock in a foreign business that operates outside the investor's home country. It is the investment made by people, businesses, or other organizations from one nation into another with the intention of acquiring a sizable stake in and control over a foreign firm (Balsalobre-Lorente et al., 2022). From a different perspective, Hamid et al. (2022) describe it as a long-term commitment and the cross-border movement of money, technology, skills, and information that serves goals such as market access, resource acquisition, cost benefits, and innovation. This type of investment can take many different forms, including Greenfield investments, and is driven by a variety of objectives, such as expanding into new markets, gaining access to resources, cutting costs, and lowering risk (Sarkodie et al., 2020).

FDI plays a significant role in a nation's economic growth. It brings in fresh resources in terms of money, technology, and knowledge, which might result in the development of jobs and a rise in productivity (Adedoyin et al., 2022). FDI can also assist in bridging the technological divide and spurring economic growth by facilitating the transfer of knowledge, expertise, and technology from developed to developing nations (Duodu et al., 2022). Similarly, the home nation also gains from FDI through market development, risk diversification, knowledge acquisition, and balance of payments improvement. Inversely, the exploitation of natural resources, the destruction of the environment, and the eviction of residents are examples of its potential drawbacks (Tan & Uprasen, 2022). Studies (e.g., Faheem et al., 2022; Nyeadi, 2022) have also indicated other factors that can impede FDI, including political instability, economic circumstances, market size, regulations, enticements, facilities, and employment opportunities.

4.3 FDI and Economic Growth

FDI is often regarded as a key driver of economic growth. However, the empirical evidence is varied, indicating that there is a negative, positive, and equal link between FDI and economic growth. The empirical evidence is classified into four hypotheses: First, FDI-led growth hypothesis, this hypothesis claims that from FDI to economic growth, there is one-way causal flow; second, growth-led FDI hypothesis states that economic growth is what drives FDI (Granger-effects FDI); third, FDI and economic growth cause one another, arguing that there is bidirectional causal link between FDI and economic growth and lastly studies demonstrate that there is no causal relationship between FDI and economic growth (neutrality hypothesis).

The endogenous growth model, which forms the basis of the FDI-led economic growth hypothesis, asserts that FDI's impacts on economic growth have been significant when combined with other variables including capital, exports, technology transfer, and human capital. These growth-spurring factors might be introduced and nurtured to stimulate economic growth through FDI. Some studies suggest that the inflow of FDI might be able to stimulate a country's economic performance through technology transfer and spill over efficiency. When indigenous enterprises can absorb the material and intangible assets of multinational corporations (MNCs) represented by FDI, spill over efficiency is assumed to emerge. The level of technology and productivity (for both labor and capital) of local producers is also projected to increase when FDI creates backward and forward linkages and when MNCs provide technical help to domestic enterprises (Borensztein et al., 1998).

The GDP-led FDI hypothesis is primarily based on the theory of MNCs in contrast to the FDI-led economic growth hypothesis. The Eclectic Theory of Dunning (1977 and 1996) holds that MNCs with certain ownership advantages invest in nations with specific geographic advantages and that both benefits may be efficiently exploited by "internalizing" output through FDI. Hence, the geographic factors, such as market size (as measured by GDP or GNP) as the most crucial element in luring FDI, are at the center of the growth-led FDI hypothesis. A high rate of economic growth will lead to an increase in FDI due to the anticipated greater level of profitability. Increased aggregate demand for investments (both local and international) will result from rapid economic expansion. Also, stronger economic success means improved infrastructure and more profitable prospects. As a result, FDI inflows into recipient nations are inversely correlated with market size.

Borensztein et al. (1998) investigated the link between FDI and economic development using 69 developing nations between 1970 and 1989 and discovered that FDI has a positive influence on economic growth and that the link is somewhat reliant on the host country's human capital availability. Similar results were found by Bengoa and Sanchez-Robles (2003) over the period 1970–1999 of 18 Latin American nations; Li and Liu (2005) in 84 nations from the year 1970 to 1999, with 21 developed and 63 developing nations represented, and Sokhanvar (2019) in European economies from the year 1995 to 2014. For FDI to be beneficial to economic growth, the host nation should have political stability, macroeconomic, as well more economic openness and policy legitimacy (Bengoa & Sanchez-Robles, 2003).

Coe et al. (1997) found a positive relationship between FDI and Economic growth, but they recommended that the host nation ought to have reached a certain level of growth or development that will aid it to gain the benefits of improved productivity. Therefore, developed nations are projected to have greater human capital and consequently profit more from FDI compared to developing nations (Li & Liu, 2005). Xu (2000), who studied United States MNCs as a route of global technology diffusion over 40 nations from the year 1966 to 1994, appears to prove this. The major findings stated that technology transfer offered by MNCs based in the United States help in productivity development within developed nations while not in underdeveloped nations. This is because majority of emerging market economies do not really meet the threshold criteria, and they may struggle to profit from foreign FDI.

Chowdhury and Mavrotas (2005) examined the causal relationship between FDI and economic growth considering three large FDI receivers mostly in underdeveloped nations, respectively, Thailand, Chile, and Malaysia, which each have different policy regime, development patterns, and macroeconomic situations from the year 1969 to 2000; according to their empirical outcomes based on Toda-Yamamoto granger-causality test for the case of Chile, it indicates that economic growth (GDP) influences FDI rather than the other way. Mah and Yoon (2010) stated that based on the market size theory, fast economic (GDP) development that develops new investment opportunities mostly in host nation might lead to greater FDI inflows. Zhang (2001) stated that the growth caused FDI concept highlights the need of enhancing market size, human capital, and infrastructural conditions to attract foreign investment. Fast economic expansion generates a high level of aggregate demand, which drives increased investment. Some empirical studies demonstrates that nations that have better infrastructure tend to attract foreign investment.

The most intriguing economic framework asserts a bidirectional causal relationship between FDI and economic development. Although it is quite possible that the significant relation between FDI and growth is the consequence of either FDI caused economic growth or economic growth caused FDI and it is possible that the two variables go together via feedback (hypothesis of feedback) (Zhang, 2001). In a data set of 80 nations, Choe (2003) employed the standard panel data causality test procedure and found a bidirectional causation between FDI and economic growth; albeit, FDI's causal influence on economic growth is limited. Narayanamurthy et al. (2009) investigated the causal link between economic growth and FDI in the BRICS nations—Brazil, Russia, India, China, and South Africa—from the year 1992 to 2007. According to the study, economic growth in Russia, Brazil, and South Africa is causally related to FDI in both directions. The analysis reveals a unidirectional causal relationship between economic growth and FDI in China and India.

Some studies discovered evidence in favor of neutral link between economic development and FDI, and some of the research concluded the causality between economic development and FDI seems to be either nonexistent or mechanical (Odhiambo, 2022). Irandoust (2001) investigated the relationship between economic growth and FDI in four OECD nations: Finland, Sweden, Denmark, and Norway and found that there is no causal relationship between economic development and FDI in Finland and Denmark, but they do speculate that the peculiar dynamics and type of FDI entering these nations may be to blame.

4.4 Climate Change

Climate change is a concept used to describe long-term changes in temperature, patterns of precipitation, and other weather-related occurrences that last for several decades or more (Arogundade et al., 2022). It is a naturally occurring phenomenon, but in recent years, human actions, including the use of fossil fuels, forest loss, and industrial operations, have dramatically accelerated the speed of climate change, causing global warming. According to Guo et al. (2023), global warming is the long-term rise in the average temperature of the earth's environment and oceans. The effects of this phenomenon on the climate system, ecosystems, and human societies are extensive. Li et al. (2022) define climate change as the long-term changes in temperature patterns and weather conditions on earth that are predominantly brought on by human activity and natural processes, with the atmospheric concentration of greenhouse gases playing a key role. These greenhouse gases, which include carbon dioxide, methane, and nitrous oxide, are produced because of various industrial, agricultural, and fossil fuel-related processes.

The consequences of climate change are widespread and include rising sea levels, greater intensity and frequency of weather events, the loss of biodiversity, and detrimental effects on human health, agriculture, and economies worldwide. Izadi and Madirimov (2023) emphasized that the most vulnerable groups, such as indigenous peoples and communities with limited resources, frequently suffer the most from these effects. Therefore, it is crucial to reduce greenhouse gas emissions by switching to renewable energy sources, enhancing energy efficiency, and encouraging sustainable land use practices to counteract these consequences of climate change (Renyong & Sedik, 2023). According to Renyong and Sedik (2023), adapting to climate change's consequences is critical by strengthening infrastructure resilience, water management, and disaster preparedness. Adaptation aims to reduce vulnerability and increase resilience by responding to and adapting to changing climatic circumstances. For instance, implementing disaster preparedness and response plans is one strategy, along with putting water management systems in place, strengthening infrastructure durability, adopting agricultural techniques adaptable to varying conditions, and so on (Barış-Tüzemen & Tüzemen, 2022).

Consequent to these facts, a coordinated global response is needed to meet the myriad issues posed by climate change since it is complicated and multidimensional. This can be achieved through collaboration and international cooperation, such as the Paris Agreement and the United Nations Framework Convention on Climate Change (UNFCCC), which serve as important global frameworks for combating climate change (Shehzad et al., 2021). According to Agyeman et al. (2022), these agreements support mitigation initiatives, adaptation measures, financial aid to poor nations, technological transfer, capacity building, and frequent monitoring and reporting of progress. To secure a sustainable future for future generations, this will aid in the reduction of emissions and adaptation to changing environmental circumstances.

4.5 The Costs and Benefits of FDI on Climate Change

The environment of a host nation may experience both advantages and hazards due to FDI. Technology transfer is one of the important advantages of FDI concerning climate change (Waqih et al., 2019). This is because foreign investors frequently adopt cutting-edge technology and techniques that support cleaner and more sustainable manufacturing processes when they transfer their firms and operations to a host nation. Due to their reputation for integrating environmental management systems and renewable energy options, MNCs are the reason for this (Li et al., 2019). Thus, by putting these technologies into practice, the host country may reduce GHG emissions and contribute to the fight against climate change.

FDI can spur green investments in renewable energy projects (Kindo et al., 2023). For instance, investors may devote money to developing renewable energy sources like hydropower, wind, and solar. These initiatives offer substitute energy choices for fossil fuel-based energy sources, lowering carbon emissions and halting climate change (Agboola et al., 2022). Similarly, Wang et al. (2022) believe foreign investors frequently have important knowledge and experience in resource efficiency, sustainable business methods, and environmental protection. As a result, this expertise may be transferred to the host nation through FDI, aiding their efforts to combat the effects of climate change. According to Marques and Caetano (2020), the transfer of skills can improve the local community's ability to create and carry out sustainable activities, promoting the long-term viability of the environment. Additionally, FDI can stimulate economic growth and generate job opportunities (Raihan, 2023). Economic expansion results might lead to the creation of funds for actions aimed at reducing and adapting to climate change. For instance, the host nation may encourage the development of green jobs, promote innovation, and aid in the shift to a low-carbon economy by investing in renewable energy infrastructure, which consequently reduces the effect of climate change (Odugbesan & Adebayo, 2020).

The idea of carbon leakage presents a problem when it comes to FDI and climate change (Muhammad et al., 2021). For instance, if the environmental restrictions in the investor's own country are strict, they can look for investment possibilities in nations with laxer environmental laws. Carbon leakage, as defined by Chen et al. (2023), is the transfer of emissions from a nation with tougher restrictions to a nation with laxer rules without a corresponding overall decrease in emissions. This may weaken international efforts to prevent climate change if not properly handled. Additionally, FDI in industries like mining and logging can lead to habitat degradation and deforestation, which negatively affect biodiversity and cause climate disruption (Bediako et al., 2022). According to Roy (2023), the extraction of these natural resources, if not managed effectively, can cause ecological harm and the loss of carbon sinks, aggravating environmental problems.

Investors solely motivated by money may favor short-term financial gains over long-term sustainability objectives. Climate change mitigation efforts may be undermined by this narrow emphasis on goals that neglect environmental concerns (Ekwueme et al., 2021). To encourage sustainable behaviors, investors must match their strategies with environmental goals. Again, dams and industrial zones are examples of large-scale FDI-related infrastructure projects that may negatively influence the environment (Ahmad et al., 2020). These projects may cause habitat loss, land degradation, and an increase in carbon emissions if they are not planned and maintained responsibly. To reduce these negative consequences, rigorous environmental standards must be put into place and include sustainable practices in infrastructure construction. FDI can potentially worsen social and economic disparities, which have ramifications for the effects of climate change. Due to the unequal distribution of the benefits and costs of climate change, impacted communities, particularly those adjacent to industrial sites, may bear the burden of pollution and environmental deterioration (Musah et al., 2022).

4.6 Nexus Between FDI and Climate Change

The nexus between FDI and Climate Change has become a topic of increasing interest in recent years. FDI indicates investments made by a foreign entity in a domestic company or project. It is often seen to increase economic growth and development in host countries. But FDI may also have a big influence on the environment, especially when it comes to global warming. One of the ways in which FDI can contribute to climate change is through the exploitation of natural resources (Ssali et al., 2019). According to Vitenu-Sackey (2020), many foreign investors seek out countries with abundant natural resources, such as oil, gas, and minerals, and invest heavily in extractive industries. This can lead to increased greenhouse gas emissions, deforestation, and other environmental damage.

Udeagha and Breitenbach (2023) revealed that FDI can contribute to climate change through the promotion of unsustainable practices. For instance, foreign investors may bring with them technologies or business models that are not environmentally friendly and may push for policies that prioritize short-term profits over long-term sustainability. Despite these risks, FDI can also be a powerful tool for mitigating climate change. According to Balsalobre-Lorente et al. (2022), foreign investors may bring technologies and expertise to help countries transition to low-carbon economies. They can also invest in renewable energy projects and other initiatives that contribute to climate change mitigation and adaptation. Ultimately, while FDI can contribute to environmental damage, it can also be a powerful force for positive change.

From a theoretical point of view, the pollution haven hypothesis suggests that international corporations tend to relocate their polluting operations from countries with strict environmental regulations to developing countries where regulations are more lenient (Hamid, Alam, et al., 2022). However, recent policies such as the Paris Agreement and Clean Air Act aim to reduce emissions globally while allowing flexibility for local changes. On the other hand, the pollution halo theory suggests that FDI can lead to improved energy efficiency and reduced pollutant emissions through spillover effects such as improved management techniques, advanced technology, and job creation. Several studies have supported this theory, showing that FDI can contribute to reducing emissions in specific regions, such as China and the Gulf Cooperation Council (GCC) nations.

FDI has been related to both economic development and increasing carbon emissions, exhibiting short-term variations as well as long-term amplifying effects. According to Tan and Uprasen (2022), FDI was not effective in reducing CO2 emissions. Faheem et al. (2022) observed a link between FDI, economic growth, and carbon emissions. Contrary to these findings, FDI inflows can lead to improved energy efficiency and reduced pollutant emissions through beneficial spillover effects, referred to as the pollution halo theory. Nyeadi (2022) found that increased FDI inflows were associated with reduced emissions, supporting the pollution halo effect. Uddin et al. (2023) discovered that FDI reduced CO2 emissions whilst Gyamfi et al. (2022) found that increased FDI had little effect on pollutant emissions in GCC nations.

4.6.1 The Pollution Haven Theory (PHH)

Copeland and Taylor developed the PHH in 1994 to investigate the link between environmental legislation, trade practices, and pollution levels. The idea postulates that in a worldwide economy, companies may move their output from nations with rigorous environmental rules to nations with fewer stringent restrictions to reduce costs and increase profits (Nejati & Taleghani, 2022). Consequently, businesses look for "pollution havens" where they may do business with fewer environmental constraints and laws (Yilanci et al., 2023). According to Nguyen-Thanh et al. (2022), the fundamental tenet of the PHH is that tougher environmental restrictions in industrialized nations raise production costs because pollution control measures must be put in place. As a result, businesses move their manufacturing to nations with laxer environmental regulations, where they may do it more affordably and without having to make significant investments in pollution control technology.

Advocates of PHH have claimed that moving polluting companies may have detrimental effects on the environment. Studies by Abbasi et al. (2023) hold the opinion that when businesses relocate their operations to nations with laxer restrictions, pollution, and ecological damage rise in such areas. This can lead to a "race to the bottom" in ecological standards as governments seek foreign investment by lowering laws (Tayyar, 2022). Additionally, some have claimed that the theory oversimplifies the many variables that affect investment choices and the placement of enterprises. Employment costs, facilitating market access, and governance stability, among other factors, also play major roles in shaping trends in investment and the placement of sectors different from those proposed by the theory (Gao et al., 2022).

Abbasi et al. (2023) showed that although there may be situations where businesses transfer to nations with laxer environmental standards, the overall influence on pollution levels is not certain. Technological improvements, alterations in customer tastes, and international initiatives to address environmental problems may all affect how businesses behave and help to lessen any possible negative consequences. For these reasons, there is a rising acknowledgement of the need for international collaboration in addressing environmental concerns, such as pollution. This includes the Paris Climate Change Agreement, which sought to establish an international framework for lowering greenhouse gas emissions and fostering sustainable development. These programs aim to standardize environmental standards and deter businesses from using lax rules to their benefit (Nguyen-Thanh et al., 2022).

4.6.2 The Pollution Halo Hypothesis

According to the pollution halo notion, pollution can have far-reaching consequences beyond its direct source (Bashir, 2022). The hypothesis holds that pollution in one place can have a halo of adverse environmental effects that radiate outward and damage a much larger territory (Wang & Luo, 2022). According to this notion, multinational firms transmit cleaner technology to host countries via FDI, which increases quality of life and lowers the impact of global warming (Nejati & Taleghani, 2022). Technology transfer may involve green technology, such as those that lower pollution or utilize renewable energy sources, or it may include highly advanced energy-saving devices that reduce the demand for traditional energy sources. Scientists have recently conducted substantial research on this idea to comprehend the effects of pollution on both a local and global scale.

The pollution halo hypothesis has been demonstrated to appear in a variety of ways, one of which is the dispersion of particles in the air (Cil, 2023). A city's pollutants from industries or automobiles, for instance, may be transported by the wind to nearby places, affecting the air quality and perhaps endangering the health of residents. Pollutants from one nation can also be transported across borders, affecting air quality in adjacent countries (Balsalobre-Lorente et al., 2022). The pollution halo concept can also be detected through water system pollution. Musah et al. (2022) claim that because polluted water might move downstream, it will impact the nearby region and the greater basin to which it belongs. Both aquatic environments and the people who depend on them for sustenance and livelihoods may suffer because of this. Given these facts, this theory is especially pertinent in the world that we live in today, as we are still dealing with the effects of global warming and degradation of the environment and the actions being taken to lessen those effects and move toward an environmentally friendly future.

4.6.3 The Environmental Kuznets Curve (EKC)

The EKC is a proposed correlation between several environmental deterioration indices and per capita income (Pata & Samour, 2022). The EKC, named after Simon Kuznets, an economist who first postulated a similar curve for wealth disparity, is a theory that proposes a link between environmental degradation and economic progress (Ben Jebli et al., 2022). According to the EKC theory, nations emphasize economic expansion and industrialization in the early phases of economic growth, frequently at the expense of their environment (Mahmood et al., 2023). However, when nations get wealthy due to a possible inflow of FDI, they can afford to invest in more environmentally friendly technology, laws, and practices that improve the quality of their surroundings.

The theory postulates that during the initial stages of economic growth, because the nature of FDI activities is not environmentally friendly, pollutants rise and environmental quality increases, but that once per capita income reaches a certain level, the trajectory reverses, and at high-income levels, growth in the economy results in improved environmental conditions (Jahanger et al., 2023). This means that environmental effects, or emissions per capita, are an inverted U-shaped function of per capita income. The inverted U-shape association between income and environmental damage suggests that countries tend to endure deteriorating environmental conditions in the initial phases of development but can reach healthier surroundings as they get wealthy (Murshed & Dao, 2022).

The EKC has also been acknowledged as a contentious idea, with many claiming that it overgeneralizes the connection between economic development and environmental damage. Given that the EKC hypothesis presupposes that all nations follow the same path of development and that environmental concerns can be remedied by merely accelerating economic growth, this assumption has not always been held in recent years, according to Farooq et al. (2022). Despite these concerns, the EKC remains an essential concept in ecological economics and is widely used to drive policy choices. Governments have recently adopted the concept of the EKC to support funding for greener technology and the advancement of sustainable development (Mahmood et al., 2023). Several studies (e.g., Pata & Samour, 2022) have discovered that income considerably influences environmental quality measures, with early degradation followed by improvement as nations expand economically. Therefore, since FDI inflow is argued to drive economic growth, it means that a rise in growth can cause environmental pollution due to changes in the climate because economic activities trigger a rise in CO2 emissions (Murshed & Dao, 2022).

4.7 Importance of FDI in South Africa

According to the Economic Report on Africa by the United Nations Economic Commission, FDI is essential for Africa's economic growth. According to international agencies like the IMF and the World Bank, attracting sizable FDI inflows can result in a sizable decrease in the issues caused by climate change

(Mohanty & Sethi, 2022). African governments have changed from aggressively soliciting foreign investment to filling resource shortfalls, fostering competition, and promoting the environment rather than creating jobs and supporting the local economy (Hamid, Alam, et al., 2022). The acceptance of neoliberal principles promoted by the World Bank and IMF, structural adjustment programs, and growing climate change-related challenges all have an impact on this transition (Borga et al., 2023). For a variety of reasons, African nations, particularly South Africa, are eager to lure FDI. These reasons include overcoming resource shortages like capital and entrepreneurship, gaining access to international markets, acquiring effective managerial skills, facilitating the diffusion of technology and innovation, and creating job opportunities (Rahaman et al., 2022).

Guoyan et al. (2022) noted that FDI has played a significant role in South Africa's economic development by bringing in essential capital investment. South Africa got $4.6 billion in FDI in 2020, down from the previous year because of the COVID-19 epidemic (Faheem et al., 2022). However, FDI in the nation has grown steadily over the past 10 years, averaging $5.8 billion per year between 2010 and 2019 (Williams et al., 2022). Due to FDI, businesses in South Africa can tap into new markets, technologies, and skills. With a total investment of $2.4 billion in South Africa in 2020, the United States was the largest investor, followed by the United Kingdom ($616 million) (Jorgenson et al., 2022). These investments have aided in boosting South African businesses' innovative capacity and global competitiveness.

Technology transfer is anticipated when overseas businesses import technology from their own nations. In terms of development, technology must spread and have an impact on local output that benefits local businesses. However, no proof exists that FDI in South Africa has significantly increased technology diffusion (Faheem et al., 2022). Foreign investment can sometimes lead to a rivalry that stunts domestic technological innovation and takes funds away from it to attract FDI (Ullah et al., 2023). FDI can aid in the transfer of management skills to local managers through the opening of new facilities, the purchase of businesses, or the outsourcing of work to nearby subcontractors. As evidenced by South Africa's Growth, Employment, and Redistribution (GEAR) strategy, which focused on luring investment in industry clusters to foster the development of local businesses, particularly as it relates to climate change issues, increased export competitiveness is therefore anticipated.

4.7.1 Initiatives Taken by South Africa to Attract FDI

Like many other continents, African governments have put in place several FDI-attracting efforts, such as financial incentives, investment treaties, and actions to promote FDI. Introducing incentives, which are political measures intended to entice globally mobile investors, is one such endeavor (Yasmeen et al., 2022). Similarly, African nations provide incentives, including tax holidays, exemptions from export and import levies, subsidized infrastructure, and restrictions on workers' rights, through initiatives like Export Processing Zones (EPZs) (Apergis et al., 2023). According to Pan et al. (2022), governments and multinational firms have differing perspectives on the significance of incentives. Corporations consider EPZs good places to invest while governments see them as a way to draw FDI.

According to Salahodjaev and Isaeva 2022, African countries have enhanced their legal frameworks for FDI by liberalizing their economies, allowing profit repatriation, and offering tax rebates and other incentives to attract investment. Numerous African nations have signed bilateral investment treaties to safeguard and encourage FDI. These agreements define the terms under which FDI may enter the host nation. For instance, since the 1980s, all governments of the Southern African Development Community (SADC) have loosened regulations for foreign investors by making it easier for them to enter, relaxing borrowing restrictions (despite the effects on foreign exchange reserves), easing ownership of land and mining concessions, and creating new public–private partnerships (PPPs) with the private sector (Nasir et al., 2019).

South Africa has recently put in place several steps to attract FDI and foster a climate that is favorable for foreign investors. Elheddad et al. (2022) claim that the government has formed organizations that aggressively market South Africa as a desirable investment destination, such as Invest South Africa (ISA) and the South African Investment Conference. These organizations inform, help, and support potential investors while showcasing the advantages and prospects of doing business in the nation. Additionally, to encourage FDI, the South African Government has recently provided potential investors with investment incentives like tax breaks, grants, and subsidies for eligible investments in priority industries, special economic zones (SEZs), and economically depressed areas (Opoku & Boachie, 2020). These incentives are designed to lower emissions and investment costs while encouraging businesses to start up or grow in South Africa. SEZs offer extra benefits such as tax rebates, reduced regulations, infrastructural development, and market access. Examples include the Coega Industrial Development Zone, Richards Bay Industrial Development Zone, and Dube TradePort.

The nation has given infrastructure development priority to draw in investment and ease commercial operations. The South African Government has reportedly made investments in telecommunications networks, energy infrastructure, transportation networks, and logistics centres (Akinlo & Dada, 2021). These infrastructure upgrades boost connectivity, save companies money, address the issue of climate change, and foster an atmosphere that helps businesses succeed. Policy measures have been put into place to make conducting business in South Africa easier and to foster a welcoming environment for investments (Shabir et al., 2022). These changes include simplifying regulatory procedures, lowering administrative obstacles, increasing transparency, and safeguarding investor rights. Additionally, efforts have been undertaken to resolve issues with governance, land reform, and labor laws to inspire trust in potential investors. In a similar vein, South Africa has prioritized education and skill development in recognition of the value of a trained workforce. The nation has developed programs to raise educational standards, expand vocational training, and match skill development with market demands. These programs seek to develop a skilled labor force that can fulfil the needs of foreign investors.

South Africa has recently pushed for PPPs to use private sector knowledge and funding for infrastructure projects (Shear et al., 2023). PPPs facilitate collaboration between public and private organizations in sectors including energy, transportation, healthcare, and education. These alliances draw investment, share risks, and hasten the building of infrastructure. According to Ahmed et al. (2022), these activities have had fruitful outcomes. For instance, despite the global economic slowdown brought on by the COVID-19 pandemic, a study from the South African Reserve Bank reveals that FDI inflows to South Africa grew from ZAR 16.8 billion in 2019 to ZAR 29.2 billion in 2020 (Ait Soussane et al., 2023). This is due to the investments being distributed among several industries, such as manufacturing, service provision, and the development of infrastructure.

4.8 Conclusion

South African economy may have transitioned away from relying on FDI and is now more dependent on local investment, government policies, and macroeconomic stability. This shows that rather than depending just on FDI, attention must be paid to a wide range of elements that might foster economic growth. Technology transfer, the creation of new jobs, and knowledge exchange are some of the side impacts of FDI. South Africa may not have tapped into its full potential in FDI spillover benefits because of several things, including insufficient infrastructure, a lack of skills within the domestic labor, and weak ties between international and domestic businesses. Policymakers can be tempted to place substantial dependence on FDI as an engine of economic growth. This might be dangerous since FDI is susceptible to external influences like instability in politics and changes in the state of the world economy. Policymakers should instead concentrate on establishing a robust domestic economy that can withstand outside shocks. It implies that to attract FDI, officials must adopt a more focused strategy. Politicians must think about focusing on certain industries or sectors that may profit from FDI rather than just concentrating on luring FDI. This may entail offering incentives to foreign companies to participate in certain sectors or making investments in infrastructure and education to encourage the growth of these sectors.

References

Abbasi, M. A., Nosheen, M., & Rahman, H. U. (2023). An approach to the pollution haven and pollution halo hypotheses in Asian countries. *Environmental Science and Pollution Research*, *30*(17), 49270–49289.

Adedoyin, F. F., Afolabi, J. O., Yalçiner, K., & Bekun, F. V. (2022). The export-led growth in Malaysia: Does economic policy uncertainty and geopolitical risks matter? *Journal of Public Affairs*, *22*(1), e2361.

Agboola, P. O., Hossain, M. E., Gyamfi, B. A., & Bekun, F. V. (2022). Environmental consequences of foreign direct investment influx and conventional energy consumption: Evidence from dynamic ARDL simulation for Turkey. *Environmental Science and Pollution Research*, *29*(35), 53584–53597.

Agyeman, F. O., Zhiqiang, M., Li, M., Sampene, A. K., Dapaah, M. F., Kedjanyi, E. A. G., Buabeng, P., Li, Y., Hakro, S., & Heydari, M. (2022). Probing the effect of governance of tourism development, economic growth, and foreign direct investment on carbon dioxide emissions in Africa: The African experience. *Energies*, *15*(13), 4530.

Ahmad, M., Jiang, P., Majeed, A., & Raza, M. Y. (2020). Does financial development and foreign direct investment improve environmental quality? Evidence from belt and road countries. *Environmental Science and Pollution Research*, *27*, 23586–23601.

Ahmed, F., Ali, I., Kousar, S., & Ahmed, S. (2022). The environmental impact of industrialisation and foreign direct investment: Empirical evidence from Asia-Pacific region. *Environmental Science and Pollution Research*, 1–15.

Ait Soussane, J., Mansouri, D., Fakhouri, M. Y., & Mansouri, Z. (2023). Does climate change constitute a financial risk to foreign direct investment? An empirical analysis on 200 countries from 1970 to 2020. *Weather, Climate, and Society*, *15*(1), 31–43.

Akinlo, T., & Dada, J. T. (2021). The moderating effect of foreign direct investment on environmental degradation-poverty reduction nexus: Evidence from sub-Saharan African countries. *Environment, Development and Sustainability*, 1–21.

Amadi, C. (2019). *FDI and economic growth in Nigeria: An analysis of the role of financial development on linkages*. Manchester Metropolitan University. Doctoral dissertation.

Apergis, N., Pinar, M., & Unlu, E. (2023). How do foreign direct investment flows affect carbon emissions in BRICS countries? Revisiting the pollution haven hypothesis using bilateral FDI flows from OECD to BRICS countries. *Environmental Science and Pollution Research*, *30*(6), 14680–14692.

Arogundade, S., Mduduzi, B., & Hassan, A. S. (2022). Spatial impact of foreign direct investment on ecological footprint in Africa. *Environmental Science and Pollution Research*, *29*(34), 51589–51608.

Balsalobre-Lorente, D., Ibáñez-Luzón, L., Usman, M., & Shahbaz, M. (2022). The environmental Kuznets curve, based on the economic complexity, and the pollution haven hypothesis in PIIGS countries. *Renewable Energy*, *185*, 1441–1455.

Balsalobre-Lorente, D., Driha, O. M., Halkos, G., & Mishra, S. (2022). Influence of growth and urbanisation on CO2 emissions: The moderating effect of foreign direct investment on energy use in BRICS. *Sustainable Development*, *30*(1), 227–240.

Barış-Tüzemen, Ö., & Tüzemen, S. (2022). The impact of foreign direct investment and biomass energy consumption on pollution in BRICS countries: A panel data analysis. *Global Journal of Emerging Market Economies*, *14*(1), 76–92.

Bashir, M. F. (2022). Discovering the evolution of pollution haven hypothesis: A literature review and future research agenda. *Environmental Science and Pollution Research, 29*(32), 48210–48232.

Bediako, F. E., Twerefou, D. K., & Codjoe, E. (2022). Effects of foreign direct investment on environmental quality in West Africa. *West African Journal of Applied Ecology, 30*(2), 86–93.

Ben Jebli, M., Madaleno, M., Schneider, N., & Shahzad, U. (2022). What does the EKC theory leave behind? A state-of-the-art review and assessment of export diversification-augmented models. *Environmental Monitoring and Assessment, 194*(6), 414.

Bengoa, M., & Sanchez-Robles, B. (2003). Foreign direct investment, economic freedom and growth: New evidence from Latin America. *European Journal of Political Economy, 19*(3), 529–545.

Borensztein, E., De Gregorio, J., & Lee, J. W. (1998). How does foreign direct investment affect economic growth? *Journal of International Economics, 45*(1), 115–135.

Borga, M., Egesa, K., Entaltsev, D., Legoff, G. M., Pegoue, A., & Rodelgo, A. S. (2023). Measuring CO2 emissions of foreign direct investment. In *Data for a greener world: A guide for practitioners and policymakers*. International Monetary Fund.

Chakrabarti, A. (2001). The determinants of foreign direct investments: Sensitivity analyses of cross-country regressions. *Kyklos, 54*(1), 89–114.

Chen, L., Guo, F., & Huang, L. (2023). Impact of foreign direct investment on green innovation: Evidence from China's provincial panel data. *Sustainability, 15*(4), 3318.

Choe, J.-I. (2003). Do foreign direct investment and gross domestic investment promote economic growth? *ResearcHGate: Review of Development Economics, 7*(1), 44–57.

Chowdhury, A., & Mavrotas, G. (2005). FDI and growth: A causal relationship (No. 2005/25). *WIDER Research Paper*. https://www.researchgate.net/publication/23566065_FDI_and_Growth_A_Causal_Relationship

Cil, N. (2023). Re-examination of pollution haven hypothesis for Turkey with Fourier approach. *Environmental Science and Pollution Research, 30*(4), 10024–10036.

Coe, D. T., Helpman, E., & Hoffmaister, A. W. (1997). North-south R & D spillovers. *The Economic Journal, 107*(440), 134–149.

Dunning, J. H. (1977). Trade, location of economic activity and the MNE: A search for an eclectic approach. In *The international allocation of economic activity: Proceedings of a nobel symposium held at Stockholm* (pp. 395–418). Palgrave Macmillan UK.

Dunning, J. H. (1996). *The geographical sources of the competitiveness of firms: Some results of a new survey*. University of Reading, Department of Economics.

Duodu, E., Oteng-Abayie, E. F., Frimpong, P. B., & Takyi, P. O. (2022). The impact of the compact with Africa initiative on foreign direct investments and environmental pollution. *Management of Environmental Quality: An International Journal, 33*(6), 1457–1475.

Ekwueme, D. C., Zoaka, J. D., & Alola, A. A. (2021). Carbon emission effect of renewable energy utilisation, fiscal development, and foreign direct investment in South Africa. *Environmental Science and Pollution Research*, *28*(31), 41821–41833.

Elheddad, M., Alfar, A. J., Haloub, R., Sharma, N., & Gomes, P. (2022). The impact of foreign direct investment (FDI) on renewable and non-renewable energy in Bangladesh: Does the global climate change emergencies required? *International Journal of Emergency Services*, *11*(3), 409–421.

Faheem, M., Hussain, S., Safdar, N., & Anwer, M. A. (2022). Does foreign direct investment asymmetrically affect the mitigation of environmental degradation in Malaysia? *Environmental Science and Pollution Research*, 1–13.

Farooq, S., Ozturk, I., Majeed, M. T., & Akram, R. (2022). Globalization and CO2 emissions in the presence of EKC: A global panel data analysis. *Gondwana Research*, *106*, 367–378.

Gao, L., Pei, T., Zhang, J., & Tian, Y. (2022). The "Pollution Halo" effect of FDI: Evidence from the Chinese Sichuan–Chongqing urban agglomeration. *International Journal of Environmental Research and Public Health*, *19*(19), 11903.

Guo, Y., Deng, J., & Liu, X. (2023). None-linear nexus between natural resources dependency, foreign direct investment, and environmental sustainability in newly industrialised countries. *Resources Policy*, *83*, 103656.

Guoyan, S., Khaskheli, A., Raza, S. A., & Shah, N. (2022). Analysing the association between the foreign direct investment and carbon emissions in MENA countries: A pathway to sustainable development. *Environment, Development and Sustainability*, 1–18.

Gyamfi, B. A., Agozie, D. Q., & Bekun, F. V. (2022). Can technological innovation, foreign direct investment and natural resources ease some burden for the BRICS economies within current industrial era? *Technology in Society*, *70*, 102037.

Hamid, I., Alam, M. S., Kanwal, A., Jena, P. K., Murshed, M., & Alam, R. (2022). Decarbonisation pathways: The roles of foreign direct investments, governance, democracy, economic growth, and renewable energy transition. *Environmental Science and Pollution Research*, *29*(33), 49816–49831.

Hamid, I., Jena, P. K., & Mukhopdhyay, D. (2022). Should China prefer more foreign direct investment inflows to environmental change? *Journal of Public Affairs*, *22*(2), e2466.

Irandoust, J. E. M. (2001). On the causality between foreign direct investment and output: A comparative study. *The International Trade Journal*, *15*(1), 1–26. https://doi.org/10.1080/088539001300005431

Izadi, J., & Madirimov, B. (2023). Effect of foreign direct investment on sustainable development goals? Evidence from Eurasian countries. *Journal of Sustainable Finance & Investment*, 1–20.

Jahanger, A., Hossain, M. R., Onwe, J. C., Ogwu, S. O., Awan, A., & Balsalobre-Lorente, D. (2023). Analysing the N-shaped EKC among top nuclear energy generating nations: A novel dynamic common correlated effects approach. *Gondwana Research*, *116*, 73–88.

Jorgenson, A., Clark, R., Kentor, J., & Rieger, A. (2022). Networks, stocks, and climate change: A new approach to the study of foreign investment and the environment. *Energy Research & Social Science*, *87*, 102461.

Kindo, M., Ouoba, Y., & Kabore, F. P. (2023). Effect of foreign direct investment on environmental quality in West Africa. *Environmental Science and Pollution Research*, 1–13.

Li, Z., Dong, H., Huang, Z., & Failler, P. (2019). Impact of foreign direct investment on environmental performance. *Sustainability*, *11*(13), 3538.

Li, X., & Liu, X. (2005). Foreign direct investment and economic growth: An increasingly endogenous relationship. *World Development*, *33*(3), 393–407.

Li, F., Zhang, J., & Li, X. (2022). Research on supporting developing countries to achieve green development transition: Based on the perspective of renewable energy and foreign direct investment. *Journal of Cleaner Production*, *372*, 133726.

Mah, J. S., & Yoon, S. C. (2010). Determinants of FDI flows into Indonesia and Singapore. *International Area Review*, *13*(1), 63–73.

Mahmood, H., Furqan, M., Hassan, M. S., & Rej, S. (2023). The environmental Kuznets curve (EKC) hypothesis in China: A review. *Sustainability*, *15*(7), 6110.

Marques, A. C., & Caetano, R. (2020). The impact of foreign direct investment on emission reduction targets: Evidence from high-and middle-income countries. *Structural Change and Economic Dynamics*, *55*, 107–118.

Mohanty, S., & Sethi, N. (2022). The energy consumption-environmental quality nexus in BRICS countries: The role of outward foreign direct investment. *Environmental Science and Pollution Research*, *29*(13), 19714–19730.

Muhammad, B., Khan, M. K., Khan, M. I., & Khan, S. (2021). Impact of foreign direct investment, natural resources, renewable energy consumption, and economic growth on environmental degradation: Evidence from BRICS, developing, developed and global countries. *Environmental Science and Pollution Research*, *28*, 21789–21798.

Murshed, M., & Dao, N. T. T. (2022). Revisiting the CO2 emission-induced EKC hypothesis in South Asia: The role of export quality improvement. *GeoJournal*, *87* (2), 535–563.

Musah, M., Mensah, I. A., Alfred, M., Mahmood, H., Murshed, M., Omari-Sasu, A. Y., Boateng, F., Nyeadi, J. D., & Coffie, C. P. K. (2022). Reinvestigating the pollution haven hypothesis: The nexus between foreign direct investments and environmental quality in G-20 countries. *Environmental Science and Pollution Research*, 1–18.

Narayanamurthy, V., Perumal, S., & Rao, K. (2009). Causal relationship between foreign direct investment and growth: Evidence from BRICS countries. *International Business Research*, *2*(4), 198–203.

Nasir, M. A., Huynh, T. L. D., & Tram, H. T. X. (2019). Role of financial development, economic growth & foreign direct investment in driving climate change: A case of emerging ASEAN. *Journal of Environmental Management*, *242*, 131–141.

Ndou, E., & Mokoena, T. (2019). Do positive bank concentration shocks impact economic growth in South Africa? Inequality. *Output-Inflation Trade-Off and Economic Policy Uncertainty*, 269–280. https://doi.org/10.1007/978-3-030-19803-9_17

Nejati, M., & Taleghani, F. (2022). Pollution halo or pollution haven? A CGE appraisal for Iran. *Journal of Cleaner Production*, *344*, 131092.

Nguyen-Thanh, N., Chin, K. H., & Nguyen, V. (2022). Does the pollution halo hypothesis exist in this "better" world? The evidence from STIRPAT model. *Environmental Science and Pollution Research*, *29*(58), 87082–87096.

Nyeadi, J. D. (2022). The impact of financial development and foreign direct investment on environmental sustainability in Sub-Saharan Africa: Using PMG-ARDL approach. *Economic Research-Ekonomska Istraživanja*, 1–23.

Odhiambo, N. M. (2022). Is export-led growth hypothesis still valid for sub-Saharan African countries? New evidence from panel data analysis. *European Journal of Management and Business Economics*, *31*(1), 77–93.

Odugbesan, J. A., & Adebayo, T. S. (2020). The symmetrical and asymmetrical effects of foreign direct investment and financial development on carbon emission: Evidence from Nigeria. *SN Applied Sciences*, *2*(12), 1982.

Opoku, E. E. O., & Boachie, M. K. (2020). The environmental impact of industrialisation and foreign direct investment. *Energy Policy*, *137*, 111178.

Pan, L., Wang, L., & Feng, Q. (2022). A bibliometric analysis of risk management in foreign direct investment: Insights and implications. *Sustainability*, *14*(12), 7078.

Pata, U. K., & Samour, A. (2022). Do renewable and nuclear energy enhance environmental quality in France? A new EKC approach with the load capacity factor. *Progress in Nuclear Energy*, *149*, 104249.

Rahaman, M. A., Hossain, M. A., & Chen, S. (2022). The impact of foreign direct investment, tourism, electricity consumption, and economic development on CO2 emissions in Bangladesh. *Environmental Science and Pollution Research*, *29*(25), 37344–37358.

Raihan, A. (2023). Exploring environmental Kuznets curve and pollution haven hypothesis in Bangladesh: The impact of foreign direct investment. *Journal of Environmental Science and Economics*, *2*(1), 25–36.

Renyong, H., & Sedik, A. A. (2023). Environmental sustainability and foreign direct investment in East Africa: Institutional and policy benefits for environmental sustainability. *Sustainability*, *15*(2), 1521.

Roy, A. (2023). *The impact of foreign direct investment, renewable and nonrenewable energy consumption, and natural resources on ecological footprint: An Indian perspective*. International Journal of Energy Sector Management.

Salahodjaev, R., & Isaeva, A. (2022). Post-Soviet states and CO2 emissions: The role of foreign direct investment. *Post-Communist Economies*, *34*(7), 944–965.

Sarkodie, S. A., Adams, S., & Leirvik, T. (2020). Foreign direct investment and renewable energy in climate change mitigation: Does governance matter? *Journal of Cleaner Production*, *263*, 121262.

Shabir, M., Ali, M., Hashmi, S. H., & Bakhsh, S. (2022). Heterogeneous effects of economic policy uncertainty and foreign direct investment on environmental quality: Cross-country evidence. *Environmental Science and Pollution Research*, *29* (2), 2737–2752.

Shear, F., Ashraf, B. N., & Butt, S. (2023). Sensing the heat: Climate change vulnerability and foreign direct investment inflows. *Research in International Business and Finance*, 102005.

Shehzad, K., Xiaoxing, L., & Sarfraz, M. (2021). Envisaging the asymmetrical association among FDI, ICT, and climate change: A case from developing country. *Carbon Management*, *12*(2), 123–137.

Sokhanvar, A. (2019). Does foreign direct investment accelerate tourism and economic growth within Europe? *Tourism Management Perspectives*, *29*, 86–96.

Ssali, M. W., Du, J., Mensah, I. A., & Hongo, D. O. (2019). Investigating the nexus among environmental pollution, economic growth, energy use, and foreign direct investment in 6 selected sub-Saharan African countries. *Environmental Science and Pollution Research*, *26*, 11245–11260.

Tan, Y., & Uprasen, U. (2022). The effect of foreign direct investment on renewable energy consumption subject to the moderating effect of environmental regulation: Evidence from the BRICS countries. *Renewable Energy*, *201*, 135–149.

Tayyar, A. E. (2022). Testing pollution haven and pollution halo hypotheses for the energy sector: Evidence from Turkey. *Business and Economics Research Journal*, *13*(3), 367–383.

Uddin, I., Usman, M., Saqib, N., & Makhdum, M. S. A. (2023). The impact of geopolitical risk, governance, technological innovations, energy use, and foreign direct investment on CO2 emissions in the BRICS region. *Environmental Science and Pollution Research*, 1–16.

Udeagha, M. C., & Breitenbach, M. C. (2023). The role of financial development in climate change mitigation: Fresh policy insights from South Africa. *Biophysical Economics and Sustainability*, *8*(1), 1.

Ullah, S., Luo, R., Adebayo, T. S., & Kartal, M. T. (2023). Paving the ways toward sustainable development: The asymmetric effect of economic complexity, renewable electricity, and foreign direct investment on the environmental sustainability in BRICS-T. *Environment, Development and Sustainability*, 1–25.

Vitenu-Sackey, P. A. (2020). Financial development, foreign direct investment and carbon emissions: A comparative study of West Africa and Southern Africa regions. *International Review of Research in Emerging Markets and the Global Economy*, *6*(1), 1550–1569.

Wang, L., Liu, G., Alkhatib, S., Wang, X., Dai, J., Abbas, S. Z., & Khan, Y. A. (2022). The impact of foreign direct investment on environment: Evidence from newly industrialised countries. *Environmental Science and Pollution Research*, *29* (47), 70950–70961.

Wang, H., & Luo, Q. (2022). Can a colonial legacy explain the pollution haven hypothesis? A city-level panel analysis. *Structural Change and Economic Dynamics*, *60*, 482–495.

Waqih, M. A. U., Bhutto, N. A., Ghumro, N. H., Kumar, S., & Salam, M. A. (2019). Rising environmental degradation and impact of foreign direct investment: An empirical evidence from SAARC region. *Journal of Environmental Management*, *243*, 472–480.

Williams, M., Abu Alrub, A., & Aga, M. (2022). Ecological footprint, economic uncertainty and foreign direct investment in South Africa: Evidence from asymmetric cointegration and dynamic multipliers in a nonlinear ARDL approach. *Sage Open*, *12*(2), 21582440221094607.

Xu, B. (2000). Multinational enterprises, technology diffusion, and host country productivity growth. *Journal of Development Economics*, *62*(2), 477–493.

Yasmeen, R., Yao, X., Padda, I. U. H., Shah, W. U. H., & Jie, W. (2022). Exploring the role of solar energy and foreign direct investment for clean environment: Evidence from top 10 solar energy consuming countries. *Renewable Energy*, *185*, 147–158.

Yilanci, V., Cutcu, I., Cayir, B., & Saglam, M. S. (2023). Pollution haven or pollution halo in the fishing footprint: Evidence from Indonesia. *Marine Pollution Bulletin*, *188*, 114626.

Zhang, K. H. (2001). How does foreign direct investment affect economic growth in China? *The Economics of Transition*, *9*(3), 679–693.

Chapter 5

Foreign Direct Investment: Kenya Case Study

Abstract

Foreign direct investments (FDIs) are regarded as investments that intend to gain persistent or long-term interests in firms based outside the investor's economy, whereas economic growth is widely believed to be an increase in the manufacturing and consumption of goods and services. This chapter focuses on how FDI affects economic growth in Kenya and potential strategies for accelerating that growth and providing direction for government and policymakers to create workable monetary and fiscal policies to increase FDI inflows into the nation and achieve higher economic growth.

Keywords: FDI; economic growth; Kenya; capital; GDP

5.1 Introduction

Foreign direct investments (FDIs) have historically been driven primarily by a need for resources. Economic theory suggests that FDI is an important component of economic advancement, especially in developing countries (Asiedu, 2006). The need for better economies, advanced technology, economic expansion, poverty reduction, and improved living standards has led to African nations working toward getting FDI injected into their economies to help achieve these. As a result of dynamism brought about by globalization, the continent has improved its processes in technology usage improvement, and this has encouraged cross-border trade by multinational corporations (MNCs) and firms. As a result of the benefits that FDI can have on economic progress, several African nations are working to attract it. This is demonstrated by the creation of the New Partnership for Africa's Development (NEPAD), which places a high priority on luring international investment to Africa (AERC Research Paper 165).

Foreign Direct Investment, 65–75

doi:10.1108/978-1-83662-900-920261005

Significant research has been conducted to ascertain whether FDI may spur economic growth in the receiving nations. While some academics contend that FDI has primarily favorable effects on developing economies, others are convinced of the contrary. Hanson (2001) believes that beneficial impacts might not be very significant. However, FDI, as acknowledged by Findlay (1978), Borensztein et al. (1998), UNCTAD (1998) and Ikiara (2002), serves as a connection to the innovation and resource gap of developing countries by providing the technical know-how, financial planning, and business acumen, facilitating access to international markets, and creating both technological and efficiency spillover effects to local businesses, provided the proper policies and business conditions are available.

5.2 Foreign Direct Investment

FDI is viewed as an essential way to foster growth in developing countries (Asiedu, 2006). The primary reason for this is that FDI helps to address the two key issues that most developing nations face. African nations struggle with a lack of resources and technological expertise, and closing the savings gap lowers the poverty rates and enhances living conditions (Nyamwange, 2009). When a party from one nation makes an investment into a company or organization in another with the hope of forming a long-term relationship, it is referred to as FDI. This happens when an investor gains at least 10% of the voting power in a company (OECD, 2002). FDIs are distinct from foreign portfolio investments, which let investors hold foreign assets without any active involvement. FDI might be made through acquiring a long-term stake or by expanding a company overseas.

The globalization trend has significantly increased the importance of FDI in recent decades, providing enormous opportunities for third-world countries to achieve better economic growth through global trade and investment. FDI is believed to benefit both foreign investors and host countries by allowing them to participate in global supply and commerce networks. For most developing nations, FDI is frequently seen as an economic stimulant (Borensztein et al., 1998; Makki & Somwaru, 2004). This is because they invest in and bring new technology and job opportunities with them. It is inherently characterized by the frequent transfer of knowledge and skills usually from their home country to the host country.

Cross-border acquisitions and mergers, strategic partnerships, and greenfield investments are just a few examples of how FDI might be implemented. The stakeholders (foreign investors and host nation) are dedicated to contributing their expertise in the local or international markets and bureaucracies, financial ability, and technical experience to the investment operation. Thus, FDI is a benefit of globalization, which is characterized by the fusion of national economic systems and international markets. This provides more information on how wealthier countries assist less developed countries in purchasing goods and equipment and utilizing natural resources for economic growth (Sacerdoti, 1997).

FDI can be categorized as vertical, horizontal, or efficiency-seeking. According to Mackton et al. (2018), FDI flows between industrial countries are horizontal, as opposed to the vertical FDI that occurs between industrialized and developing nations (Almfraji & Almsafir, 2014). Horizontal FDI refers to an investment that occurs in the same industry as that of a business that runs or provides services in its country of origin, but it concentrates on generating for the original or local markets rather than exporting most of its production to the host country (Maskus, 2002). It intends to profit from a new market, which is a typical FDI motivation. This is a common type of investment made by MNCs, which frequently have production facilities in multiple countries and thus want to take benefits of economies of scale by leveraging local workforce, land, as well as other resources.

Vertical FDI, on the other hand, refers to MNCs that divide production processes spatially. MNCs vertically separate the production chain by outsourcing several production phases to other regions, hence the term "vertical." The idea is that the production process is divided into phases, each with its own set of input prerequisites. When production costs differ between regions, it makes sense for a company to divide its production process (Protsenko, 2004). This type of FDI is more likely to result in employment transmissions and reductions in job safeguards than horizontal FDI (Maskus, 2002). As a result, when evaluating FDI flows between industrial and developing nations, the link between trade flows and FDI flows is complimentary rather than substitute.

Efficiency-seeking FDI or optimization FDI develops, expands, and modernizes a company's production, increasing its efficiency. Efficiency-seeking FDI reduces or eliminates internal or/and external inefficiencies that prevent the firm from reaching its goals. It aims to improve producer and/or consumer productivity, which boosts returns on investments. FDI can do this by introducing efficient technology and/or the know-how (Dunning, 1993). Macro-level complementarity exists, but a substitutive relationship exists at the industry and product level, which is resolved by evaluating the interplay between trade and FDI inflows at the aggregate and micro level.

5.3 Economic Growth

When compared between two periods in time, economic growth is the expansion of a country's capacity to produce products and services. To measure economic growth, one can use nominal terms that account for inflation or real terms that are inflation-adjusted. Economic expansion is typically correlated with developments in technology. An economy's capacity to create more goods and services as well as its potential to raise the standard of living for its population are both considered benefits of economic growth. Economic development is the process by which an economy's real national income and per capita income rise over a comparatively long period of time, and economic growth is a positive result of that process. As a result, economic growth can be summed up as a process that involves interwoven changes in the fundamental components of supply and in the composition of demand, ultimately resulting to an increase in the net national product of a nation (Khadenje, 2015).

High economic growth rate is often characterized by:

- High rates of ideological, political, and social change: These include the process of general urbanization and the adoption of "modernization's" institutions, values, and ways of thinking.
- High rates of growth in population and per capita output: Over the previous 200 years, annual growth rates in the now-developed nations have averaged almost 2% for per capita output and 1% for population. The per capita output would therefore double over the course of about 36 years.
- High economic structural transition rates: This is characterized by shifts from agriculture to manufacturing and then from manufacturing to services. The contribution of services to GDP rises along with a nation's economic development.
- Propensity to trade: Some believe that trade drives economic growth, while others believe that trade follows economic growth. International trade, according to Stiglitz and Charlton (2007) in *Fair trade for all*, was a significant factor in the industrialization of East Asian economies, including India and China, at various points in the 20th century, as well as North American and Australian economies in the 19th century.

Even though global productivity has increased dramatically over the past years, there has been a very uneven distribution of economic growth. According to an analysis of the world map, most high-income nations can be found in North America and Western Europe. Japan, Australia, New Zealand, and a few oil-producing nations in the Middle East are additional high-income nations. Furthermore, the disparity between the richest and poorest 20% of the world's population continues to grow. The disparity could be attributed to:

- Physical and human resource endowments: Most developing countries, especially in Africa, are poorly endowed and desperately need investment from abroad.
- Climate difference: It is observed that most developed nations are in temperate countries. Most poor developing countries suffer from extreme heat and humidity that lead to rapid soil depreciation and deterioration, hence low agricultural activities.
- Population size, distribution and growth: High population growth that is not accompanied by corresponding investments means that there is a decline in capital per person in these countries leading to lower or negative economic growth/development.
- Stability and flexibility of political and social institution: Conflicts involving culture, religion, and ethnicity still exist in some developing nations such as Sudan, Ethiopia, and Eritrea. In addition, there are some developing nations

with unstable governments. Political unrest hinders the expansion and development of the economy.

5.4 FDI and Economic Growth

There are numerous ways that FDI affects economic growth. Firstly, it is a successful method of transferring technology from developed economies with sound financial foundations to underdeveloped countries (Blomstrom & Perssion, 1983; Caves, 1974). This is because international businesses seeking to establish a presence in other nations must choose the best technological environment to support their operations. The introduction of new technologies benefits not just the companies and the industries in which they operate but also the host nations. As a result, the host nations also get access to technology, which has enormous advantages that ultimately lead to economic progress.

MNCs can establish alliances with local businesses or even a physical presence in the host nations by opening branches there via FDI. Contingent on the prospects that appeal to investors, investments can be made in a variety of sectors (Fan & Dickie, 2000). When this occurs, production levels in the corresponding industries will grow significantly. Additionally, this will result in a rise in imports and exports, generating higher income. Since the investors are also in business, they will gain from this income in addition to the host nation (Chia, 1995).

FDI also increases the value of human capital (Lahiri & Ono, 2003). MNCs are always particularly interested in the affordable labor force if they are considering an investment in a certain nation for their operations to run smoothly and according to plan. However, it is not always simple to locate enough highly skilled labor in the host nation. As a result, they must go above and beyond to provide on-the-job training to hire talented workers. FDI develops human capital in this way. The skilled workforce that is created is advantageous to both the investor and the host nation since it will stay behind if the company or multinational decides to change its operations or reduce FDI in the future. FDI has a variety of effects on economic growth, and these effects largely depend on a nation's national income, human capital, domestic financial development, and trade openness, among other things.

Scholars like Blomström et al. (1994) and Javorcik (2004) ascertain that increased competitiveness and supply spillovers are major ways that FDI has positive benefits on the host country's economy. Given that productive FDI is invested in long-term assets, it should result in steady and long-lasting capital flows. When these resources are injected into the economy of a nation, they help to increase aggregate demand and, consequently, economic growth. Due to the competition that foreign investors of FDI can bring about, local businesses tend to be more productive. Amadi (2019) contends that another benefit of FDI is the creation of jobs, whereas others fervently contend that FDI has significant detrimental effects on the host nation's economy (Colen et al., 2009), and Lipsey (2004) contends that there is no consistently positive correlation between FDI and economic growth. Thus, it is possible to say that FDI's contribution to economic growth may be unclear. Nevertheless, FDI can be considered as a precipitate for economic expansion, productivity improvement, wealth generation, and technological advancement, which leads to the creation of job opportunities, innovation, improvement of local labor's skills, and global integration (Amadi, 2019).

5.5 FDI and the Kenyan Economy

Kenya was a common East African investment destination in the 1960s and 1970s, but the state's economy performed poorly in the years and decades that followed. Kenya's combination of politically motivated economic policies, widespread corruption, government misconducts, subpar public services, and poor infrastructure has discouraged FDI since the 1980s. Kenya has been a relative underperformer in attracting FDI over the last three decades. Although Kenya's performance in attracting FDI has improved slightly since the middle of the last decade, it still lags compared to neighboring countries like Tanzania and Uganda in dollar terms, even though these countries are smaller economies (Kinyanjui, 2014). However, the country is increasing its attention to the measures that could actively encourage FDI inflows. The unique combination of its location advantages can create assets that the country can offer prospective investors.

The influence of FDI on the Kenyan economy has been enormous. It can never be understated how the quality of life in Kenya has been improved because of FDI. We can always point to things that nowadays appear simple such as the introduction and use of cell phones which are now a common sight in almost the entire country. The construction of new roads and the introduction of computers in schools, especially as promoted by the government through various curricula implemented by the Ministry of Education right from primary education all the way to universities, have been a great revelation in easing technology access. Without a doubt, technology, energy, and infrastructure are some of the sectors that have been impacted the most through activities arising from foreign investment in Kenya.

In terms of the country's economic development, FDI is a major player and contributor. The progress can be seen and pointed out in all pillars that drive the progress of Kenya. We can clearly trace the influence from the Overseas Private Investment Corporation (OPIC), which established a subsidiary in Kenya in 1950 (the first FDI).

Kenya's GDP has had a boost from foreign investment mostly through the acquisition of items from local businesses or putting money into new initiatives. Undoubtedly, the results were seen in the form of job creations and growth in exports to the international markets. It is therefore very critical for Kenya's economy to try in its own very right to attract foreign investors who will invest in local firms and spur growth of the various trades and industries. This will not only benefit the locals but also regional markets because the resulting goods and services will be consumed both locally and regionally, and the international markets will receive a share of the perks.

The United States has been traditionally investing in manufacturing and agricultural sectors, in addition to FDI from countries such as Canada, China, and South Africa. This has more so been made possible through various available pacts and agreements that enable such flow of investments; for example, the African Growth and Opportunity Act (AGOA) has been a key instrument. China has over the recent years grown to be a major player in Kenya through continued target and focuses on building infrastructure, such as roads, railway lines, improvement of ports, and hydroelectric dams. We have also seen an interest from China to develop the Kenyan agricultural, food-processing, packaging, textile machinery, medical equipment, hardware and tools, and automobile and spare parts sectors.

The economic, political, and social impacts of FDI in Kenya can be broken down into three categories. FDI has been used to enhance the quality, quantity, and variety of products and services accessible to customers in a competitive market economy like Kenya. FDI's impact on politics may be less evident, but it is no less significant. A lot of foreign investors get involved in the politics of a country where they invest (Bayar, 2016). It is possible for foreign investors to be involved by trying to exert influence on local governments for the government to prefer their corporate interests above those of the local population. Foreign companies may try to persuade local officials to allow a factory to be built in Kenya—if they fear opposition from local inhabitants who oppose it on environmental grounds—by offering them money or other forms of support. If this plan becomes effective, it benefits the company's stockholders as well as its employees, but if it fails, it could have detrimental effects on the parties involved.

A report by the United Nations Conference on Trade and Development (UNCTAD) shows that a country's growth rate can be increased by as much as 5% if it has access to FDI (Diouf & Hai, 2017). In addition, FDI has a positive impact on a country's export revenues, which can increase by as much as 30%. As a matter of fact, in 2016, Kenya happened to be the host of the 14th UNCTAD assembly. We will appreciate that the declarations by the participating states, captured in the general recommendations, declaration number 13 through to number 30, highlights the key role that this body plays in promoting FDI (UNCTAD, 2016).

According to the UNDP, FDI has accounted for around 10% of Kenya's GDP growth over the past decade. It has traditionally been a matter of great concern in a world that is making strides in promoting equity and equality that women's employment rates are still lower than men's across all age groups. FDI has tried to address and bridge this gap and has, in turn, enabled the development of more jobs for women than would have been otherwise possible. "Substantial economic growth is predicted during this period"; therefore, "foreign direct investment in Kenya is expected to increase significantly over the coming decade" (UNDP).

Kenya has been interested in attracting more FDI for some time now, and there are many reasons why FDI inflows should be encouraged into the country

(Jurakulovna, 2020). First and foremost, Kenya and Kenyans need jobs; a lack of employment opportunities is one of the biggest issues facing the Kenyan people today. By attracting more FDI through increased foreign investment, Kenya will be able to create more jobs for its citizens and attract talented workers from around the world. Reviving the manufacturing industry in Kenya should be a key priority in this move because it stimulates growth of other sectors in the process. For example, in 2008, a consortium called KenGen opened a geothermal power plant in Mombasa County with funding from the Chinese government. The project created nearly 1,000 jobs for construction workers and provided training for others who were employed by the company or served as mentors for younger workers who wanted to learn more about this type of work. By creating new jobs and providing training opportunities, FDI helps develop Kenya's workforce so that it can better compete in global markets.

5.6 Does Kenya Have a Problem of FDI?

It is widely acknowledged that economic growth is reliant on both domestic and international capital (Uwazie et al., 2015). Consequently, the amount of FDI inflow is determined by the pace of growth of the economy of the country seeking FDI. Having foreign direct inflows and observing its impact on the economy are two different things. OECD (2002) argues that "FDI contributes positively to income growth and productivity if the host country has achieved a certain level of absorptive capacity."

Kenya's level of FDI has been low and stagnating, much below its potential, and there has been a concerning trend of foreign investors leaving Kenya and heading elsewhere. However, there have been conflicting reports about the specific effects that FDI has on the economy, and the decreasing levels of FDI inflows have necessitated the deployment of numerous structural and regulatory measures or several adjustments. There are ongoing efforts being done, such as the 2008-launched 2030 Vision, to ensure that Kenya becomes a middle-income economy with sustainable growth of 10% and above and the Big 4 agenda, which is a 5-year plan under the pillars: manufacturing, food security, affordable housing, and universal health coverage (Big4, 2020).

5.7 Conclusion

The ability of Kenya to attract FDI has played a role in the country's development. Since its independence in 1963, FDI inflows have continuously expanded, putting the country at the top of the list of African nations receiving FDI as of 2017. Kenya could be a potential alternative for investors wishing to expand into Africa.

In general, although with certain exceptions, FDI in Kenya has had a favorable effect on the country. In addition to providing funding for small enterprises and entrepreneurs, FDI can be a catalyst for the development of new technologies and processes. It also serves as a platform for the development of economic ties between developed and developing countries. However, FDI can have a negative influence on the Kenyan economy. Many local workers may lose their jobs or be made unemployed as a result of foreign corporations looking for low-cost labor. There are also many who suggest that foreign investors should instead invest in renewable energy sources like wind and solar instead of coal, which contributes to climate change.

Additionally, FDI has helped to diversify the economy, grow the market, and create jobs for the Kenyan populace. Kenya's infrastructure has also benefited from FDI infusions. Some of these include telecommunications, electricity, and transportation; others include a rise in the degree of development. As a result, it has become easier for the enterprises to export their products. The infusion of FDI into Kenya's economy has also been essential in propelling the country forward in terms of growth. Many Kenyans have seen a rise in their standard of living and income because of this development.

Government spending on infrastructure has been one method of realizing these advantages. Kenya's economic growth has been bolstered by the government's investment in infrastructure, which has reduced poverty. Several persons who were previously out of job have found work because of a rise in demand for their services from local businesses. Because the country's reliance on FDI has grown, so has Kenya's approach to luring it in. It is increasingly imperative for companies operating in Kenya to interact with local partners and suppliers who can help them gain access to resources. The country has become a magnet for multinational firms looking to set precedence in Africa. Companies looking to enter new markets like a progressive regulatory structure, low tax rates, and open labor market in the host nation. There has been a huge increase of FDI in Kenya since its independence because of the country's political stability and business-friendly atmosphere. Foreign ownership or control of land or public utilities or infrastructure projects is unrestricted as a result, as is foreign ownership in general. Kenya will pique the interest of multinational firms in search of new markets.

The country should participate in bilateral and multilateral trade agreements to open the economy and improve the quality of the exports by allocating more resources to development, especially in the country's outlying regions. Additionally, to inspire more confidence in international investors, the government needs to improve current policies and political will in the fight against corruption. These measures can make FDI more alluring and hence support economic growth.

The country has also been heavily reliant on agriculture as its major source of income. Erratic weather conditions have led to reduced exports, and land degradation has led to poor quality of produce, resulting in reduced prices in international markets. FDI can be channeled to promote feasibility in agricultural studies so that product quality can be increased. Additionally, Kenya can divert FDI to create and promote manufacturing industries to increase job employment opportunities.

References

Almfraji, M. A., & Almsafir, M. K. (2014). Foreign direct investment and economic growth literature review from 1994 to 2012. *Procedia - Social and Behavioral Sciences*, *129*(129), 206–213. https://doi.org/10.1016/j.sbspro.2014.03.668

Amadi, C. (2019). *FDI and economic growth in Nigeria: An analysis of the role of financial development on linkages*. Doctoral dissertation. Manchester Metropolitan University.

Asiedu, E. (2006). Foreign direct investment in Africa: The role of natural resources, market size, government policy, institutions and political instability. *The World Economy*, *29*(1), 63–77.

Bayar, Y. (2016). Impact of foreign direct investment inflows on environmental pollution in Turkey. *New Trends and Issues Proceedings on Humanities and Social Sciences*, *2*(2), 23–29. https://doi.org/10.18844/gjhss.v2i2.409

Big4 Delivery (2020). *The Big 4 - Empowering the Nation* [online]. https://big4.delivery.go.ke/

Blomström, M., Kokko, A., & Zejan, M. (1994). Host country competition, labor skills, and technology transfer by multinationals. *Review of World Economics*, *130*, 521–533.

Blomstrom, M., & Perssion, H. (1983). Foreign investment and spillover efficiency in an underdeveloped economy: Evidence from the Mexican manufacturing industry. *World Development*, *11*, 493–501.

Borensztein, E., De Gregorio, J., & Lee, J.-W. (1998). How does foreign direct investment affect economic growth? *Journal of International Economics*, *45*(1), 115–135. https://doi.org/10.1016/s0022-1996(97)00033-0

Caves, R. E. (1974). Multinational firms, competition and productivity in host country. *Economica*, *41*, 176–193.

Chia, S. Y. (1995). The international procurement and sales behavior of multinational enterprise. In *Corporate links and foreign direct investment in Asia and the Pacific*. https://doi.org/10.4324/9780429501296

Colen, L., Maertens, M., & Swinnen, J. (2009). *Do bilateral investment treaties attract FDI to developing countries?* Working LICOS Centre for Institutions and Economic Performance, KU Leuven.

Diouf, M., & Hai, Y. L. (2017). The impact of Asian foreign direct investment, trade on Africa's economic growth. *International Journal of Innovation and Economic Development*, *3*(1), 72–85. https://doi.org/10.18775/ijied.1849-7551-7020.2015.31.2004

Dunning, J. H. (1993). *Multinational enterprises and the global economy*. Addison-Wesley.

Fan, X., & Dickie, P. M. (2000). The contribution of foreign direct investment to growth and stability: A post-crisis ASEAN-5 review. *ASEAN Economic Bulletin*, *17*(3), 312–323. https://doi.org/10.1355/ae17-3f

Findlay, R. (1978). Relative backwardness, direct foreign investment, and the transfer of technology: A simple dynamic model. *Quarterly Journal of Economics*, *92*(1), 1–16.

Hanson, G. H. (2001). *Should countries promote foreign direct investment?* G-24 Discussion Paper 9. United Nations Conference on Trade and Development.

Ikiara, M. M. (2002). *Impact of foreign direct xinvestment (FDI) on technology transfer in Africa: Conceptual issues and a research agenda*. Special Paper Series No 6. African Technology Policy Studies Network.

Javorcik, B. S. (2004). Does foreign direct investment increase the productivity of domestic firms? In search of spillovers through backward linkages. *The American Economic Review*, *94*(3), 605–627. https://doi.org/10.1257/0002828041464605

Jurakulovna, J. G. (2020). The impact of direct foreign investment on the economic and social development of Uzbekistan. *International Journal of Psychosocial Rehabilitation*, *24*(4), 6374–6382. https://doi.org/10.37200/ijpr/v24i4/pr2020447

Khadenje, M. D. (2015). *The effect of foreign direct investment on economic growth in Kenya* Doctoral dissertation. University of Nairobi.

Kinyanjui, S. (2014). The impact of terrorism on foreign direct investment in Kenya. *International Journal of Business Administration*, *5*(3). https://doi.org/10.5430/ijba.v5n3p148

Lahiri, S., & Ono, Y. (2003). Export-oriented foreign direct investment and local content requirement. *Pacific Economic Review*, *8*(1), 1–14. https://doi.org/10.1111/1468-0106.00179

Lipsey, R. E. (2004). Home- and host-country effects of foreign direct investment. In *Challenges to globalization: Analyzing the economics* (pp. 333–382). University of Chicago Press.

Mackton, W., Odondo, A., & Nyongesa, D. (2018). Real effective exchange rate volatility and its impact on foreign direct investment in Kenya. *Asian Journal of Economics, Business and Accounting*, *6*(4), 1–20. https://doi.org/10.9734/ajeba/2018/38008

Makki, S. S., & Somwaru, A. (2004). Impact of foreign direct investment and trade on economic growth: Evidence from developing countries. *American Journal of Agricultural Economics*, *86*(3), 795–801.

Maskus, K. E. (2002). Intellectual property rights and foreign direct investment. *SSRN Electronic Journal*. https://doi.org/10.2139/ssrn.231122

Nyamwange, M. (2009). *Foreign direct investment in Kenya.*

OECD. (2002). *'Foreign direct investment for development: Maximising benefits, minimising costs': An Overview*. Organisation for Economic Co-Operation and Development.

Protsenko, A. (2004). *Vertical and horizontal foreign direct investments in transition countries*. Department of Economics, University of Munich.

Sacerdoti, G. (1997). Press, bilateral treaties and multilateral instruments. *Journal of International Economic Law*, *269*, 261–287.

Stiglitz, J. E., & Charlton, A. (2007). *Fair trade for all: How trade can promote development*. Oxford University Press.

UNCTAD. (1998). *World Investment Report*. United Nations, New York.

United Nations Conference on Trade and Development. (2016). *Declaration of Civil Society to UNCTAD XIV*. United Nations.

Uwazie, I. U., Igwemma, A. A., & Nnabu, B. E. (2015). Causal relationship between foreign direct investment and economic growth in Nigeria: 1970-2013. *International Journal of Economics and Finance*, *7*(11), 230. https://doi.org/10.5539/ijef.v7n11p230

Chapter 6

Foreign Direct Investment: Nigeria Case Study of the Manufacturing Sector

Abstract

Globalization efforts have continued to expand with the aid of foreign direct investment (FDI) inflows from the developed region to developing economies. The inflow of FDI presents a huge economic opportunity for developing countries like Nigeria to stimulate local manufacturing productivity through the flow of capital, expertise, and critical technology. However, the extent to which the inflow of FDI promotes local productivity remains uncertain owing to the mixed findings in literature. This chapter x-rays the effect of FDI inflows on domestic investment in the manufacturing sector.

Keywords: FDI; Nigeria; manufacturing sector; manufacturing productivity; economic development

6.1 Introduction

Globalization now promotes cross-border trade, especially between multinational companies (MNCs). Through this type of investment, the term foreign direct investment (FDI) became popular among developing nations. FDI is the kind of investment that occurs over borders wherein a foreign investor acquires a long-term stake and considerable power in an enterprise in another economy (Belloumi & Alshehry, 2021). Lately, developing nations have considered FDI a valuable pillar of their economic growth strategies. According to Yahia et al. (2018), this is probably because FDI brings capital, technology, marketing, and management. There are concerns that FDI can fill up gaps and shortage of financial resources, marketing, technology, skills, and know-how, which are believed to be capable of improving the economy (Danmola et al., 2017).

Abu and Abd Karim (2016) suggest that FDI can also indirectly help increase domestic investment in sectors such as manufacturing productivity and creating

Foreign Direct Investment, 77–92

Published under exclusive licence by Emerald Publishing Limited
doi:10.1108/978-1-83662-900-920261006

jobs in developing economies. The argument is that foreign capital from the inflow of FDI can fill the gap in local investment, boost productivity, increase competition, and create managerial and technological spillovers in the host country. The inflow of FDI to developing economies reached about 524 billion USD at the end of 2023, although it fell by 9% from the previous year (UNCTAD). However, for Nigeria, the inflow of FDI has continued to dwindle in the last decades. Between 2010 and 2011, FDI inflow to Nigeria rose from 6.03 billion USD to 8.84 billion USD, but this size of FDI inflow plummeted to about 0.78 billion USD in 2018, but the inflow of FDI increased to 3.31 million USD in 2021 but also declined to −0.9 USD billion in 2022.

Even though the FDI inflow for Nigeria has been dwindling, how has it driven domestic investment in Nigeria that spurs local productivity within the manufacturing sector? This is because the inflow of FDI to Nigeria is expected to come with technology, technical know-how, and even healthy competition that can spur local productivity. Since FDI inflow is even dwindling in Nigeria, meaning that some areas that FDI must drive in the Nigerian economy directly remain open, such an open areas, especially in the manufacturing sector, are expected to be developed by local entrepreneurs, which consequently can stimulate a rise in domestic investment and general economic development.

Regrettably, Nigerian domestic investment in terms of manufacturing output development over three decades remains poor, thereby contributing minimally to the performance of the Nigerian economy (Danmola et al., 2017). For instance, in real terms, the manufacturing sector's contribution to Nigeria's GDP decreased to N1.5 trillion in the second quarter of June 2023. This indicates a quarterly decrease of 17.24% as compared to the N1.8 trillion contribution reported in the first quarter of 2023. How has FDI inflow driven domestic investment in the manufacturing sector in Nigeria is critical for examination to understand the intricate dynamics between FDI and domestic investment to guide domestic policy measures to support manufacturing sector development in Nigeria.

Considering the central role FDI plays in developing economies in terms of augmenting domestic investment and productivity in the manufacturing sector, there is a need to rethink Nigeria's approach to bringing and captivating FDI. Despite the global inclination toward a higher level of FDI, Nigeria has experienced a depressing trend in FDI inflow since the beginning of the last decade (Miao et al., 2021; Mounde, 2017). Sharma et al. (2022) and Olusegun (2021) noted that the reduction in inward FDI investments also explains the loss of critical technologies and market expansion opportunities, coupled with the need for policymakers and business leaders to create an environment for FDI growth.

Therefore, the role of FDI inflow in stimulating local productivity in the manufacturing industry becomes clear with the help of technology transfer, knowledge sharing, and competition stimulation (Aigheyisi, 2017). Nevertheless, the falling FDI inflows now cast doubt on the need to take a proactive approach to draw and retain foreign investors. Sharma et al. (2022) emphasizes that it would require fixing the physical deficits, harmonizing the regulatory processes, and creating a business environment for green investment. Nigeria can thus successfully rejuvenate its manufacturing sector, attract more domestic investment, and emotionally boost the economy and development by harnessing the advantages of FDI.

Nonetheless, the fact that there are dwindling investments in both local and manufacturing industry output denotes that effective and holistic policy intervention should be devised to reduce the industrial-base sluggish development in Nigeria to a minimal level. While FDI seems to be a remedy, it can also be vital to empower local entrepreneurs, ensure access to finance and technology, protect innovations, and enhance skills to drive local productivity, thereby stimulating the local manufacturing sector (Idoko & Taiga, 2018). This can be achieved by creating synergies between FDI and domestic investors to tap into the untold potential within the local manufacturing sector of Nigeria to create employment, among other things (Eze et al., 2019). Fundamentally, a holistic plan focused on creating targeted policies, building strategic partnerships, implementing required reforms, and ensuring that there is a system of checks and balances for future development for all generations to come is fundamental.

6.2 Foreign Direct Investment Inflow in Nigeria

FDI influx in Nigeria refers to the movement of funds from foreign companies into the country to start new businesses, purchase existing ones, or make long term investments in various areas of the Nigerian economy. FDI is a significant type of foreign investment that supports international commerce, knowledge transfer, and economic integration. Emako et al. (2022) showed that FDI is a crucial driver of global economic growth and development. The trajectory of FDI inflows to Nigeria in US dollars from 1985 to 2022 is depicted in Fig. 1, demonstrating how erratic and unstable FDI inflows into Nigeria has been.

Fig. 1 shows Nigeria's FDI inflow trend over the specified period. Before this trend, Nigeria has seen a rise in FDI inflow since 1970, notwithstanding some notable fluctuations. FDI inflow, for example, rose from $205 million in 1970 to $470 million in 1975. There was a decrease in FDI inflows from 1976 to 1980. By the end of 1989, FDI inflows to Nigeria had risen significantly from $193 million in 1986 to $1.88 billion. The abrupt surge in FDI inflows during that period can be ascribed to several investment-promoting federal government initiatives, including the lifting of restrictions on foreign investors and their participation in the upstream and downstream oil sub-sectors (Amade et al., 2022; Adelakun & Ogujiuba, 2023). Fig. 1 illustrates how FDI inflows into Nigeria increased between 1991 and 1994. This was mostly caused by increased government action to encourage foreign investment in the economy.

FDI flow increased further before seeing a notable decline between 1997 and 1999. This was the time of transition from military to democratic governance. By 2000, FDI inflows had improved, with net inflows exceeding $1.14 billion. Between 2002 and 2005, Nigeria's FDI inflow continued to expand, rising from $1.87 billion to $4.98 billion. According to Okafor (2012) and Osabohien et al. (2020), one likely explanation for this is enhanced foreigners' trust in the domestic economy due to the transition from military to democratic rule. Additionally, during this time, Nigeria's economy was able to draw in foreign investment due to several economic changes and incentives provided to foreigners. FDI inflows to Nigeria totaled $8.19 billion in 2008. Most FDIs in the nation went into the extractive, oil and gas, and communication industries. As a result, the economy is still not very diversified, with 95% of export revenue coming from oil exports and less than 2% coming from the industrial sector (Kunle et al., 2014). In 2010, the amount of FDI inflow decreased due to the negative impact of the global financial crisis, although this was particularly apparent in the portfolio investment module.

FDI influx to the nation was around $775 million in 2018, compared to $2.41 billion in 2017. This difference indicates a decline in FDI inflow because of the austerity measures implemented in 2018. FDI inflows decreased to $186 million in 2022 from $3.31 billion in 2021. Several causes contributed to Nigeria's fall in FDI inflows, which fell from $3.31 billion in 2021 to $186 million in 2022. As noted by Akinwalere and Chang (2023), policies that boost trade have a better economic growth effect than investment policies, according to the trade-led growth theory. Amade et al. (2022) also support this statement, reaffirming that FDI is negatively related to economic growth. Zoramawa and Kiru (2022) explain that natural resources and openness to trade are key factors that attract FDI. These factors likely contributed to the decline in FDI in Nigeria and the impact of trade policy and austerity measures.

In the mid-1980s, Nigeria's FDI inflows were not high, indicating that foreign investors preferred a cautious approach. The uptrend from 1989 to $4.282087862 is due to investor confidence, market turnaround, and other market conditions. The government may have implemented policies that promoted economic

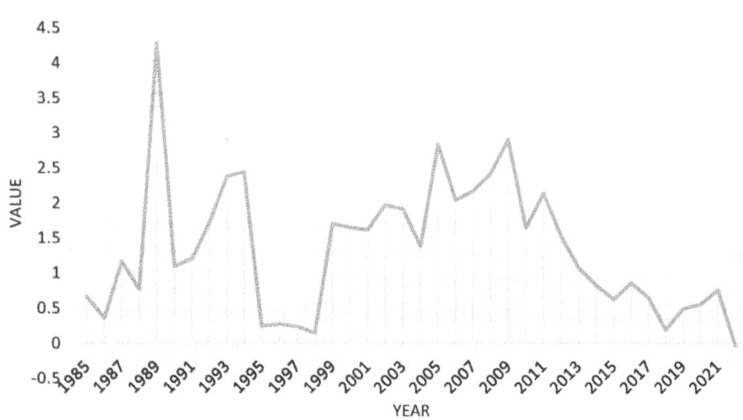

Fig. 1. FDI Inflow(net) in Nigeria, 1985 to 2022, in US$. *Source:* authors'.

stability and attracted foreign capital. This period likely saw a diversification of sectors, with perhaps a focus on oil and natural resources, which have traditionally been significant contributors to Nigeria's FDI.

The modest upturn in 2019 and 2020 indicates initiatives to tackle issues and establish laws to draw in foreign capital. The significant rise in 2021 ($0.75156918) points to a resurgence of interest, either because of advantageous economic circumstances or focused policy measures. However, the negative figure in 2022 ($−0.039522367) raises concerns and shows a net outflow is affected by external reasons, policy changes, or economic issues that require additional investigation to develop effective improvement solutions.

6.3 Overview of the Manufacturing Sector in Nigeria

In the modern world, a country's manufacturing sector is utilized to assess its economic effectiveness (Nyor & Chinge, 2014). However, after crude oil was discovered in Nigeria in the late 1950s, the nation turned its focus from being a leading developing industrial production base to producing crude oil (Banjoko et al., 2012); this jeopardized the nation's economic activities and increased the unemployment rate. Due to a persistent noneconomic approach and a flagrant disregard for other economic sectors like agriculture, tourism, mining, and manufacturing, the underutilization of these potentials has made the nation's widespread poverty, low individual standards of living, and rising unemployment worse (Okon & Osesie, 2017). Nigeria, the largest country in Africa, has long been considered a country endowed with abundant human and material resources. Manufacturing is a component of the industrial sector, which includes processing, mining, quarrying, and crafting. Thus, according to Okon and Osesie (2017), manufacturing is converting raw materials into finished commodities, intermediate goods, or producer goods.

The manufacturing sector has been a vital sector for economic development in many developing countries, including Nigeria. It acts as a catalyst in transforming the economic structure of countries from simple, slow-growing, and low-value activities to more productive ones (Nwosa, 2018). However, the Nigerian manufacturing sector's output has been sluggish over the years, particularly when compared with other sectors of the economy (Giwa et al., 2020). Using the index of manufacturing output, the manufacturing sector expanded between 1970 (the year the civil war ended) and 1982 (see Fig. 2). Manufacturing grew at a faster average annual rate in the second half of the 1970s than it did in the first, starting to pick up speed in the first half of the 1980s. Manufacturing started to decrease after 1982. Nigeria's manufacturing sector has so far produced a good number of commodities for the country. Studies like Tonuchi and Onyebuchi (2019) have revealed recently that Nigeria exports items to foreign nations. Nowadays, Nigerians buy products created in their country. In 1994, the industrial sector's performance showed a minor improvement, with an industry growth index of 20.92. 2010 was the year with the least growth for the sector, with an industrial growth index of 6.55 (see to Fig. 2). This results from the nation's over reliance on imports. In 2021, the government's tactics of promoting domestic manufacturing and prohibiting specific imported goods have resulted in a 14.61 growth index.

The Nigerian manufacturing sector, seen in the trend in Fig. 2, has witnessed a series of fluctuations and unstable growth, which has been reflected in its share of Gross Domestic Product (GDP) and the economy. As pointed out by Ajide et al. (2022), the problems associated with the manufacturing sector persisted despite the government's efforts to establish the National Economic Empowerment Development Strategy (NEEDS), which emphasized the relevance of rising manufacturing sector performance. Due to the dominance of the food, beverage, tobacco, beer, spirit, and textile sectors over the manufacturing activity structure, the industrial growth structure was primarily oriented toward the consumer goods industries. The consumer products industry dominates both value addition and employment (Banjoko et al., 2012). According to Eze et al. (2019), by 1985, the durable consumer goods sectors, which had started to grow quickly in the middle of the 1970s, had not yet had a major influence. Likewise, the manufacturing of value addition was not significantly aided by the transportation, machinery, equipment, mental fabrication, chemicals, energy, or engineering sectors (Oburota & Okoi, 2017). The manufacturing sector's performance saw a steep downturn in 1984 because of the drop in global oil prices. Uma et al. (2019) claim that this poor performance reveals the sector's underlying weakness, which had been mainly shielded from competition by the Import Substitution Industrialization (ISI) program the nation enacted following its independence in 1960. The pyramid tariff structure, which has gradually higher taxes on imports of consumer products and relatively low rates on imports of capital and intermediate goods, therefore became emblematic of the ISI process.

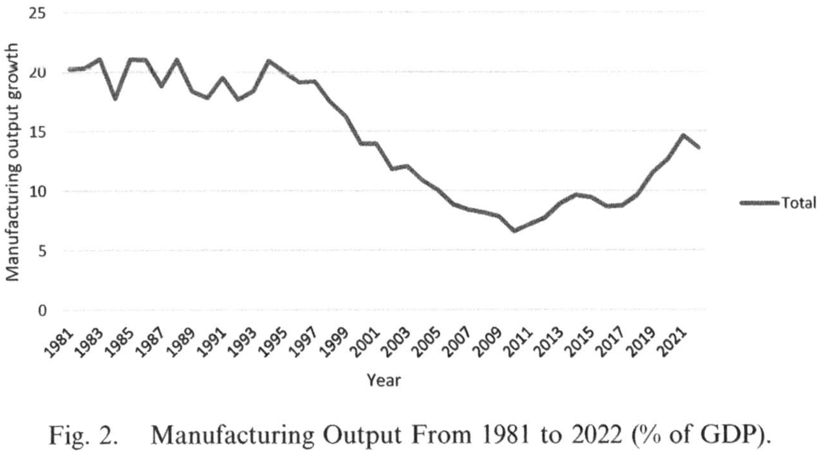

Fig. 2. Manufacturing Output From 1981 to 2022 (% of GDP).
Source: authors'.

According to Nyor and Chinge (2014), there was a notable decrease in import substitution in the manufacture of nondurable consumer products under the SAP (Structure Adjustment Program), but a small rise in import substitution in the production of durable consumer goods. This demonstrated that most of the foreign money earned in the auction market went to the manufacturing sector. Usually, 70–80% of auction proceeds go into industrial expansion, particularly for raw materials, equipment, and replacement parts; the remaining portion is used for final consumer items. Numerous factors contribute to the industrial sector's subpar performance; such as, trade restrictions in industrialized nations, the economy's overall dismal macroeconomic performance, which results in low aggregate demand, lower demand for local producers due to subpar products, and the flood of relatively cheaper imports (Oburota & Okoi, 2017; Olusegun, 2021; Tonuchi & Onyebuchi, 2019). Domestic manufacturers' high prices are partly attributable to higher costs, inefficient and aging equipment, poor infrastructure, and the currency (naira) depreciation. The Nigerian government has taken proactive steps to improve the productivity level of the sector, such as adopting an import-substitution industrialization strategy (Uma et al., 2019). However, the 2014 Nigeria Industrial Revolution Plan (NIRP) and the 2017 Economic Recovery Growth Plan (ERGP) failed to achieve the desired levels of growth and development.

6.4 The Role of Manufacturing Sector Development on the Nigerian Economy

Nigeria's primary economic activity is agriculture, but in recent years, rapid growth has been seen in the services sector (Ebire et al., 2018). While the manufacturing sector is usually considered the most significant contributor to productivity, its contribution could be better. Leading service sectors like software, business processing, finance, and tourism may be at the edge of development, while the manufacturing role will gradually shrink. Still, empirical research shows that the change from agriculture to manufacturing and services is the correct structural transformation (Djokoto, 2021). It is argued that manufacturing effectively creates an economy that grows faster and shares wealth.

Manufacturing is a prime area for the prosperity of Nigeria's economy since it is essential for developing and opening the economy. Manufacturing provides more direct jobs requiring more production, assembly, and quality control workers. Such jobs allow more stable employment and offer more wages to more people (Ndugbu et al., 2017). The manufacturing sector has strong backward and forward linkages, and multiple employment opportunities. These interactions will strengthen the economy in the long run as more jobs are added.

Manufacturing creates job opportunities, increases the workforce and consumer spending power, and promotes economic activities by increasing demand for goods and services across various industries (Yahia et al., 2018). It expands Nigeria's export base and boosts GDP by stimulating further action along the value chains, from raw materials to finished goods (Duramany-Lakkoh et al., 2021). Manufacturing also strengthens economies by cascading growth in other sectors.

Other important benefits of manufacturing make it the best driver of economic growth in emerging economies. These include the huge potential for scale economies, the generally inverse relationship between prices and demand for manufactured goods, and the possibility of increasing exports to developed countries (Danladi et al., 2015; Nyor & Chinge, 2014; Obasi, 2023). Mesagan and Ezeji (2016) contended that manufacturing aids in achieving a just equilibrium between the production of commodities for export and local rivalry for imported products. In the end, converting resources into completed items will increase their worth, lessen our reliance on a particular industry, and lessen our susceptibility to outside shocks.

Manufacturing has unique characteristics that make this sector exert a greater influence on price stability, even if agriculture and services also have an impact on CPI. One example, Asaleye et al. (2018) claim, is that because manufacturing entails several production and distribution phases, businesses may simplify their supply chains and lower unit costs and consumer pricing. It also gains from economies of scale, which enable mass manufacturing and reduce unit costs and product pricing. For example, according to Akinmulegun and Akinde (2019), the purchase of used cars in Nigeria in 2021 accounted for 3.7% of all imports, indicating that many Nigerians cannot afford to buy a new car. Nevertheless, the establishment of Innoson Vehicle Manufacturing Company is shifting the scenario since new vehicles' prices are going down (Chukwu & Nduka, 2022).

Nigeria's manufacturing industry faces the same problems: the lack of infrastructure, inadequate access to capital, the unfriendly business environment, and limited market integration. Miao et al. (2021) claim that insufficiency in infrastructure, especially in power supply and transportation, augments operation costs and hinders competitiveness. The country's higher production costs and usage of emergency power generators are worsening these problems. In addition, the absence of efficient rail systems will increase operating costs (Adejumo & Asongu, 2020). Through policy measures, the manufacturing sector credit is being pulled in; however, banking credit is unattractive to manufacturing companies. Hence, internal revenue generation is the crucial source for their operation, which limits their potential and competitiveness in the regional and international markets (Oduola et al., 2022). The chaotic business environment, full of inconsistent policies and regulations that are usually changed too often, lowers investor confidence and complicates attracting domestic and foreign direct investment (Eze et al., 2019). Also, security problems bring along uncertainty that consequently makes the economy unstable. For this purpose, the government should remove bureaucracy, create conditions for long-term investments, and invest in infrastructure projects. Nwosa (2018) pointed out this will make manufacturers concentrate on innovation, expansion, and job creation, thus boosting economic growth. Infrastructure development is also pivotal in diversifying the manufacturing sector.

6.5 The Role of FDI on Local Manufacturing Sector Development

Manufacturing is essential for producing goods and services, job creation, and economic growth in developing countries. All over the world, it is common for countries to advance their productive sectors by investing more or attracting FDI that delivers new technologies and innovations and creates jobs. Nigeria, which mainly produces oil, has a magnet for FDI, which has consequently influenced the growth of the manufacturing sector.

FDI transfers technology and management skills to host countries, boosting productivity and economic growth (Amadi, 2019; Miao et al., 2021). Nevertheless, Nigeria has constantly increased and declined FDI inflows and outflows, averaging USD 53 billion in 2013 and an all-time low in 2011 due to political disruptions in several transition countries (Afolabi et al., 2019). This has caused a plunge in the investment attractiveness of the whole area, and some investors have been suspending their operations or withdrawing their investments.

In Nigeria, foreign investment can be traced to the colonial era when the colonialists were mainly focused on developing their economies by exploiting the country's resources. The discovery of oil in 1956 encouraged MNCs, which led the Nigerian government to implement various strategies and policies that can be used to incentivize FDI (Giwa et al., 2020). Conversely, literature has shown that the growth-stimulating effect of FDI on the manufacturing sector is country-specific, such that certain nations having better business climates will likely attract more FDI inflows. Consequently, the influence of FDI on the domestic manufacturing industry is significant.

FDI significantly impacts the local manufacturing sector through access to cash, technology, management skills, and external markets. This contributes to economic growth and industrial upgrading. FDI contains capital investment, advanced technology, and managerial competence, which can help local manufacturing firms improve their productivity and efficiency. The injection of funds allows local manufacturers to modernize their production processes, adopt new technologies, and improve their product quality to succeed in domestic and international markets (UNCTAD).

Moreover, FDI establishes connections between foreign affiliates and local suppliers, subcontractors, and service providers. These connections build local supply chains, facilitate technology transfer, and spark the growth of similar industries. In addition, local manufacturing can benefit by accessing new markets, specialized inputs, and workforce skill development opportunities, resulting in increased employment and more income generation (World Bank). According to Borensztein et al. (1998), FDI stimulates domestic investment, fosters exports, and transfers managerial and technological skills – all beneficial for economic growth, particularly in emerging nations. Furthermore, Blomström and Kokko (1997) emphasized FDI's role in fostering positive spillover effects that help the local manufacturing sector, such as knowledge transfer and skill upgrading.

Nonetheless, some believe that the capacity of developing countries to attract foreign investment is a function of the presence of natural resources, their market sizes, the level of political stability, and other macroeconomic stimulus (Orji et al., 2015). This invariably suggests that supporting local manufacturing firms is not one of the attractions of FDI. Little wonder the Nigerian manufacturing sector, despite having a vast potential for economic development, still struggles and cannot attract the spillover effect of FDI through technology and knowledge transfer. FDI inflow to Nigeria has focused largely on the extractive industry instead of the manufacturing sector (Ojo & Ololade, 2013).

On the contrary, many schools of thought are of the view that the failure of the manufacturing sector was a result of a lack of modern capital equipment, over-dependency on the external sector for the supply of inputs, weak demand for the manufacturing sector's products. low export market, and the inability of the sector to create forward and backward linkages with the rest of the economy (Ojo & Ololade, 2013). Perhaps, encouraging mergers or outright acquisitions by foreign MNCs, which are an element of FDI, would enhance the development of the manufacturing sector.

The enhancing effect of FDI on the manufacturing sector appears to be country-specific, as it varies from one country to another; while the effect could be positive to some, to others, it can be adverse (Borensztein et al., 1998). Alluding to this theory, some school of thought asserts that contrary to the overbearing belief in the development tenet, the growth-stimulating effect of FDI is not automatic but stems from country-specific factors. Hence, a country with a better conducive business environment is more likely to attract more FDI inflows. Although presently, the Nigerian manufacturing sector cannot support economic development, the sector remains particularly important in the process of industrialization because of its multi-dimensional benefits to the development process while being the most attention-grabbing market in the continent of Africa (Adejumo, 2013).

6.6 How Has Foreign Direct Investment Driven Manufacturing Sector Performance in Nigeria

With the influx of FDI, Nigeria's manufacturing sector has been immensely boosted in terms of the provision of capital, technology, expertise, and market access. These investments have improved competitiveness, productivity, employment, and technical innovations, thus increasing output and chances of trade in both international and domestic markets (Ndugbu et al., 2017). FDI flows have expanded and renovated manufacturing facilities, leading to increased output and competitiveness. FDI has enhanced Nigeria's manufacturing sector through increased productivity, employment creation, and technological advancement. In addition, knowledge and skill transmission have enhanced productive procedures and product quality. Nevertheless, the long-term effects of FDI on Nigeria's manufacturing sector have diverse perceptions. Some studies stipulate a negative long-term effect, while others claim a positive but insignificant impact. Fig. 3 best demonstrates this influence and how it helps develop the manufacturing sectors of Nigeria.

The graph in Fig. 3 represents the FDI and the output of the manufacturing sector in Nigeria. The fluctuating nature of FDI inflows and output within the manufacturing sector can be a clear example of the general dynamicity of the global and local economies. For instance, in the period, FDI flows into Nigeria tended to follow the pattern of output growth in the manufacturing sector during a ten-year transition that spanned the 1980s and early 1990s. This period also marked an unprecedented coordination in the inflow of foreign capital, which in turn promoted the development of the manufacturing sector by introducing new technologies and the enlargement of production capacity and employment. The year-to-year positive correlation is just a confirmation of the truth that, as far as investment goes, it creates manufacturing activities and ascending economies.

On the other hand, toward the end of the nineties, a big factor that altered the decision between FDI inflows and manufacturing output was completely different. The manufacturing sector clearly encounters various other factors, such as policy instabilities, deficient infrastructures, or stringent regulations. Anetor (2019) noted that this innovation suggests an adjusted perception of manufacturing firms' development, where it is not always possible to guarantee their growth through FDI unless other aspects of the economy and institutions are considered.

The early 2000s were the period when FDIs and manufacturing sector outputs were back on the list. These are the signs of both the existence and possible positive externality of the link between foreign investments and industrial development. The efficiency with which the government addressed the economic environment and implemented specific policies to encourage and support investors may have facilitated the uptrend. The period represents why it is necessary to be a relevant business and a good policy framework if you want to be the best first effects of FDI through manufacturing.

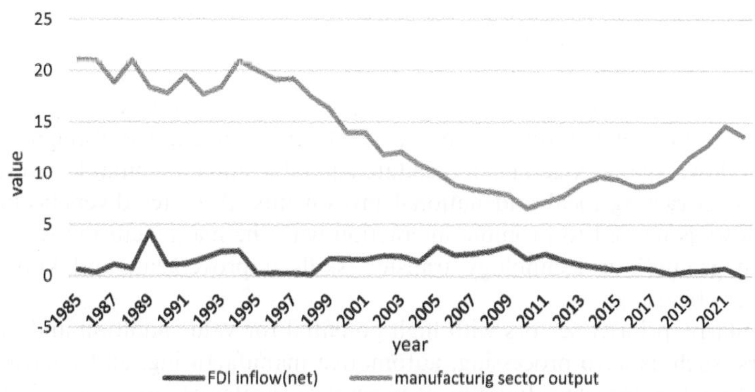

Fig. 3. FDI and Manufacturing Sector Output From 1985 to 2022. *Source:* authors'.

The global financial crisis in 2008 invited a steep plummet in FDI inflows to Nigeria. Thus, there was a significant drop in the manufacturing industry's productivity in Nigeria. FDI inflow during this period might have led to the shrinking of the manufacturing sector, after which the sector's fragility toward global economic shocks re-emerged (Oduola et al., 2022). That FDI volatility for Nigerian manufacturing, especially within the past few years, is still a matter of concern; however, this sector still possesses the power to surmount even the most complicated difficulties. Although what is particularly clear is the fact that FDI has been contributing to an increase in manufacturing sector output since 2010, it is high time for the authorities to dedicate their time and efforts to the creation of investor-oriented programs and policies that will help the sector to grow (Ndugbu et al., 2017).

Nevertheless, the positive FDI inflow direction signifies a profound inquiry into what contributed to this shift. In line with the study of Miao et al. (2021), finding out the reasons behind this situation is a priority to policymakers to tackle the impediments that are hindering the great works from being done well and the later performance of the sector, the manufacturing sector in Nigeria.

6.7 Conclusion and Recommendations

Diversification of FDI can be initiated through infrastructure development, relaxation of regulation, and encouraging skills growth and technology transfer. Again, policy coherence, institutional strengthening, and governance administration must be enhanced to win and exploit investor trust and increase investment inflows. To this end, addressing these issues and creating a participative and cooperative environment will help Nigeria meet its target of high FDI inflows and enhance productivity, leading to sustainable economic development and prosperity.

There is a need for strategic measures to uncover potential values of FDI that will make industrial growth and economic development sustainable. For instance, Nigeria's FDI policy should focus on comprehensive reforms, aiming to increase the investment climate and improve the quality of the business environment. This includes streamlining bureaucratic procedures, cutting red tape, and consolidating institutions to create an environment for foreign capital inward flow. Again, Nigeria can facilitate equitable and commutable investment settings, attracting local and national investments. A better diversification of FDI flows is needed to promote interaction with the manufacturing sector and lay the ground for technology transfer, skills improvement, and knowledge spillover effects.

Similarly, priority sectors with high potential for value addition and income earners, such as agro-processing, automotive manufacturing, and pharmaceuticals, should be targeted. Investment promotion strategies, fiscal incentives, and sector-specific policies can be used to foster investment in these sectors. The government should focus on capacity building and upgrading existing facilities for the development of the manufacturing sector and, at the same time, to promote productive FDI. Ultimately, policymakers ought to strongly emphasize inclusive growth strategies and development programs that designate some of the FDI shares for the distribution of wealth between rich and poor, consequently lifting households out of poverty. This objective will be achieved through policies that lead to job creation, skills development, and value chain inclusivity across geographical and socio-economic spaces.

There is need to enhance the future impact of FDI on the country's economic growth. Among the main measures are adopting strategies to promote FDI into sectors of the economy more productive such as manufacturing and be more transformative in terms of adding value. This involves, among other measures, stimulating specially oriented investment, urging regulatory harmonization, and capturing the attention of potential foreign investors to the areas in which they, as aforesaid, can employ their advice, technology, and capital. Strategic alliances between foreign investors and local manufacturing industries make FDI output and productivity more productive. Also, lawmakers could begin with actions geared toward knowledge transfer, technology diffusion, joint ventures, research partnerships, and capacity-building programs. Consequently, the manufacturing sector's productivity is affected by measures that positively reinforce the coherence of policies. Therefore, authorities should implement a transparent legal system that safeguards assets and contracts, thereby creating a favorable environment for foreign investors.

References

Abu, N., & Abd Karim, M. Z. (2016). The relationships between foreign direct investment, domestic savings, domestic investment, and economic growth: The case of Sub-Saharan Africa. *Society and Economy*, *38*(2), 193–217.

Adejumo, A. V. (2013). Foreign direct investments and manufacturing sector performance in Nigeria, (1970-2009). *Australian Journal of Business and Management Research*, *3*(4), 39.

Adejumo, A. V., & Asongu, S. A. (2020). *Foreign direct investment, domestic investment and green growth in Nigeria: Any spillovers?* (pp. 839–861). Springer International Publishing.

Adelakun, J., & Ogujiuba, K. (2023). A comparative analysis of the determinants of foreign direct investment: The case of top ten recipients of foreign direct investment in Africa. *Economies*, *11*(10), 244.

Afolabi, A., Laseinde, O. T., Oluwafemi, I. J., Atolagbe, O. D., & Oluwafemi, J. F. (2019, December). Correlation between manufacturing sectors and foreign direct investment. *Journal of Physics: Conference Series*, *1378*(3), 032005.

Aigheyisi, O. S. (2017). The effect of foreign direct investment on domestic investment in Nigeria: Any role for financial development and human capital? *Amity Journal of Economics*, *2*(2), 1–20.

Ajide, F. M., Dada, J. T., & Olowookere, J. K. (2022). Shadow economy and foreign direct investment in Nigerian manufacturing industry. *International Journal of Economics and Business Research*, *23*(2), 156–180.

Akinmulegun, S. O., & Akinde, J. A. (2019). Financial deepening and manufacturing sector performance in Nigeria (1981-2017). *Journal of Economics and Finance, 10* (4), 18–27.

Akinwalere, S., & Chang, K. (2023). The determinants of foreign-direct-investment (FDI) inflows in Nigeria. *The Journal of Developing Areas*, *57*(4), 91–105.

Amade, M. A., Mohammed, I., Ibisanmi, E. V., Owolabi, A. T., & Joshua, U. (2022). Interaction between domestic investment foreign direct investment and economic growth in Nigeria. *Ömer Halisdemir Üniversitesi İktisadi ve İdari Bilimler Fakültesi Dergisi*, *15*(2), 261–275.

Amadi, C. (2019). *FDI and economic growth in Nigeria: An analysis of the role of financial development on linkages.* Doctoral dissertation. Manchester Metropolitan University.

Anetor, F. O. (2019). Foreign direct investment inflows and real sector: A vector autoregressive (VAR) approach for the Nigerian economy. *The Journal of Developing Areas*, *53*(3).

Asaleye, A. J., Adama, J. I., & Ogunjobi, J. O. (2018). Financial sector and manufacturing sector performance: Evidence from Nigeria. *Investment Management and Financial Innovations*, *15*(3), 35–48.

Banjoko, S. A., Iwuji, I. I., & Bagshaw, K. (2012). The performance of the Nigerian manufacturing sector: A 52-year analysis of growth and retrogression (1960–2012). *Journal of Asian Business Strategy*, *2*(8), 177–191.

Belloumi, M., & Alshehry, A. S. (2021). The causal relationships between corruption, investments and economic growth in GCC countries. *Sage Open*, *11*(4). https://doi.org/10.1177/21582440211054425

Blomström, M., & Kokko, A. (1997). *How foreingn investment affects hose countries* (No. 1745). World Bank Publications.

Borensztein, E., De Gregorio, J., & Lee, J. W. (1998). How does foreign direct investment affect economic growth? *Journal of International Economics*, *45*(1), 115–135.

Chukwu, K. O., & Nduka, J. A. (2022). Manufacturing sector and economic development of Nigeria. *Journal of Emerging Trends in Management Sciences and Entrepreneurship*, *4*(2), 111–128.

Danladi, J. D., Akomolafe, K. J., Babalola, O., & Oladipupo, A. R. (2015). Globalisation and the Nigerian manufacturing sector. *Journal of Law, Policy and Globalization*, *41*, 202.

Danmola, R. A., Olateju, A. O., & Aminu, A. W. (2017). The impact of foreign direct investment on the Nigeria manufacturing sector: A time series analysis. *European Scientific Journal*, *13*(31), 521–556.

Djokoto, J. G. (2021). Level of development, foreign direct investment and domestic investment in food manufacturing. *F1000Research*, *10*. https://doi.org/10.12688/f1000research.28681.3

Duramany-Lakkoh, E. K., Jalloh, M. S., & Jalloh, A. (2021). Foreign direct investment and manufacturing sector in Sierra Leone: A vector auto-regression analysis approach. *Journal of Mathematical Finance*, *11*(4), 620–650.

Ebire, K., Onmonya, O., & Inim, V. E. (2018). Effects of the determinants of foreign direct investment in Nigeria: Error correction mechanism. *Asian Journal of Economics and Empirical Research*, *5*(2), 155–164.

Emako, E., Nuru, S., & Menza, M. (2022). The effect of foreign direct investment on economic growth in developing countries. *Transnational Corporations Review, 14* (4), 382–401.

Eze, A. A., Nnaji, M., & Nkalu, N. C. (2019). Impact of foreign direct investment on manufacturing sector output growth in Nigeria. *International Journal of Applied Economics, Finance and Accounting, 5*.

Giwa, B. A., George, E. O., Okodua, H., & Adediran, O. S. (2020). Empirical analysis of the effects of foreign direct investment inflows on Nigerian real economic growth: Implications for sustainable development goal-17. *Cogent Social Sciences, 6*(1), 1727621.

Idoko, C. U., & Taiga, U. U. (2018). Effect of foreign direct investment (FDI) on manufacturing output in Nigeria (1981–2016). *Advances in Social Sciences Research Journal, 5*(5).

Kunle, A. M., Olowe, S. O., & Oluwafolakemi, F. O. (2014). Impact of foreign direct investment on Nigeria economic growth. *International Journal of Academic Research in Business and Social Sciences, 4*(8), 234.

Mesagan, E. P., & Ezeji, A. C. (2016). *The role of social and economic infrastructure in manufacturing sector performance in Nigeria*. University Library of Munich.

Miao, M., Borojo, D. G., Yushi, J., & Desalegn, T. A. (2021). The impacts of Chinese FDI on domestic investment and economic growth for Africa. *Cogent Business & Management, 8*(1), 1886472.

Mounde, W. L. (2017). Causal relationship between foreign direct investment and manufacturing output in Nigeria. *International Journal of Advanced Studies in Business Strategies and Management, 5*(2), 233–267.

Ndugbu, M. O., Duruechi, A. H., & Ojegbe, J. S. (2017). Macroeconomic policy variables and foreign direct investment in Nigeria. *IIARD International Journal of Banking and Finance Research, 3*(2), 112–136.

Nwosa, P. I. (2018). Foreign direct investment in Nigeria: Its role and importance in industrial sector growth. *Acta Universitatis Danubius. OEconomica, 14*(2), 41–52.

Nyor, G. A., & Chinge, A. D. (2014). The impacts of industrial policies on the manufacturing sector in Nigeria: An assessment. *Research on Humanities and Social Sciences, 4*(21), 111–120.

Obasi, K. J. (2023). Manufacturing: The key to economic growth and shared prosperity in Nigeria. *Economic and Policy Review, 21*(1), 41–46.

Oburota, C., & Okoi, I. (2017). Manufacturing subsector and economic growth in Nigeria. *British Journal of Economics, Management & Trade, 17*(3), 1–9.

Oduola, M., Bello, M. O., & Popoola, R. (2022). Foreign direct investment, institution and industrialisation in Sub-Saharan Africa. *Economic Change and Restructuring*, 1–30.

Ojo, A. S., & Ololade, O. F. (2013). An assessment of the Nigerian manufacturing sector in the era of globalization. *American Journal of Social and Management Sciences, 5*(1), 27–32.

Okafor, H. O. (2012). Do domestic macroeconomic variables matter for foreign direct investment inflow in Nigeria. *Research Journal of Finance and Accounting, 3* (9), 55–67.

Okon, E. O., & Osesie, S. W. (2017). Hazards of manufacturing sector and economic growth in Nigeria. *International Journal of Social Sciences, Humanities and Education, 1*(1), 1–16.

Olusegun, F. A. O. (2021). Determinants and sustainability of manufacturing sector performance in Nigeria: The roles of selected macroeconomic variables. *Applied Finance and Accounting*, *7*(2), 31–40.

Orji, A., Anthony-Orji, O. I., Nchege, J. E., & Okafor, J. (2015). Manufacturing output and foreign direct investment in Nigeria: A new evidence. *International Journal of Academic Reserach in Economics and Management Sciences*, *4*(4).

Osabohien, R., Awolola, O. D., Matthew, O., Itua, O. Q., & Elomien, E. (2020). Foreign direct investment inflow and employment in Nigeria. *Investment Management and Financial Innovations*, *17*(1), 77–84.

Sharma, S., Saxena, A. K., & Paul, S. N. (2022). Role of foreign direct investment inflows in the development of BRICS: A study of forecasting of FDI inflows from 2018 to 2028. *International Journal of Business Innovation and Research*, *28*(3), 410–419.

Tonuchi, J. E., & Onyebuchi, N. A. (2019). Economic diversification in Nigeria: The role of agriculture and manufacturing sector. *International Journal of Research in Electronics and Computer Engineering*, *7*(3), 916–919.

Uma, K. E., Obidike, P. C., Chukwu, C. O., Kanu, C., Ogbuagu, R. A., Osunkwo, F. O., & Ndubuisi, P. (2019). Revamping the Nigerian manufacturing sub-sector as a panacea for economic progress: Lessons from South Korea. *Mediterranean Journal of Social Sciences*, *10*(4), 111.

Yahia, Y. E., Liu, H., Khan, M. A., Shah, S. S. H., & Islam, M. A. (2018). The impact of foreign direct investment on domestic investment: Evidence from Sudan. *International Journal of Economics and Financial Issues*, *8*(6), 14002.

Zoramawa, L. B., & Kiru, A. T. (2022). An impact assessment of foreign direct investment and government expenditure: Empirical evidence on Nigerian economy 1970 to 2021. *African Journal of Management and Business Research*, *5*(1), 23–36.

Chapter 7

Foreign Direct Investment: Nigeria Case Study of the Natural Gas Sector

Abstract

Foreign Direct Investment (FDI), a global capital activity, has the capacity to promote economic growth, investment development, and efficiency. This chapter x-rays the business environment for FDI in the Nigerian Natural Gas Industry. Nigeria's inflow of FDI has significantly decreased in recent years. This dramatic decline of almost 60.4% demonstrates the necessity for the Nigerian government to start addressing the obstacles to foreign investment, particularly in the gas sector. This chapter highlights the difficulties facing the natural gas industry in Nigeria and how they affect FDI influx, as well as the status and trends of FDI inflow. A major factor in attracting FDI is policy and regulatory frameworks, with regulations like the National Gas Policy and the Petroleum Industry Act (PIA) designed to boost the industry. However, policy framework in Nigeria has not been adequately implemented and enforced because of weak government, corruption, and lack of continuity in government regime. Economic diversification, accountability and openness, prohibition of gas flaring, addressing security and insurgency challenges, and strengthening macroeconomic framework are recommended areas of improvement.

Keywords: FDI; Natural gas sector; geopolitical factors; socioeconomic and regulations; Nigeria

7.1 Introduction

Nigeria's abundant natural gas reserves position it as an attractive destination for global investors. As a result, the gas industry is essential in propelling the country's economic growth. However, Nigeria grapples with significant challenges, such as inadequate infrastructure, high inflation, unstable currency exchange rates, etc. These challenges must be carefully considered as they have a

Foreign Direct Investment, 93–112

doi:10.1108/978-1-83662-900-920261007

direct impact on investment decisions and the overall economic stability of the nation. Along with other social factors like understanding the demographic makeup and labor market dynamics, effective community engagement aimed at building trust and transparency, thus mitigating potential obstacles, helps investors in assessing market size and growth trajectories, thereby raising their confidence in the sustainability of their investments over time.

More so, several factors like appropriate regulatory and legal frameworks, which are indispensable for safeguarding businesses and addressing disputes, emphasize the importance of compliance with international standards. These factors collectively influence the investment decisions of potential investors, especially when combined with other intricate issues like political stability, transparency in regulations, and technological advancements. Thus, to effectively handle these complex challenges, an extensive approach that integrates economic, social, political, technological, and legal aspect is critical in boosting investor confidence, attracting foreign direct investment (FDI), and unlocking the full potential of Nigeria's natural gas resources for sustainable development.

The energy requirements, sociopolitical structure, sustainability issues, and technical improvements have all had an impact on the global natural gas business (Aigheyisi & Oligbi, 2020). Global investment movements known as FDI have the potential to support the expansion of an economy, investment creation, and competitiveness (Höysniemi, 2022). In recent years, it is widely accepted that foreign investment is the main propellant of development in economies (Nwuke, 2021). According to Financial Times Limited's FDI Report 2012, the global percentage of FDI initiatives grew by 5.6% in 2011, which was more rapidly growing above a rise of 3% in 2010. The anticipated capital investment linked to FDI projects increased by 1.2% to $860 billion in 2011 from a 14.5% decline in 2010, signaling the start of a rebound for greater capital-intensive industries (Ademiloye et al., 2020). Meanwhile, the worldwide flows of FDI were expected to expand in 2017 and reach $1.8 trillion in 2018, although they did not reach the projected value before the recession rise in 2019. The UNCTAD yearly report from 2018 indicates a significant increase in the percentage of global FDI stock relative to gross domestic product (GDP) over the period spanning from 1990 to 2017. Notably, this percentage rose from 9.58% to 39.24%, as stated in the UNCTAD report. This trend indicates a growing reliance on FDI as a proportion of global economic output during the specified time frame, which reflects the increasing interconnection and integration of economies worldwide. In advanced nations, the ratio climbed from 9.32 to 43.79, whereas in developing nations, it soared from 12.86 to 32.58 (Daka, 2022). Global FDI declined by 12% in 2022 to $1.3 trillion following a substantial increase in 2021, which was mostly because of combining global issues, such as the war in Ukraine, rising costs of food and energy, and soaring government debt (NBS, 2022). Most advanced nations saw the downturn, with FDI dropping by 37% to $378 billion. However, investment movements to developing nations have increased by 4%, although inconsistently, with most of the investment going to a small number of major developing nations, while those with weaker economies saw a fall. FDI in the natural gas and refinery sectors stimulates various exports, including petrochemicals.

The world's nations are fiercely competing with one another for export-oriented FDI (Charles et al., 2023). A considerable amount of FDI has previously been made in natural gas development, manufacture, liquefying, and infrastructure for shipping. In the context of the quantity of newly developed investments made between 2019 and 2022, the fossil fuel and natural gas industry ranked 23rd among all FDI sectors. About 0.6% of all greenfield development FDI worldwide is in the coal and natural gas sector (Sunday, 2023). Meanwhile, the last 10 years have seen a radical shift in foreign investment regulation as authorities, especially in nations that are developing or emerging, have lifted numerous barriers to the inflow and outflow of capital from their respective countries (Bajrami & Zeqiri, 2019). According to UNCTAD, developing nations must address and deal with an increasing yearly investment shortfall to meet the sustainable development goal (SDG) by 2030.

Nigeria stands out as the top FDI-attracting nation in West Africa (Kimiagari et al., 2023). According to the World Trade Organization's (WTO's) global export records, the top five countries in terms of net natural gas sales in 2011 were as follows: Saudi Arabia (8,167), Nigeria (2,242), Kuwait (2,343), UAE (2,309), and Russia (7,504), in 1,000 barrels per day. Approximately $18 to $20 billion in investment could be made in Nigeria's oil and gas industry as corporations look to accelerate ongoing initiatives owing to better conditions and revive already discontinued ones (Osunmiyiwa & kalfagianni, 2016). The major fuel that propels Nigeria's financial engine is natural gas. It is essential to the current state of the Nigerian economy (Daka, 2022). Due to the natural gas industry's significant contribution to the Nigerian economy, certain steps are being taken to encourage foreign investors to participate (Ademiloye et al., 2020). This rationale explains why there are so many foreign investors in Nigeria's natural gas sector. In Q2 2023, Nigeria imported $1.03 billion in total, a little less compared with the $1.13 billion imported in the first quarter of that year and 32.9% less than the $1.54 billion imported in the same time in 2022 (Langerak, 2023). It is also important to note that the number for Q2 2023 is the poorest since Q2 2021. An additional analysis of the Nigerian Bureau of Statistics (NBS) data shows that borrowing accounted for 74.9% of the entire capital importation over this time frame, which was when most foreign inflows into the nation occurred (NBS). Meanwhile, 8.4% of the total came from FDI ($86.03 million), and 10.4% came from foreign portfolio investments ($106.85 million). At the time, foreign portfolio investments, at $106.85 million, represented 10.4% of the total, whereas FDI, at $86.03 million, contributed for 8.4% (Charles et al., 2023).

The trust of stakeholders and the likelihood of forming partnerships in the natural gas business are influenced by the transparency, consistency, and comprehensibility of regulations governing the natural gas sector. Specifically, the clarity and uniformity of legislation regarding authorization procedures, tax regulations, and environmental standards play important roles (Adejumo, 2013). In essence, when governments take positive steps to encourage investment and when a country is politically stable, it tends to attract more foreign investment, as it makes it easier for businesses to set up, and foreign companies are more likely to be confident to want to operate within their borders (Aminu & Suraya, 2020). Effective exploration, extraction, manufacturing, and delivery of natural gas were reported by (Sunday, 2023) to depend on having sufficient amenities, which include electrical energy, transportation, and broadband connections. Insufficient facilities can make operations highly expensive and make investments less appealing. Regarding suppliers of natural gas, a connection with domestic as well as global markets is essential. Export contracts, market dimensions, projections for demand, export facilities, and other variables all have an impact on possible revenue flow and choice of investments. However, Ademiloye et al. (2020) reported that macroeconomic variables that affect the natural gas business's general investment environment and confidence among investors include growth in GDP, the rate of inflation, foreign exchange rates, and financial stability. Technological innovations in the fields of exploration, the extraction procedure, and manufacturing can improve the economic viability and profitability of natural gas business processes, which in turn can draw FDI (Yusuff et al., 2023). Therefore, to create an appealing economic atmosphere that encourages foreign investment in Nigeria's natural gas industry, it is imperative that these aspects be thoroughly evaluated and addressed.

Nigeria's natural gas industry has the potential to be a beacon of foreign investment attraction, characterized by steady FDI inflows, strong economic growth, and sustainable development. Also, the business environment is supposed to be conducive, stable, transparent, and efficient across economic, social, political, technological, and legal domains. Investors also perceive Nigeria as a promising destination that promotes long-term partnerships and mutual success (Titus et al., 2023). However, the reality diverges significantly from this ideal. Recent years have witnessed a sharp decline in FDI inflows to Nigeria's natural gas sector, reflecting broader challenges within the business environment. Economic instability, social unrest, political uncertainty, technological constraints, and legal ambiguities collectively deter foreign investors, undermining the industry's potential for growth and development.

The Nigerian government has implemented various reforms and initiatives as well as regulatory framework and policies to address these challenges, including economic restructuring, social empowerment programs, political stability efforts, technological advancements, and legal reforms (Ademiloye et al., 2020; Wenche et al., 2017). Despite these measures, the investment climate remains unfavorable, with persistent barriers hindering investor confidence and participation. Foreign investors continue to face obstacles such as declining foreign exchange liquidity, regulatory inconsistencies, community tensions, technological deficiencies, and legal uncertainties. These challenges exacerbate the decline in FDI inflows, leading to missed opportunities for economic expansion, job creation, and infrastructure development. Moreover, the exodus of foreign oil corporations from Nigeria further worsens the situation, which signals a concerning trend of divestment and market decline.

Existing literature has identified the general challenges foreign investors encounter in Nigeria's natural gas sector. However, there are still gaps in fully comprehending how these challenges interact with various aspects of the business environment, such as economics, social factors, politics, technology, and legal frameworks, particularly concerning FDI. There is a lack of a thorough analysis that brings together all these factors and one that identifies the precise obstacles that impede FDI inflows. As a result, there is a significant gap in knowledge within academic and policy circles regarding the topic.

The objective of this chapter is to identify specific barriers hindering investment attraction and recommend tailored approaches and strategies to overcome them, ultimately to provide valuable insights for policymakers, stakeholders, and investors that will enable them to make informed decisions. By doing so, it promotes a more favorable environment for sustainable FDI and the growth of Nigeria's natural gas sector.

7.2 What Is Natural Gas?

Natural gas, primarily composed of methane, is a vital energy source from underground reservoirs, often coexisting with oil. The comprehensive process of exploration, extraction, and utilization constitutes the natural gas industry, which plays a vital role in global energy provision. The natural gas industry is an integral part of modern energy systems, providing essential energy for various needs globally (Gielen & Boshell, 2019). Composed mainly of methane (CH_4), natural gas is a versatile fuel used in electricity generation, heating, cooking, and various industrial applications (Chala et al., 2018). It is categorized into conventional sources, which refer to gas found in reservoirs trapped beneath impermeable rock formations in a manner that allows for relatively straightforward extraction, as well as unconventional sources, that is, gas reserves that are trapped in geological formations that are more complex or challenging to extract from. For example, shale formations, coal beds, or other unconventional sources requiring advanced drilling techniques like hydraulic fracturing (or "fracking"), horizontal drilling, or other innovative methods (Mahmud et al., 2020).

The exploration and extraction of natural gas involves sophisticated processes such as geological surveys, seismic imaging, drilling, and other innovative techniques (Sahu et al., 2020). After extraction, raw natural gas undergoes processing to remove impurities and extract valuable hydrocarbons to prepare it for transportation and distribution (Kumar et al., 2017). Transportation of processed natural gas occurs through pipelines, liquefied natural gas (LNG) tankers, or compressed natural gas vehicles, which facilitates distribution to end-users worldwide (Chala et al., 2018). This transportation network is vital for connecting production centers with consumption hubs, primarily through cost-effective and reliable pipeline networks spanning continents.

Natural gas finds widespread adoption across various sectors, including power generation, heating, industrial processes, and transportation, due to its affordability, efficiency, and lower emissions compared to other fuels (Safari et al., 2019). Despite its many advantages, concerns persist regarding environmental impacts, including methane leakage, carbon dioxide pollution, and the side effects of extraction processes (Field et al., 2014). Hence, effective regulation and sustainability measures are crucial for managing these challenges and ensuring the continued viability of natural gas as an energy source.

7.3 Global Energy Market Dynamics: Nigeria's Position

The limited availability of energy resources contrasts sharply with the increasing global demand for natural gas. The energy industry is influenced by various factors, including market forces, societal and political factors, technological advancements, sustainability considerations, and regulatory frameworks. These factors interact in complex ways, influencing how the energy market is structured and how decisions are made within the sector. The global energy market is influenced by a wide range of dynamic factors, as highlighted by Kimiagari et al. (2023). Moreover, the ongoing issues of environmental degradation and air pollution, particularly from greenhouse gases like carbon dioxide and methane, are driving a notable transition toward more environmentally friendly and energy-efficient choices in the global energy market. This shift includes a growing preference for natural gas, recognized for its cleaner combustion compared to coal and oil, as a fossil fuel option. Worldwide, distribution networks, economic structures, and trends in investment are being altered by this shift (Nitte, 2023). The distribution networks can be disrupted, and global energy prices can be impacted by international conflicts and wars in important oil-producing countries, such as the Middle East and Eastern Europe.

International rivalries have a substantial impact on the dynamics of the global energy market, as Basiru (2022) highlighted. Geopolitical concerns and national strategic objectives affect energy cooperation, trade alliances, and development initiatives. For instance, the terms of international partnership may be shaped by competition for control over pipeline routes or energy sources. A common basis for agreements or trade disputes between competing nations is their geopolitical goals, resource access, and energy requirements. International competitiveness influences trades, investment decisions, and terms of collaboration in the energy sector, which in turn affects the trends of the global energy market. The energy transition towards cleaner and more sustainable energy sources has significant implications in all geopolitical ramifications (Fadekunayo & Abdulrasheed, 2023). Global energy demand is still rising despite initiatives to encourage climate change mitigation and conservation of energy. These trends are mostly due to development in cities, rising populations, and business growth, especially in developing countries.

Striking a balance between growing energy demand and sustainability concerns remains a major concern in the global energy sector. To meet this challenge, nations are incorporating a wide range of energy sources into their electrical grids. For long-term sustainability, the significance of diversifying energy sources and lowering reliance on fossil fuels. Similarly, the energy markets are significantly shaped by laws and regulations, which impact investment decisions, competitive rivalry, and technological progress. The implementation of legislation aimed at enhancing efficiency guidelines, green power implementation, carbon taxation, and reducing greenhouse gas emissions significantly affects the structure of the market (Liu et al., 2020).

Nigeria maintains a prominent place in the global energy industry, particularly in the oil and gas sector (Merkulov et al., 2020). It is a major player in the international oil and gas industry and stands as one of Africa's major oil producers. With exports mostly directed to consumers in Asia, Europe, and North America, the nation contributes significantly to the supply of oil worldwide due to its substantial reserves and production capacity (Zou et al., 2022). Considerable prospects for local consumption, foreign markets, and expenditures on energy-to-power projects are presented by the exploitation of its natural gas potential (International Gas Union, 2022). Over an extended period projection report, World Oil Vision 2045, the world's demand for oil is expected to rise from 82.5 million barrels of fuel per day (bpd) to 104.4 million bpd within the next the period from 2021 to 2026.

Like many other countries, Nigeria relies heavily on fossil fuel-based energy systems, which raises concerns about climate change and the depletion of resources in years to come (Arowolo & Perez, 2020). The modern global fossil fuel environment, nevertheless, emerges as a perpetually changing stage rather than one that follows set standards (Aigheyisi & Oligbi, 2020). Several reasons drive this shift, notably advances in technology, the need to address global warming, and evolving international relationships. All along, the entire value supply chain, from drilling and manufacturing to refinements, LNG manufacturing, and crude oil, Nigeria's power industry presents appealing possibilities for investment. To realize the maximum effectiveness of its hydrocarbon supplies, the federal government of Nigeria has been seeking to modernize regulatory structures, revamp the sector, and draw in foreign investment (Botao et al., 2023).

7.4 Natural Gas Industry in Nigeria: Current Status and Trends

Nigeria's natural gas sector plays an essential role in the country's economic performance, self-sufficiency in energy, and equitable growth. Nigeria is home to some of the world's greatest confirmed natural gas reserves, with estimates of over 200 trillion cubic feet (tcf) (Basiru, 2022). According to research, natural gas output in the nation has steadily increased over time, propelled by rising domestic consumption, expanding industry, and advancements in natural gas infrastructure and developments (Eniekezimene, 2020).

The extraction, development, and exploration of natural gas in Nigeria are primarily undertaken by major local and foreign oil corporations (IOCs), further highlighting the sector's importance (Agu & Nyatanga, 2020). Nigeria now has natural gas reserves that account for more than 5% of global reserves, and its untapped gas potential remains substantial (Charles et al., 2023). The authorities have been enacting laws and providing benefits to promote the consumption of natural gas as a greener and more effective fuel than other fossil fuels like coal and diesel (Bassey & Ekong, 2019). Moreover, the Nigerian government has implemented various initiatives to encourage the use of natural gas for electricity production, such as the Gas Revolution Industrial Park and the Nigerian Gas Master Plan. These efforts aim to increase the share of natural gas in the country's energy mix while reducing reliance on alternative sources like oil and diesel. Supported by investments in gas infrastructure, such as pipelines and processing facilities, Nigeria has emerged as a significant exporter of LNG, with production facilities concentrated on Bonny Island in Rivers State, and LNG is exported from these plants, run by Nigeria LNG Limited (NLNG), to consumers in Asia, Europe, and the Americas.

The average daily output of gas in November 2020 averaged 5.134 billion cubic feet, which meant that 6.09% was flared and 93.9% used for exporting melted natural gas (LNG), 32.7% for gas re-injection and gas lift make-up, 16.28% for the nation's gas sales, 6% for fuel gas, 5.12% for the Escravos Gas-to-Liquid project, and 1.46% for natural gas liquids or liquefied petroleum gas (LPG).

Between 2001 and 2017, Nigeria exported over 13 trillion standard cubic feet of LNG, as reported by the Nigeria Liquefied Natural Gas (NLNG) Corporation (Eze et al., 2019). By 2017, Nigeria held the fourth position globally in the export of fossil fuel products and services, contributing more than 7% to the total global gas exports (Bajrami & Zeqiri, 2019). Within the African natural gas industry, the nation plays a significant role, accounting for 29% and 21% of the continent's gross reserves of petroleum and natural gas, respectively, in 2018 (Charles et al., 2023). Nigeria's substantial proven reserves rank ninth in the world; nevertheless, the gas sector remains underdeveloped, with supply to reserves at only about 1% of total output. The country possesses 202 tcf of proven but undeveloped gas reserves, with an exploitable potential of 139.4 tcf (Yusuff et al., 2023). Nigeria's gas sector has demonstrated the possibility to be an important supplier in the developing global natural gas market, given that the country's natural gas deposits are now valued at 182 tcf with an expected growth rate of over 70% by 2025 (Anderson, 2021).

Despite challenges such as the increasing capacity of key gas-producing countries like Australia and Qatar, Nigeria's gas sector is expected to maintain steady growth, with a projected compound annual growth rate (CAGR) of 1.39% from 2024 to 2029 according to Wakili (2017) who also emphasize that at a CAGR of 1.39%, the Nigerian natural gas sector is projected to rise from 4.60 billion cubic meters every day in 2024 to 4.93 billion cubic feet per day by 2029. However, the COVID-19-related worldwide production processes downturn in 2020, along with the mandatory shutdown and worldwide constraints, have lowered the medium-term forecast for the energy industry in Nigeria (World Bank, 2020). Nigeria's gas potential was projected to increase to 210.8 tcf (trillion cubic feet) by 2022 with sufficient investment in gas development, making Nigeria the continent's gas superpower. Yet, one of the biggest trends for 2023 is the restriction of the world's natural gas supplies (Agbunase & Charity, 2023). Another significant trend affecting the natural gas sector is a rise in inflation, as it is expected that oil consumption would exceed current levels notwithstanding tighter supplies, leading to a resurgence in pipeline investment (Amuda et al., 2023).

7.5 Foreign Direct Investment in the Nigerian Natural Gas Industry

The primary drivers of economic expansion and growth on a macroeconomic scale include FDI and several other key factors such as foreign currency exchange rates, economic transparency, and government investment. Achieving sustainable growth hinges upon a government's ability to maintain equilibrium among these factors, ensuring their effective management and support (Abiola, 2019). In Nigeria's natural gas sector, foreign investors are paying more attention to social and environmental consciousness in their business activities (Ndukwu et al., 2020). They are also following global standards and standards of excellence in governance of the environment, stakeholder engagement, and environmentally conscious growth (Alabi, 2019). Research has shown that FDI positively impacts many external marketplace elements, including total foreign currency merchandize sales, imports of materials, and shipments of natural gas.

Nigeria's natural gas industry is experiencing significant development, largely driven by FDI, which brings in capital, facilitates information transfer, builds new infrastructure, generates employment, and fosters economic expansion (Animigha et al., 2023). According to recent data from Nigeria's National Bureau of Statistics (NBS), foreign investment inflows into Nigeria's energy sector reached $0.75 million in the first quarter of 2023, marking a 22.95% increase from the $0.61 million recorded in the same period in 2022. However, this figure represents a substantial decline compared to the $2.26 million reported in the fourth quarter of 2022, showing a decrease of 66.81% in the first quarter of 2023. According to Ajala and Charles (2023), in an NBS report, the total capital imported into Nigeria during the first quarter of 2023 amounted to $1.133 billion, reflecting a decrease of $279.97 billion compared to the same period in 2022.

In a similar report, Nigeria attracted $47.60 million in FDI in the first quarter of 2023, marking a significant decline of 69.28% compared to the previous year. Nigeria's economic growth is severely hampered by corruption, which both domestic and foreign investors frequently point out as a major impediment to conducting business there. The country's ranking in the Transparency International 2021 Corruption Perceptions Index fell to 154 out of 180 countries, showing a slight decrease from its position of 149 out of 175 countries in 2020 (Akiri et al., 2016).

7.6 Factors Influencing Foreign Direct Investment in the Nigerian Natural Gas Industry

7.6.1 Regulatory Environment

The natural gas sector's attractiveness to investors and ease of doing business are significantly influenced by the details, reliability, and transparency of regulatory frameworks, which encompass permits, tax policies, and investment incentives (Danjuma, 2021). Nigeria's natural gas industry has witnessed several legislative and regulatory changes in the past decade aimed at promoting investment, enhancing the business environment, and encouraging accountability and transparency (Asghari, 2016).

One of the significant policy advancements in Nigeria's oil and gas sector is the passage of the Petroleum Industry Bill (PIB) in 2021, which aims to enhance the industry's legal framework, promote transparency and accountability, and attract investment (Akinwalere & Kirk, 2023). The Nigerian Content Development and Monitoring Board (NCDMB) Act governs the activities of the NCDMB, aiming to enhance local content and capabilities while encouraging Nigerian participation in the natural gas industry (Animigba et al., 2023). The Act mandates energy companies operating in Nigeria to prioritize local products and services, while providing training and employment opportunities to Nigerian citizens. Moreso, to improve the efficiency of licensing and regulatory processes, the Department of Petroleum Resources (DPR) has implemented various initiatives, including the establishment of a virtual licensing platform and an open bidding procedure for oil and gas licenses. These measures aim to streamline regulatory procedures, enhance transparency, and attract more investors to the Nigerian natural gas sector.

7.6.2 Political Stability and Security

Social stability, legal system robustness, and political security play key roles in shaping FDI trends within the natural gas sector. Political turmoil, instability, and security risks can deter international investors and jeopardize long-term investment opportunities (Acquah & Ibrahim, 2020). Nigeria has an appealing economic prospect and market size yet struggles to attract the necessary FDI inflows for sustained economic growth. This challenge is often attributed to the elevated investment risks and diminished investor confidence stemming from prevalent insecurity and political instability.

Research has shown that host economies characterized by strong democratic accountability and favorable investment climates tend to attract considerably higher levels of FDI. Notably, factors such as corruption, inadequate legislative frameworks, and a lack of democratic accountability and investment attractiveness significantly impact FDI inflows into Nigeria's natural gas sector. Corruption stands out as a major deterrent to growth in revenue in Nigeria, as both domestic and foreign investors frequently cite it as a significant barrier to conducting business in the country.

7.6.3 Infrastructural Development

The effective development, extraction, handling, and marketing of natural gas rely heavily on the availability and quality of essential systems such as power supplies, gas transmission lines, LNG stations, transportation routes, and manufacturing structures (Ezeanya & Azubuike, 2023). In any economy, the presence of infrastructure such as electricity, telecommunications, well-maintained roads, internet facilities, and rail networks reduces business operating costs, thereby increasing the net return on investment. This favorable investment environment inspires more foreign investors to establish their ventures in the economy, as the primary goal of any investment is to maximize the return on invested capital.

Nigeria faces various challenges with its transportation system, including limited capacity, traffic congestion, and poorly maintained roads, railways, and ports. These issues act as deterrents to FDI by increasing operational risks, complexities, and high administrative costs for natural gas projects (Ezeanya & Azubuike, 2023). Improving transportation infrastructure can enhance the appeal of the natural gas industry by reducing traffic congestion and enhancing supply chain efficiency. To attract and retain FDI in Nigeria's natural gas sector, addressing infrastructural challenges, promoting the adoption of technological advancements, strengthening the legal framework, and ensuring social and environmental awareness are critical steps to be taken, to create an environment conducive for FDI (Amadi, 2019).

7.6.4 Technology and Innovations

Access to modern technologies and innovative practices in extraction, processing, and distribution significantly enhances the appeal of the natural gas industry to international investors (Charles et al., 2023). For instance, advancements in seismic imaging techniques have transformed the exploration process, enabling more precise identification of potential gas reserves deep beneath the earth's surface. Similarly, innovative drilling technologies like horizontal drilling and hydraulic fracturing have unlocked previously inaccessible natural gas deposits, thereby broadening the industry's scope for growth and profitability.

Collaborations with academic institutions and technology suppliers play a key role in driving competitiveness and technical advancements within the natural gas sector (Animigha et al., 2023). Research partnerships between universities and industry stakeholders have led to the development of novel extraction techniques that optimize resource recovery while mitigating environmental impact. Moreover, engagements with technology suppliers have facilitated the adoption of cutting-edge technological equipment and software solutions, thus boosting operational efficiency and safety across the natural gas value chain. Initiatives aimed at enhancing digitalization and automation in natural gas operations have yielded tangible benefits, including increased productivity and cost savings, thereby enhancing the sector's global competitiveness.

7.6.5 Geopolitical Influences on FDI in Nigeria's Natural Gas Industry

In Nigeria, the impact of political instability on FDI inflows is still an essential concern (Kufre & Koyejo, 2023). Political uncertainty discourages FDI, but economic development makes the country more appealing to FDI. Despite its sizable industry and appealing economy, Nigeria struggles to draw in the FDI required to achieve rapid growth in its economy (Nyande et al., 2020). It was shown that a decline in FDI into the nation was correlated with a surge in terrorist acts. Nevertheless, categorized research revealed that the impact of a terrorist attack on FDI inflows to different industries varies (Obiora et al., 2018). Nigeria still has prospects, but its investment environment has been compromised by fraud in the financial sector, ethical upheavals, unstable geopolitical circumstances, and a lack of diversifying their portfolios (Aigheyisi & Oligbi, 2020).

7.7 Natural Gas Infrastructure Development in Nigeria: Opportunities and Challenges

Nigeria's natural gas sector offers promising opportunities. Developing innovation, providing substantial financial assistance, and utilizing its enormous natural gas reserves are all essential to realize the industry's potential. This not only drives Nigeria's economic advancement but also contributes to broader goals of environmental preservation and ensuring energy security across the African continent (Akinrele, 2016). The gas sector provides opportunity for fiscal diversification, revenue generation, and economic sustainability in addition to meeting the country's energy demands domestically (Melvin et al., 2022). Natural gas utilization in Nigerian supports job growth and economic diversity.

However, it has been argued that the infrastructure needed for shipping and distributing natural gas effectively is lacking in Nigeria. For effective shipment, the chain of gas facilities must be expanded (Oyewunmi, 2019). Similarly, there is shortage of ample funding for the initial petroleum and gas advancements required because of the government's conflicting political and social objectives toward which it must allocate its monetary assets. For this reason, the sector is unable to adequately fund its priorities according to the relevant joint venture/ joint contract of operation (Antoinette & Jeroen, 2017).

7.8 Policies and Regulatory Structure: Impacts on FDI in Nigeria's Natural Gas Sector

The PIB, which was passed in 2021, is one of the major policy advancements in Nigeria's natural gas industry. The PIB seeks to improve the industry legal structure, encourage responsibility and transparency, and attract investments. The NCDMB Act is another crucial regulatory framework that governs the natural gas industry in Nigeria (Adam, 2020). This Act seeks to promote local resources and competence while encouraging Nigerians and Nigerian-owned businesses to work in the natural gas industry.

7.9 Importance of Foreign Direct Investment in the Nigerian Economy

FDI drives the growth of a host nation, especially by addressing challenges like insufficient internal savings, investing, and foreign exchange shortages. It brings in actual revenue and stimulates the economy of the country (Eze et al., 2019). There have been discussions in research over the impact of FDI on economic development. Whereas certain analysts believe that FDI has a beneficial impact on the nation's economy, others argue that FDI has a negligible and insignificant effect (Anfofun et al., 2013).

FDI supplies capital to fund infrastructure projects, manufacturing, investment in technology, and business expansion in Nigeria. These investments create jobs, boost the economy, and help alleviate extreme poverty. FDI serves as a conduit for the dissemination of innovation, knowledge transfer, and the exchange of technology and skills between foreign investors and local businesses. The integration of cutting-edge technologies, advanced managerial techniques, and scientific expertise leads to enhanced performance, effectiveness, and productivity across enterprises (Danjuma, 2021). This synergy of innovation and expertise can manifest in several ways, such as automated processes, data-driven decision making, quality management system (Kimiagari et al., 2023).

Funds from FDI create an opportunity for a host nation to carry out huge developments in fields like information technology, electricity, and logistics, which help to improve infrastructural development. Adequate infrastructure usually lowers the cost of operations and improvements in outputs, thereby leading to the attraction of investments into country. Through the development of jobs in both direct and indirect ways in a variety of industries, FDI creates opportunities for employment in Nigeria, which helps to reduce unemployment, economic hardship, and social inequality (Acquah & Ibrahim, 2020). Nigerian businesses can reach global marketplaces and take part in worldwide supply chains due to the presence of foreign investors, who also contribute logistics and knowledge of foreign markets (Akiri et al., 2016).

FDI helps countries with fewer amenities by improving infrastructure and diversification of economies outside of big cities. In Nigeria, this would help to achieve a balanced economic growth throughout various regions; as a result, there will be a reduction in disparities of development between the regions, and taxes and revenue from FDI are used to finance government spending on social amenities, economic growth, welfare programs, etc. A consistent income from FDI into Nigeria would boost the economy and reduce the reliance on petroleum revenue, which usually fluctuates (Yusuff et al., 2023). By encouraging the establishment of multinational corporations, banks, insurance firms, and other businesses in Nigeria's financial sector, FDI helps develop the economy by increasing access to financial services, by enhancing financial intermediaries, better market liquidity, etc., and thereby leading to economic growth in the country (Alabi, 2019).

7.10 Conclusion

Different variables, such as market dynamics, infrastructure constraints, operational inefficiencies, and geopolitical risks, have affected FDI inflows into Nigeria's natural gas business. Global gas price swings, geopolitical unrest, and uncertainty in policy are all factors contributing to the volatility of FDI inflows. Nigeria holds substantial quantities of natural gas, making it a prominent participant in the worldwide natural gas industry. However, Nigeria has difficulties such irregular output levels, high gas flaring rates, and volatile exports despite its vast reserves. These problems have impacted the industry's appeal to foreign capital and have added to swings in FDI inflows. The National Gas Policy and the Petroleum Industry Act (PIA) are the two major policy and regulatory frameworks enacted. Enforcement of these acts could have a big impact on FDI inflow and the natural gas industry's overall growth in Nigeria.

FDI in Nigeria has been severely affected by insurgency and terrorism, especially the activities of Boko Haram sect. This has created an environment of fear and insecurity that discourages foreign investors. Nigeria's economy has grown because of FDI; however, problems like high unemployment and poverty rates still exist. This implies that these social problems could require more than FDI to solve. Although Nigeria's natural gas industry has an opportunity to grow significantly and have a big economic impact, to fully realize this potential and draw in more FDI, it is imperative that issues with amenities legislation, security, and socioeconomic growth be addressed.

7.11 Recommendations

7.11.1 Strengthen Accountability and Openness

To guarantee transparency and accountability in the natural gas sector, the government should put policies in place. This entails open financial operations, activities, and regulatory frameworks to decrease corruption and increase investor confidence (Okoro & Egbunike, 2017). Kwarto et al. (2024) posited that this strategy had been successfully adopted by the US, Australian, and Canadian governments. Canadian, the US and Australian governments have established several regulatory agencies, including the National Energy Board and the Gas Association, to encourage transparency and responsibility in the country's gas industry. Canada recorded 165.2 billion cubic meters (BCM) of gas production in 2020 with a 32% increase by 2040 because of this measure (Janzwood & Millar, 2022). Australian gas production reached 149.8 Bcm in 2022 because of transparency and openness in operation (Sage et al., 2024). Due to the implementation of this recommendation, the average daily production of natural gas in the United States increased by 4% in 2023 to 5.0 billion cubic feet (Bcf/d).

7.11.2 Diversification of Economy

In Nigeria, diversifying the economy is a highly practical way to lessen reliance on the oil and gas industry. According to Idowu and Awe (2014), this can promote stability, maintain long-term economic growth, and draw in additional investment. Economic diversification was argued by Okoye et al. (2022) to reduce risk, enable better utilization of resources, and improve innovation and technology advancement. The Nigerian government should consider diversification of the economy into other viable sectors like agriculture and technology. This will help in creating multiple channels of investment opportunities and lead to an increase in FDI inflow into the country.

7.11.3 Prohibition of Gas Flaring

Adopt measures to stop gas flaring, as this can maximize the value of natural gas reserves economically and spur economic expansion (Madodjemu et al., 2019). Prohibiting gas flaring was reported by Kabara and Amirthalingam (2020) to have an advantageous impact on the natural gas industry and FDI inflow, especially when it comes to environmental advantages, resource conservation, and regulatory compliance. There should be enforcement of existing regulations to adequately combat gas flaring in Nigeria. Also, punishment should be established to prosecute those found guilty of this act. Implementation of these recommendations would reduce long-term deterioration of the ecosystem caused by gas flaring, increase total production and exportation of gas to overseas, and greatly improve FDI inflow into the country.

7.11.4 Address Security and Insurgency Challenges

The Nigerian government needs to act proactively to resolve security issues and create a more secure environment for international business. Improving intelligence gathering, information sharing, and counterterrorism measures are some of the steps involved in this. It is imperative that Nigeria tackle its security and insurgency issues to draw FDI and foster the expansion of the natural gas industry. It necessitates a comprehensive strategy that addresses underlying social and political challenges, promotes economic development, and incorporates security measures. This will make foreign investors to consider Nigeria as a safe nation to invest.

7.11.5 Strengthen Macroeconomic Framework

Provide a solid macroeconomic environment to promote GDP expansion, FDI expansion, and job creation. This entails preserving transparent regulations, a stable economy, and effective administration (Bisiriyu & Bankole, 2020). Strong fiscal and monetary policies, along with a robust macroeconomic framework, can improve economic predictability and stability. This may boost investor confidence and draw additional FDI to the natural gas industry of Nigeria. The fluctuation of exchange rates can be lessened with financial backing of a stable macroeconomic environment, which lowers the risk for foreign investors and increases the appeal of natural gas sector investments.

References

Abiola, A. (2019). Determinants of foreign direct investment in Nigeria: A structural VAR approach. *International Journal of Applied Economics*, *16*(1), 22–38.

Acquah, A. M., & Ibrahim, M. (2020). Foreign direct investment, economic growth and financial sector development in Africa. *Journal of Sustainable Finance and Investment*, *10*(4), 315–334.

Adam, K. K. (2020). The impact of petroleum tax incentives on foreign direct investment inflow: Evidence from Nigeria. *International Journal of Energy Economics and Policy*, *10*(4), 516.

Adejumo, A. V. (2013). Foreign direct investments and manufacturing sector performance in Nigeria (1970-2009). *Australian Journal of Business and Management*, *3*(4), 39–56.

Ademiloye, I. B., Olofinjana, A., Yusuf, B. M., & Adeoye, O. S. (2020). Renewable energy resources in Nigeria as panacea to electricity inadequacy: A review. *International Journal for Research in Electronics & Electrical Engineering*, *6*(6), 1–14.

Agbunase, C. A., & Charity, E. (2023). The evolution of gas development and utilization in Nigeria. *KB Law Scholars Journal*, *1*(1), 1–23.

Agu, O. C., & Nyatanga, P. (2020). An investigation into the crude oil price pass-through to economic growth in Nigeria. *Acta Universitatis Danubius - Œconomica*, *16*(1).

Aigheyisi, O. S., & Oligbi, B. O. (2020). Energy poverty and economic development in Nigeria: Empirical analysis. *KIU Interdisciplinary Journal of Humanities and Social Sciences*, *1*(2), 1–15.

Ajala, R. B., & Charles, I. E. (2023). National security and foreign direct investment in Nigeria (2005 -2022). *Economic Journal: Scientific Journal of Accountancy, Management and Finance*, *3*(3), 122–135.

Akinrele, A. (2016). The current impact of global crude oil prices on Nigeria—an overview of the Nigerian petroleum and energy sector. *The Journal of World Energy Law & Business*, *9*(5), 313–345.

Akinwalere, S., & Chang, K. (2023). The determinants of foreign-direct-investment (FDI) inflows in Nigeria. *The Journal of Developing Areas*, *57*(4), 91–105. https://www.muse.jhu.edu/article/908648

Akiri, S. E., Vehe, B. M., & Ijuo, A. O. (2016). Foreign direct investment and economic growth in Nigeria: An empirical investigation. *IIARD International Journal of Economics and Business Management*, *2*(5), 1–12.

Alabi, K. O. (2019). The impact of foreign direct investment on economic growth Nigeria experience. *Open Journal of Applied Science*, *9*, 372–389.

Amadi, C. (2019). *FDI and economic growth in Nigeria: An analysis of the role of financial development on linkages* Doctoral dissertation. Manchester Metropolitan University.

Aminu, H. J., & Suraya, M. (2020). An asymmetric effect of economic growth, foreign direct investment and financial development on the quality of environment in Nigeria. *The Journal of Management Theory and Practice (JMTP)*, 5–13.

Amuda, Y. J., Shafiqul, H., and Umashankar, S. (2023) *Comparative review of energy, crude oil, and natural gas for exchange markets in Nigeria, India, 16* (7) 3151.

Andersen, G. (2021). *Petroleum industry act, (2021): The road to compliance for upstream companies*. https://www.mondaq.com. Accessed on February 20, 2024

Anfofun, A. A., Gambo, J. S., & Suleiman, T. (2013). Estimating the impact of foreign direct investment in Nigeria. *International Journal of Humanities and Social Science*, *3*(17), 1–12.

Animigha, B. T., Ayatse, F. K., & Igwe, A. (2023). Foreign direct investment: An impetus for economic growth in developing nations (evidence from Nigeria). *International Journal of Public Administration and Management Research*, *8*(5), 30–39.

Antoinette, G. S., & Jeroen, F. W. (2017). Geopolitical drivers of foreign investment in African land and water resources. *Land Grabbing in Africa*, 8–25.

Arowolo, W., & Perez, Y. (2020). Market reform in the Nigeria power sector: A review of the issues and potential solutions. *Energy Policy*, *144*, 111580.

Asghari, M. (2016). National security and economic growth. *Iranian Economic Review*, *21*(4), 905–924.

Bajrami, H., & Zeqiri, N. (2019). Theories of foreign direct investment (FDI) and the significance of human capital. *International Journal of Business and Management*, *7*(1), 11–24.

Basiru, M. (2022). Nigeria's vulnerability to global oil dynamics and politics. *International Journal of Social Science Research and Review*, *5*(11), 135–144.

Bassey, G. E., & Ekong, U. M. (2019). Energy consumption and inflation dynamics in Nigeria: An ARDL cointegration approach. *Energy Economics Letters*, *6*(1), 37–52.

Bisiriyu, S. O., & Bankole, K. O. (2020). Foreign direct investment, economic growth and unemployment in Nigeria. *Jalingo Journal of Social and Management Sciences*, *2*(4), 51–61.

Botão, R. P., Hirdan, K. M., & Edmilson, M. S. (2023). Global gas and LNG markets: Demand, supply dynamics, and implications for the future. *Energies*, *16* (13), 5223. https://doi.org/10.3390/en16135223

Chala, G., Abd Aziz, A., & Hagos, F. (2018). Natural gas engine technologies: Challenges and energy sustainability issue. *Energies*, *11*(11), 2934. https://doi.org/10.3390/en11112934

Charles, O. M., Ifeoma, C. N., Ogochukwu, C. O., Chuka, U. I., & Williams, A. N. (2023). The impact of foreign direct investment and oil revenue on economic growth in Nigeria. *Studia Universitatis „Vasile Goldis". Arad–Economics Series*, *33* (3), 61–85.

Daka, T. (2022). Nigeria will end fuel importation from mid-2023, says NNPC boss. The guardian. European Union External Action. *Energy diplomacy*. https://www.eeas.europa.eu/eeas/energy-diplomacy_en

Danjuma, I. (2021). Insurgency, political risk, and foreign direct investment in Nigeria: A sectorial analysis. *CBN Journal of Applied Statistics*, *12*(2), 27–57.

Eniekezimene, F. A. (2020). Determinants of foreign direct investment in Nigeria: An empirical investigation. *Asian Journal of Economics, Business, and Accounting*, *17* (2), 73–84.

Eze, A. A., Nnaji, M., & Nkalu, N. C. (2019). Impact of foreign direct investment on manufacturing sector output growth in Nigeria. *International Journal of Applied Economics, Finance and Accounting*, *5*(2), 55–64.

Ezeanya, E. V., Azubuike, C. F. (2023). Globalization and economic development: A study of Nigeria 2010-2021, *Globalization* *7*(5), 13-24.

Fadekunayo, A., & Abdulrasheed, I. (2023). Unlocking renewables amid rentierism: Market constraints to Nigeria's energy transition. *Energy Research & Social Science*, *104*, 103248.

Field, R. A., Soltis, J., & Murphy, S. (2014). Air quality concerns of unconventional oil and natural gas production. *Environmental Sciences: Processes & Impacts*, *16* (5), 954–969. https://doi.org/10.1039/c4em00081a

Gielen, D., & Boshell, F. (2019). The role of renewable energy in the global energy transformation. *Energy Strategy Reviews*, *24*(24), 38–50. https://doi.org/10.1016/j.esr.2019.01.006

Höysniemi, S. (2022). Energy futures reimagined: The global energy transition and dependence on Russian energy as issues in the sociotechnical imaginaries of energy security in Finland. *Energy Research & Social Science*, *93*, 102840. https://doi.org/10.1016/j.erss.2022.102840

Idowu, O. O., & Awe, A. (2014). Foreign direct investment in Nigeria. *International Journal of Liberal Arts and Social Science*, *2*(9), 71–87.

International Gas Union. (2022). *IGU World LNG Report 2022*. https://www.igu.org/publications/igu-world-lng-report-2022/. Accessed on February 12, 2024

Janzwood, A., & Millar, H. (2022). Bridge fuel feuds: The competing interpretive politics of natural gas in Canada. *Energy Research & Social Science*, *88*, 102526.

Kabara, M. Y., & Amirthalingam, K. (2020). Foreign direct investment (FDI) and policy inconsistence in Nigeria (1970-2016). *Colombo Journal of Multi-Disciplinary Research*, *5*(1–2).

Kimiagari, S., Mahbobi, M., & Toolsee, T. (2023). Attracting and retaining FDI: Africa gas and oil sector. *Resources Policy*, *80*, 103219.

Kufre, J. U., & Koyejo, O. (2023). Nigeria's inflation in the era of liquefied natural gas exports: Insights from 2000-2021 ARDL cointegration analysis. *American Journal of Economics and Business Innovation*, *2*(3), 192–201.

Kumar, S., Srivastava, V. C., & Nanoti, S. M. (2017). Extractive desulfurization of gas oils: A perspective review for use in petroleum refineries. *Separation and Purification Reviews*, *46*(4), 319–347. [online]. https://doi.org/10.1080/15422119.2017.1288633

Kwarto, F., Nurafiah, N., Suharman, H., & Dahlan, M. (2024). The potential bias for sustainability reporting of global upstream oil and gas companies: A systematic literature review of the evidence. *Management Review Quarterly*, *74*(1), 35–64.

Langerak, L. (2023). *Fuel transition for gas turbines: In a changing European energy landscape*. https://www.researchgate.net/publication/376508021_Energy_Diplomacy_and_Strategic_Engagements_Nigeria's_role_in_Shaping_the_Global_Energy_Landscape

Liu, Y., Shi, X., & Laurenceson, J. (2020). Dynamics of Australia's LNG export performance: A modified constant market shares analysis. *Energy Economics*, *89*, 104808.

Madodjemu, M., Ekpobodo, R. O., & Omoroghomwan, Q. (2019). Foreign investors as a means of socio-economic development of Nigeria. Образование и Црaво, 172–177.

Mahmud, H. B., Ermila, M., Bennour, Z., & Mahmud, W. M. (2020). *A review of fracturing technologies utilized in shale gas resources*. IntechOpen. https://www.intechopen.com/chapters/72128. Accessed on Mar 7, 2024

Melvin, U., Eko-Raphaels, Porwekobowei, A., Dubem, V. E., Araoye, O., & Ajiboye, R. A. (2022). Natural gas logistics, utilization and impact on Nigeria's economic health: A simple empirics. *International Research Journal of Economics and Finance*, *10*, 98–105.

Merkulov, V. I.; Skripnuk, D. F.; Kulik, S. V. (2020). Analysis of world LNG production capacity. In *IOP conference series: Earth and environmental science*; IOP Publishing: 2020; Volume *539*, p. 012057. NBS. 2019. Nigerian gross domestic product Report Q3. Abuja: National Bureau of Statistics.

National Bureau of Statistics. (2022). *Nigeria multidimensional poverty index*. https://ophi.org.uk/publications/Nigeria-MPI-2022.

Ndukwu, M. C., Onwude, D. I., Bennamoun, L., Abam, F. I., Simo-Tagne, M., Horsfall, I. T., & Briggs, T. (2020). Nigeria's energy deficit: The challenges and Eco-friendly approach in reducing the energy gap. *International Journal of Sustainable Engineering*, *14*, 1842546.

Nitte, I. S. (2023). Global energy transition and its implications on energy security in Nigeria: A critical review. *Ezra International Journal Of Climate And Resource Economic Review (Crer)*, *11*(1), 1–9.

Nwuke, K. (2021). *Nigeria's petroleum industry act: Addressing old problems, creating new ones. Africa in focus*. Brookings Institution.

Nyande, F., Chen, Y., Joseph, K., & Sow, D. (2020). Geopolitical risks (GPRs) and foreign direct investments: A business risk approach. *Global Journal of Management and Business Research*, *20*(1), 1–9.

Obiora, G. O., Glauco, De V., & Yun, L. (2018). The impact of FDI on Nigeria's export performance: A sectoral analysis. *Journal of Economic Studies*, *45*(5), 1088–1103.

Okoro, E. G., & Egbunike, P. A. (2017). Impact assessment of foreign direct investment, oil revenue on economic prosperity in Nigeria. *Journal of Academic Research in Economics*, *9*(2).

Okoye, L. U., Adeleye, B. N., Okoro, E. E., Okoh, J. I., Ezu, G. K., & Anyanwu, F. A. (2022). Effect of gas flaring, oil rent and fossil fuel on economic performance. *The case of Nigeria, Resources Policy*, *77*, 102677.

Osunmuyiwa, O., & Kalfagianni, A. (2016). Transitions in unlikely places: Exploring the conditions for renewable energy adoption in Nigeria. *Environmental Innovation and Societal Transitions*, *22*, 26–40. https://doi.org/10.1016/j.eist.2016.07.002

Oyewunmi, T. (2019). The evolving international gas market and energy security in Nigeria. In *Energy in Africa: Policy, management and sustainability* (pp. 117–145). PwC Nigeria. 2021. The Petroleum Industry Act: Redefining the Nigerian oil and gas landscape.

Safari, A., Das, N., Langhelle, O., Roy, J., & Assadi, M. (2019). Natural gas: A transition fuel for sustainable energy system transformation? *Energy Science & Engineering*, *7*(4). [online]. https://doi.org/10.1002/ese3.380

Sage, V., Patel, J., Hazewinkel, P., Ain, Q. U., Wang, F., Yang, Y., & Kozielski, C. L. (2024). Recent progress and techno-economic analysis of liquid organic hydrogen carriers for Australian renewable energy export–A critical review. *International Journal of Hydrogen Energy*, *56*, 1419–1434.

Sahu, C., Kumar, R., & Sangwai, J. S. (2020). Comprehensive review on exploration and drilling techniques for natural gas hydrate reservoirs. *Energy & Fuels*, *34*(10), 11813–11839. [online]. https://doi.org/10.1021/acs.energyfuels.0c02202

Sunday, A. K. (2023). Industrial output growth and foreign direct investment in Nigeria. *Future Business Journal*, *9*(1), 58.

Titus, K. O., Fabian, N., & Nkechiwetalu, N. (2023). Creating a strategic business and environmental management framework for entry and exit in the oil and gas sector: A case study of Nigeria. *International Journal of Innovative Business Strategies*, *9*(1), 572–581.

Wakili, I. (2017). *Nigeria: Mambilla power project gets $5.79bn for takeoff. Daily Trust (Abuja)*. https://allafrica.com/stories/201708310060.html. Accessed on February 12, 2024

Wenche, A., Tuomas, A., Kirsi, A., Andreas, Ø., & Bjørn, A. (2017). Project sustainability strategies: A systematic literature review. *International Journal of Project Management*, *35*(6), 1071–1083.

World Bank. (2020). *World development indicators 2020*. World Bank.

Yusuff, J. A., Shafiqul, H., & Umashankar, S. (2023). Comparative review of energy, crude oil, and natural gas for exchange markets in Nigeria, India and Bangladesh. *Energies*, *16*(7), 3151.

Zou, Q., Yi, C., Wang, K., Yin, X., & Zhang, Y. (2022). Global LNG market: Supply-demand and economic analysis. In *IOP conference series: Earth and environmental science* (Vol. 983, p. 012051). IOP Publishing.

Chapter 8

Foreign Direct Investment: Sri Lanka Case Study on the Environment

Abstract

This chapter focuses on the intricate dynamics between foreign direct investment (FDI), industrialization, and their collective impact on the environment. As the world grapples with the challenges of sustainable development, this chapter is poised to offer multifaceted benefits to academia, policy formulation, corporate practices, and international environmental agendas. The expansion of FDI in Sri Lanka has experienced substantial growth since the commencement of economic restructuring in 1977. The government of Sri Lanka views continued increases in FDI inflows as a vital element in its efforts to promote and stimulate economic development. The insights derived from this chapter possess the potential to reshape policy decisions at both national and international levels. By examining the complex interplay between FDI-driven industrialization and environmental consequences, policymakers will gain a deeper understanding of the trade-offs involved. Multinational corporations (MNCs) play a pivotal role in shaping global economic trends and environmental impacts. The chapter can serve as a guide for MNCs in adopting environmentally responsible practices during their operations. As FDI often represents a vital avenue for economic progress for developing nations, insights into the potential environmental implications of rapid industrialization spurred by FDI are imperative.

Keywords: FDI; Sri Lanka; industrialization; environment degradation; sustainable development

8.1 Introduction

Foreign direct investment (FDI) is playing an increasingly essential role in economic growth because of economic globalization. At the same time,

Foreign Direct Investment, 113–132

Published under exclusive licence by Emerald Publishing Limited
doi:10.1108/978-1-83662-900-920261008

difficulties with environmental protection are fast becoming a worldwide issue because of the rise of FDI (Amendolagineet al., 2019). Both industrialization and FDI play crucial roles in the economic growth of developing countries, and their significance cannot be underestimated. FDI is particularly acknowledged as a key driver of economic growth, owing to its positive impact on financial resources, trade integration, technology infusion, human capital development, and economies of scale in target markets (Amadi, 2019; Belloumi, 2014). However, alongside the numerous benefits brought about by FDI and industrialization, both processes possess the potential for environmental degradation due to their heavy reliance on natural resource production and exploitation. As the Asia-Pacific region experiences substantial economic and technological growth, FDI is increasingly regarded as a major conduit for technology transfer; thereby influencing recipient countries' economic and environmental landscapes.

Consequently, it becomes essential for developing nations to devise policies that attract FDI and promote industrial advancement without compromising the environment and the well-being of their inhabitants (Kawai & Naknoi, 2016). A growing amount of focus is being directed into how the quality of the environment of the country receiving FDI is affected by these investments. In recent decades, there has been a notable rise in documented instances of environmental deterioration as recorded in various international publications (Shahbaz et al., 2018). This phenomenon can be attributed to the pervasive rise in economic activity that has ensued from the process of globalization (Huwart & Verdier, 2013).

Sri Lanka has enjoyed consistent economic growth since it opened its doors to the world business community, which has allowed the country to become more globally competitive. Also, the expansion of the economy has been significantly aided by the inflow of direct investment from overseas. However, just as there are two sides to a coin, there is also a negative component to the fact that the ecosystem is deteriorating before our own eyes. Making the development of FDI and the environment work together in harmony is one of the most pressing challenges we face today. To conduct a proper analysis of the FDI-environment problem, it is therefore important to integrate theoretical methodologies with empirical methods. Many scholars and specialists study the relationship between FDI, industrialization, and the environment with yet inconsistent results. Thus, the environmental effects of FDI remain unknown.

This chapter compares FDI, industrialization, and the host country's environment. The fact that FDI is a major part of globalization raises environmental concerns. This matters if global data show a rapid rise in FDI and carbon dioxide (CO_2) emissions. The purpose of this chapter is to dive into the complicated interaction between FDI, industrialization, and the environment in host nations, highlighting the possible positive and negative consequences, and the role of laws and regulations in reducing environmental repercussions.

The increasing flow of FDI in various countries has generated concerns regarding its environmental implications in relation to industrialization. FDI is widely recognized as a catalyst for economic growth, technological advancement, and job creation. However, it is important to note that if FDI is not adequately managed in a sustainable manner, it can also contribute to environmental degradation and resource depletion (Wang et al., 2022). FDI and industrialization have complex environmental effects due to several variables. To accomplish sustainable development goals and address major environmental issues, the global community must understand and properly address the relationship between FDI and the environment (Kang & Lee, 2011).

Understanding the complex relationship between FDI and the environment in economic, social, and environmental contexts is difficult. Understanding how FDI affects environmental outcomes is essential to creating targeted and empirically backed policies that maximize its advantages and minimize its negatives. FDI, including Greenfield firms, acquisitions, and cross-border mergers, may have environmental impacts that must be considered. We must also recognize that environmental laws and enforcement affect the environmental impacts of FDI. Understanding how different nations' environmental policies affect investment decisions and environmental consequences is crucial to creating regulatory frameworks that encourage environmentally responsible investments (Erdogan, 2014).

FDI may help the environment by spreading technologies and promoting sustainable production. The assessment of these prospects and advocating for environmentally friendly investments that support sustainable development goals can help create a more environmentally conscious and sustainable economy. Another important consideration is the prospect of unequal environmental impacts from FDI. Environmental justice problems arise when FDI activities cause unequal environmental degradation for some people in a nation. These inequalities must be addressed to guarantee that FDI benefits all sections of society. Understanding the complex relationship between FDI, industrialization, and the environment is the focus. This involves identifying the elements that affect this link and creating strategies and regulations to promote environmentally conscious investment while exploiting FDI's potential for sustainable development. Research and analysis are needed to inform evidence-based government and international efforts to balance economic development and environmental preservation. The global community may seek and manage FDI more sustainably and environmentally by understanding and addressing these challenges.

In recent years, there has been a growing interest and concern over the correlation between FDI and the environmental conditions of the country in which it is hosted. The ongoing process of globalization and international economic integration has had a profound impact on the contemporary global landscape (Hao et al., 2021). Within this context, FDI has emerged as a prominent catalyst for economic growth and development, benefiting both developed and developing nations alike. The imperative to preserve environmental integrity has emerged as a pressing necessity in the contemporary day. The reason for this can be attributed to the various adverse effects caused by the increasing amounts of CO_2, which is the primary component of greenhouse gases (GHGs) (Raymond et al., 2013).

There is growing recognition that FDI can have major environmental repercussions on the recipient countries, in addition to economic benefits. This chapter reviews and evaluates the current research and scholarly literature on the environmental impact of FDI by synthesizing findings from a variety of studies to reveal the intricacies of this association and identify recurring patterns and trends that can improve understanding. The chapter examines FDI and its environmental implications utilizing theoretical frameworks and conceptual models. The Pollution Haven Hypothesis (PHH), Porter Hypothesis (PH), and Environmental Kuznets Curve (EKC) are examined to determine how they help us comprehend FDI and the environment. The chapter explores how FDI may cause pollution, resource exploitation, deforestation, and GHG emissions and analyses situations where FDI has led to cleaner technology and sustainable practices.

8.2 Theoretical Linkage Between FDI and the Environment

The scholarly discourse surrounding the relationship between environmental restrictions and the attractiveness of FDI has garnered significant attention from scholars, as seen by the work of Santos & Forte, 2021. One key observation is that MNCs often prioritize countries with comparatively relaxed environmental restrictions for investment purposes, as cost considerations play a significant role in the selection of a host nation. The term used to describe this occurrence is known as the PHH (Assamoi et al., 2020). Consequently, there is a notable inclination among businesses to be drawn toward developing nations, since they consider these countries to have less rigorous environmental regulations when making judgments about where to invest (Cole et al., 2017).

The subsequent hypothesis pertains to the phenomenon known as the Pollution Halo Effect. As an illustration, if a MNC with advanced technological capabilities opts to invest in a region that possesses lower levels of technological advancement, it is deemed beneficial if the latter region aids in the mitigation of pollution. However, if the corporation chooses to relocate to a less regulated area and the resultant pollution in that region leads to an escalation in pollution levels, it is considered detrimental (Cole et al., 2017).

Another theoretical perspective posits the occurrence of a phenomenon referred to as the "race to the bottom" (RTB), wherein recipient nations endeavor to relax domestic environmental rules to attract FDI (Cole et al., 2017).

The fourth theoretical framework under consideration is the EKC, which postulates a correlation between economic advancement and environmental conditions. This chapter looks at the influence of FDI on the facilitation of industrialization. The primary argument posits that economic development will result in higher incomes, prompting wealthier population segments to advocate for the implementation of environmental rules and improved environmental quality. Consequently, this will lead to a decrease in pollution levels (Zugravu-Soilita, 2017).

The fifth theoretical perspective within the realm of environmental regulation theory is the PH-based mechanism. This perspective posits that the implementation of well-crafted environmental regulations serves as a catalyst for innovation, thereby mitigating the financial burden associated with regulatory compliance and ultimately enhancing the financial performance of firms (Porter & Van der Linde, 1995). Despite the abundance of scholarly literature on the topic, it is worth noting that the Pollution Halo Effect is not primarily focused on environmental legislation. Additionally, the concept of Real-Time Bidding (RTB) can be seen as an expansion of the PH.

The EKC framework is centered on the examination of dynamic processes that vary in response to temporal fluctuations and the prevailing circumstances within the host nation. In summary, the primary hypotheses that the host country's environmental legislation centers around are the PHH and the PH.

8.2.1 Environmental Kuznets Curve

The application and discussion of the EKC in relation to FDI and its environmental consequences have also been observed. According to Mahmood et al. (2019), the theory posits that as nations attract greater levels of FDI and undergo economic expansion, there is an initial increase in environmental degradation. However, as these countries attain higher levels of prosperity, the rate of environmental degradation eventually diminishes. The scale effect, conversely, is observed to have detrimental implications for the environment since it is associated with the expansion of the economy, indicating that greater economic output corresponds to elevated levels of pollution. It is noteworthy to mention that the magnitude of the impact indirectly raises the discussion surrounding the EKC (Ridzuan et al., 2022).

Lau et al. (2014) employed the limits testing approach and Granger causality methodology to assess the validity of the EKC hypothesis in Malaysia during the period from 1970 to 2008. The results provide empirical evidence supporting the validity of the EKC hypothesis in Malaysia. This validity is observed in both the short- and long-term while considering the influence of two additional explanatory variables, namely FDI and Trade, which were also observed to contribute to the deterioration of environmental conditions.

Furthermore, substantial evidence exists to support the notion of a reciprocal relationship between CO_2 emissions and economic growth, as well as between FDI and economic growth. The scale effect, however, is regarded as detrimental to the environment due to its association with an expansion in the magnitude of the economy, indicating that increased production results in elevated levels of pollution. It is noteworthy to add that the consideration of scale impact inherently raises the discussion surrounding the EKC (Ridzuan et al., 2022).

Moreover, the degradation of the environment is influenced by factors such as energy consumption, diversity of exports, FDI, and income levels. According to Adamu et al. (2019), there is evidence suggesting that income has a positive and major impact on environmental degradation. This supports earlier research showing that income positively and significantly affects carbon emissions. Many studies have shown that FDI may worsen environmental conditions in the countries where it is received. This may be caused by a variety of circumstances, such as the movement of ecologically damaging industries from affluent to developing nations to take advantage of lax environmental regulations and cut costs. Even with economic growth and higher incomes, "pollution havens" may increase pollution in recipient nations (He & Yao, 2016).

It is possible that the EKC hypothesis does not adequately explain the environmental disparity associated with FDI (Wang et al., 2023). FDI may improve the environment by expanding the economy. However, this growth may increase environmental inequality between rich and vulnerable groups. FDI gains may not be distributed fairly, raising environmental justice concerns. The wide range of host country characteristics and the diversity of FDI may limit the applicability of the EKC in FDI. Due to corporate diversity, investment types, and foreign investor goals, environmental impacts might vary greatly. Thus, a general association between FDI, economic growth, and environmental quality may oversimplify their complex dynamics (Marques & Caetano, 2020). While depending purely on wealth per capita to predict environmental progress, the EKC ignores technical transfer, institutional capacity, and environmental law enforcement. The receiving nation's environmental impacts from FDI depend on the above factors.

8.2.2 Pollution Haven Hypothesis

The PHH is an economic theory that suggests corporations may choose to shift their operations to nations with less stringent environmental legislation and enforcement to reduce their environmental compliance costs (Singhania & Saini, 2021). The hypothesis posits that the process of globalization and international trade could potentially result in a relocation of sectors that generate high levels of pollution from industrialized nations to developing nations, where environmental regulations are comparatively less rigorous. Consequently, it is plausible that certain emerging nations may encounter a rise in pollution levels when they attract FDI and undergo industrialization (Gill et al., 2018).

Terzi and Pata (2020) examined the correlation between environmental regulations and FDI and found empirical support for the notion that firms operating under more stringent environmental rules in their home countries exhibited a tendency to spend a greater amount in countries with comparatively lax environmental laws. In contrast, Havranek & Irsova, 2011 conducted an analysis using data from Latin American nations and concluded that countries with less stringent environmental restrictions did not exhibit a substantial ability to attract FDI.

The PHH posits that MNCs can opt to allocate their investments in nations characterized by less stringent environmental rules, aiming to capitalize on reduced expenses associated with compliance and more relaxed pollution control measures (Yang et al., 2018). The exact correlation between environmental policy, production location, and subsequent trade flows is a topic that is now under debate and is of significant interest. The PHH is a matter of significant concern. It posits that the reduction of trade barriers allows multinational enterprises (MNEs) that engage in polluting activities to relocate their production operations to regions with less stringent environmental regulations (Bulus & Koc, 2021). This phenomenon has the potential to reshape the geographical distribution of economic activity and subsequently impact trade patterns by establishing favorable environments for companies that contribute to pollution (Cai et al., 2016).

FDI has been found to have a positive correlation with resource extraction, pollution, and environmental deterioration. Nevertheless, certain instances have revealed that the impact of industrialization on the environment was determined to be statistically inconsequential (Chirilus & Costea, 2023). FDI can displace indigenous communities and degrade ecosystems in economically disadvantaged nations. Mining and hydroelectric infrastructure may deforest or alter watercourses. Industrial agriculture and urbanization also degrade natural environments. However, the relationship between FDI and natural habitat degradation is complex and depends on many factors, including the industry or project, location, and regulatory framework. FDI can also increase resource competition, raising prices and reducing resource access for indigenous populations.

The hypothesis posits that the desire for financial gain may prompt firms to transfer their pollution-intensive operations to nations with lenient environmental regulations, hence potentially establishing places that serve as "pollution havens." The relationship between the PHH and FDI is rooted in the investment choices made by MNCs (Bulus & Koc, 2021). FDI is a term used to describe the financial investment made by a firm based in one country into another one. This investment typically entails the formation of new activities or the acquisition of assets within the host country. A Public Health and Human Rights study suggests that MNCs have the potential to choose investment opportunities in developing nations that possess less stringent environmental rules. This strategic decision is primarily driven by the objective of reducing production costs and minimizing expenses related to environmental compliance.

8.2.3 The Porter Hypothesis

The PH, established by economist Michael E. Porter in 1991, posits that well-structured environmental rules have the potential to have favorable economic consequences for businesses and foster innovation (Ambec & Barla, 2006). The hypothesis presents a counter argument to the prevailing belief that environmental restrictions impose only negative consequences on businesses. It posits that strict regulations can incentivize enterprises to allocate resources toward the development and adoption of cleaner technology and sustainable practices (Wagner, 2003). Consequently, this can lead to an improvement in their overall competitiveness.

Within the realm of FDI, the PH posits that environmental restrictions implemented by host countries have the capacity to exert an influence on the attraction and behavior of foreign investors. Nations that possess robust and effectively implemented environmental rules may be regarded as more appealing investment locations for environmentally conscientious investors. The implementation of rigorous environmental rules can cultivate an atmosphere conducive to fostering innovation and the advancement of environmentally sustainable technologies. Foreign investors who are interested in entering countries that have robust environmental rules may exhibit a greater inclination to embrace cleaner and more sustainable practices to adhere to local norms (Franckx, 2015). By allocating resources toward the adoption of more environmentally friendly technologies, these corporations have the potential to enhance their ecological standing and secure a competitive edge within the domestic market of the host country.

Moreover, the PH posits that the implementation of rigorous environmental rules has the potential to generate favorable market prospects for companies that specialize in environmental technologies and sustainable products (Brännlund & Lundgren, 2009). Foreign investors have the potential to recognize and capitalize on possibilities in host countries that have robust environmental policies by offering environmentally friendly goods and services. This can result in an influx of FDI as these businesses seek to tap into and benefit from these specific market segments.

The PH presents a more optimistic viewpoint about the influence of environmental rules on FDI choices. However, it is crucial to acknowledge that not all international investors may exhibit the same level of responsiveness toward environmental policy. The influence of environmental rules on the attractiveness of FDI can differ based on various factors, including the specific industry, investment type, and the overall economic climate within the host nation. The PH posits that environmental restrictions have the potential to stimulate innovation and enhance competitiveness for enterprises, especially those involved in FDI. The implementation of rigorous and carefully crafted environmental regulations inside host nations has the potential to attract international investors that prioritize environmental sustainability. This, in turn, can stimulate the adoption of cleaner technology, resulting in positive outcomes for both the economy and the environment.

8.2.4 The Pollution Halo Effect

The "Pollution Halo Effect" in the context of FDI refers to a phenomenon where foreign-owned firms operating in a host country are perceived to have superior environmental practices and performance compared to their domestic counterparts. This positive perception creates a metaphorical "halo" around foreign companies, suggesting that they are inherently more environmentally responsible and committed to sustainable practices. The Pollution Halo Effect is an important aspect of the broader discussion on the impact of FDI on the environment (Kamal et al., 2021).

Several factors contribute to the emergence of the Pollution Halo Effect. First, MNCs often have established a reputation for adhering to higher environmental standards in their home countries. This reputation can extend to their operations in host countries, leading to the perception that foreign firms are more environmentally conscious and compliant. Second, foreign investors, particularly those with a focus on environmental, social, and governance (ESG) criteria, may prioritize environmentally responsible practices when making investment decisions. As a result, they might be more inclined to invest in foreign-owned firms with perceived better environmental performance, further reinforcing the perception of the Pollution Halo Effect. Third, MNCs often bring advanced technologies, managerial practices, and cleaner production methods to their overseas operations. These best practices, which may not be as prevalent among domestic firms, contribute to the positive perception surrounding the environmental behavior of foreign companies.

However, it is essential to approach the Pollution Halo Effect with caution. While some foreign-owned firms may indeed exhibit better environmental practices, the environmental performance of FDI firms can vary significantly depending on their sector, home country, the host country's regulations, and specific industry practices. Not all foreign firms necessarily outperform their domestic counterparts in terms of environmental sustainability. Moreover, the Pollution Halo Effect may also have implications for environmental governance in the host country. The positive perception of foreign firms' environmental behavior could potentially lead to complacency among regulatory authorities, assuming that foreign companies are already operating responsibly. This could result in less stringent monitoring and oversight, enabling some foreign firms to exploit the perception and engage in subpar environmental practices.

In conclusion, the Pollution Halo Effect is the perception that foreign-owned firms in a host country exhibit superior environmental practices compared to domestic companies. While this perception can have positive implications in terms of encouraging environmentally responsible practices in FDI, it is crucial to recognize that the environmental performance of foreign firms can vary. Striking a balance between recognizing responsible foreign investors and maintaining robust environmental regulations and monitoring is vital to ensure sustainable and responsible FDI practices that benefit both the host country and the global environment.

8.3 The Impact of FDI on Environment Degradation in Developing Countries

FDI has emerged as a pivotal catalyst for fostering economic growth and promoting development in underdeveloped nations. Nevertheless, in addition to its potential advantages, FDI has also elicited apprehensions regarding its environmental implications (Eskeland & Harrison, 2003). In the pursuit of industrialization and economic expansion, it is crucial to comprehend the correlation between FDI and environmental deterioration. In this section, we offer a thorough examination of current scholarly studies regarding the influence of FDI on environmental degradation in developing nations.

Numerous theoretical frameworks have been posited to examine the correlation between FDI and environmental degradation in developing nations. The PHH posits that companies are inclined to invest in nations that have less stringent environmental regulations to minimize the expenses associated with compliance and to encourage operations that result in pollution (Copeland & Taylor, 2004). This theory posits that FDI inflows may result in heightened levels of environmental degradation inside host nations that possess lax environmental regulations.

Furthermore, according to Eskeland & Harrison, 2003, it is suggested that the PHH is unequivocal just inside a very simplified model. In a more realistic framework, the impact of regulatory measures on foreign investment may vary, exhibiting either positive or negative outcomes. This variation is contingent upon the interdependencies between abatement efforts and capital allocation.

On the other hand, the PH posits that FDI has the potential to stimulate innovation and facilitate the uptake of more environmentally friendly technology, hence resulting in enhanced environmental outcomes (Porter & Van der Linde, 1995). This perspective argues that the adoption of ecologically sustainable practices has the potential to improve competitiveness and productivity, hence establishing a favorable correlation between FDI and environmental quality.

The findings of empirical studies investigating the influence of FDI on environmental degradation in developing nations have produced inconclusive results. Several research have provided empirical support for the PHH. Dasgupta et al. (2002) discovered a positive correlation between FDI inflows and elevated levels of CO_2 emissions in specific developing nations.

Alternative research endeavors have presented empirical support for the PH. Zhang et al. (2020) provided evidence supporting the notion that FDI in China has a favorable impact on the assimilation of more environmentally friendly technology, resulting in a reduction of air pollution levels. In a similar vein, Mottaleb et al. (2017) revealed a favorable correlation between FDI in the manufacturing sector of Bangladesh and environmental compliance, leading to a reduction in pollution levels. The operations of MNCs through FDI primarily lead to higher levels of GHG emissions and other pollutants that cause climate change (Zugravu-Soilita, 2017).

There are numerous elements that exert an effect on the correlation between FDI and environmental degradation in emerging nations. The environmental outcome can be considerably influenced by many characteristics of FDI, including the sector in which the investment is made and the origin of the investment. Industries characterized by a heightened potential for pollution, such as extractive industries, may exert a more pronounced influence on the environment. Environmental regulations and institutional capacity in the host country also affect the outcome.

The literature on FDI and environmental degradation in emerging nations is diverse. Some studies suggest that FDI harms the environment, whereas others show the opposite. Numerous theoretical frameworks and conflicting empirical findings underscore the need to understand the contextual factors that affect the environmental effects of FDI in developing nations. Policymakers should improve environmental legislation, technology transfer methods, and sustainable practices for FDI to boost economic growth and protect the environment. FDI increases CO_2 emissions, especially in countries with natural resources and lax environmental rules. This highlights the forecast that GHG and other ozone-depleting petrol emissions could rise from 25% to 90% between 2000 and 2030, causing serious health risks to the host country due to climate change.

One potential rationale for the variability shown in the empirical findings among various research might be attributed to disparities in the scope and methodological approach employed. The empirical method to examine the correlation between FDI and the environment may be analyzed from two distinct viewpoints. One approach pertains to the examination of whether firms opt to establish their operations in countries with lower environmental standards. This is achieved through the utilization of industry-level data, measurements of environmental stringency, and assessments of pollution intensities across investment of capital industries (Blanco et al., 2011). Another perspective explored in scholarly literature has focused on the influence of FDI on the environment. It is anticipated that pollution levels will rise as corporations establish their presence in other nations. Within this context, there is an argument posited that pollution levels have the potential to serve as a surrogate measure for the degree of environmental strictness (Blanco et al., 2011).

8.4 The Impact of FDI on CO_2 Emissions in Host Countries

Numerous peer-reviewed studies show that FDI can significantly impact CO_2 emissions in developing economies. FDI often transfers technologies, resources, and experience, changing the receiving country's industry and energy use. These changes may affect the host country's ecology (Potterie & Lichtenberg, 2001). Many studies suggest a positive relationship between FDI and CO_2 emissions. FDI may boost industrialization and economic growth in emerging nations. Industrial expansion may increase energy consumption and fossil fuel use, which increases CO_2 emissions. Hence, the need for governmental actions to mitigate environmental impacts.

Other research suggests that FDI and CO_2 emissions are inversely related. These studies suggest that FDI could enable greener technology and methods. These measures could boost energy efficiency and environmental sustainability in the host nation. According to Du et al. (2010), FDI in clean technology enterprises may reduce CO_2 emissions. This suggests that foreign investment could promote sustainable growth. Strong environmental policy and regulatory frameworks can encourage sustainable FDI. Consequently, this can reduce the environmental impact of economic growth and development.

In summary, the impact of FDI on CO_2 emissions in developing nations depends on many factors, including FDI characteristics, recipient country policy, and industrial structure. FDI and the environment can interact positively and negatively, emphasizing the need for policy actions to steer FDI toward sustainable trajectories that reduce environmental harm.

8.5 The Impact of FDI on Air Pollution in Host Countries

Several peer-reviewed studies have demonstrated that FDI affects air pollution in emerging nations. FDI often brings new technologies and monetary infusions that might change the recipient nation's production and environmental regulations. Industrial processes release more pollutants into the atmosphere due to FDI. According to Javorcik (2004), FDI can increase air pollution in the short run. This is largely due to FDI's increased industrialization and energy use, which often uses environmentally hazardous manufacturing methods.

Another perspective is that FDI may reduce air pollution. FDI can help companies embrace cleaner technologies and better management methods, improving environmental performance. Wheeler and Mody (1992) found that FDI helps emerging nations adopt cleaner and more efficient technology. This adoption reduces pollution. This supports the idea that foreign investors may be more environmentally conscious than indigenous enterprises. Thus, this may reduce industrialization's environmental implications.

Many studies show that host nation policies moderate the relationship between FDI and air pollution. Efficient environmental regulations and policies can steer FDI toward environmentally friendly practices. Policies that encourage cleaner manufacturing methods and renewable energy sources may reduce air pollution from FDI-related industrial activities. Damania et al. (2003) underline the importance of policy frameworks in fostering sustainable development in the context of FDI and the environment. FDI may initially increase pollution due to industrialization, but its ability to promote cleaner technology and practices suggests a viable approach to air pollution when accompanied by appropriate government measures.

8.6 The Impact of FDI on Freshwater Withdrawals in Host Countries

Several academic studies examine how FDI affects freshwater withdrawals in developing nations. FDI often changes industrial and agricultural operations, affecting freshwater usage in the recipient countries. According to Shaffer and Zhang (2004), FDI in water-intensive industries can significantly increase freshwater extraction. Such investments boost industrial activity and agricultural practices. These businesses use a lot of water for manufacture and production, straining area freshwater supplies. However, other research implies that FDI can improve water use and governance. When FDI embraces new technology and water conservation and efficiency best practices, it can reduce excessive freshwater withdrawals. Koop and Tole (2018) suggest that FDI could help agricultural companies adopt modern irrigation and water management technology. This optimizes water use and reduces waste.

The impact of host nation policy on FDI and freshwater withdrawals is crucial. Sustainable water management regulations may encourage FDI in water conservation. Implementing strict policies that require water conservation and set benchmarks for optimal water use may reduce FDI's burden on freshwater resources. Sadoff et al. (2015) support the idea that comprehensive water resource regulation methods are needed to manage FDI. However, FDI in freshwater extraction in developing nations depends on the sector, knowledge transfer, and regulatory environment. By increasing industrial and agricultural water use, FDI may increase water scarcity. It also presents an opportunity to improve sustainable water management through efficient procedures and supportive policies.

8.7 The Impact of FDI on Forest Depletion in Host Countries

Many peer-reviewed studies have explored the impact of FDI on forest depletion in developing nations. FDI often changes land use and industrial operations, which might affect deforestation in the recipient country. Achten et al. (2008) found that FDI in agro-industrial sectors promotes commercial agriculture, which often causes deforestation and forest degradation. Land use for agriculture and industry can stress forest ecosystems, causing deforestation and biodiversity loss. However, some research suggests that FDI could improve sustainable forestry and forest resource protection. Forest protection can benefit from responsible and sustainable FDI. Foreign investors can use sustainable logging and replanting. Dinda (2018) examines responsible FDI in sustainable forest management. The author emphasizes the importance of strict legislation and sustainable investment strategies for conservation success.

To mitigate the effects of FDI on forest depletion, host nation policy is crucial. Environmental regulations and effective governance may help divert FDI to sustainable forestry. Sustainable land use, reforestation, and biodiversity protection strategies may mitigate the negative effects of FDI on forest ecosystems. Studies like Angelsen (2008), which evaluate policy frameworks, emphasize the importance of proactive policy actions in achieving sustainable development goals in FDI and forestry.

The effects of FDI on deforestation in developing nations depend on the investment, land use, and regulation. FDI can promote industrial and agricultural growth and aggravate deforestation, but it can also help conserve forests. Responsible practices and good regulation can achieve this.

8.8 FDI and Industrialization

The intricate relationship between FDI, industrialization, and the environment constitutes a complex nexus that holds profound implications for both economic growth and ecological sustainability. FDI, characterized by the sand resources by foreign entities in a host country, has been a potent driver of industrialization, contributing to the expansion of manufacturing and production capacities (Athukorala & Menon, 1996). While FDI brings with it the potential for technological transfer, increased employment, and enhanced economic performance, its impact on the environment has become a central concern. The process of industrialization, fueled by FDI, often involves resource-intensive activities that contribute to energy consumption, waste generation, and pollution (Gui-Diby & Renard, 2015). As industries expand, they demand more natural resources, energy inputs, and infrastructure development, thereby exerting pressure on ecosystems and contributing to GHG emissions and other pollutants. This intricate interplay underscores the dual nature of FDI-driven industrialization: it propels economic progress but concurrently poses risks to environmental integrity.

The environmental repercussions of FDI-induced industrialization can manifest in various ways; water bodies can be polluted with untreated industrial effluents, soil quality can degrade due to improper waste disposal, and air quality can deteriorate due to increased emissions (Opoku & Boachie, 2020). Additionally, resource extraction for industrial processes can lead to deforestation and habitat destruction, further compromising biodiversity and ecological balance. These environmental challenges are particularly pronounced in developing economies where regulatory frameworks and enforcement mechanisms may be less stringent. Nonetheless, it's important to recognize that the relationship between FDI, industrialization, and the environment is not inherently negative. Technological advancements and innovation resulting from FDI can introduce cleaner production methods, more efficient energy use, and improved waste management techniques. These advancements, when effectively adopted, can mitigate environmental harm and promote sustainable industrial practices (Voumik & Ridwan, 2023). Moreover, FDI can facilitate the transfer of knowledge, expertise, and environmentally friendly technologies to host countries, bolstering their capacity to address ecological challenges.

Recognizing this intricate interplay, policymakers face the challenge of striking a balance between capitalizing on FDI's potential for economic advancement and safeguarding the environment. Effective policies can incentivize FDI inflows that align with sustainable development goals, encouraging investments in industries that prioritize resource efficiency, pollution reduction, and ecological preservation (Kobrin, 1976). Regulatory frameworks should be designed to enforce environmental standards and ensure responsible business conduct, holding FDI-driven industries accountable for their environmental impact.

In conclusion, the relationship between FDI, industrialization, and the environment is multifaceted and dynamic, encompassing both opportunities and risks. A comprehensive understanding of this relationship is essential for crafting policies that promote economic growth without compromising the planet's ecological well-being. Through judicious management of FDI inflows, fostering technological innovation, and implementing robust environmental regulations, it becomes possible to harness the potential of FDI-induced industrialization while nurturing a sustainable future for generations to come.

8.9 FDI and Environment in Sri Lanka

FDI can help developing countries like Sri Lanka achieve rapid economic growth by bridging the gap between domestic savings and investment and importing the latest technology and management know-how from industrialized countries. As a result, it is easy to understand why many developing countries are looking for innovative ways to attract FDI inflows. Some developing countries have been successful in attracting FDI, while others have not. This is due to how a country handles the elements that influence FDI inflows (Ravinthirakumaran et al., 2015). FDI in Sri Lanka has been steadily increasing over the years, bringing both opportunities and challenges for the environment. As a developing nation, Sri Lanka attracts FDI in various sectors, including manufacturing, services, infrastructure, and tourism. While FDI can contribute to economic growth, job creation, and technological advancements, it also raises concerns about its impact on the environment (Waqih et al., 2019). The environmental implications of FDI in Sri Lanka are multifaceted.

FDI can bring in advanced technologies and best practices, leading to the adoption of cleaner and more environmentally friendly production methods. This technology transfer can contribute to improving environmental performance in industries and support Sri Lanka's efforts to transition to a more sustainable and green economy (Sabir et al., 2020). However, certain FDI projects may also pose environmental risks. Large-scale infrastructure development and tourism ventures may lead to deforestation, habitat destruction, and land-use changes, impacting ecosystems and biodiversity. Moreover, industries attracted by FDI, such as manufacturing and mining, can contribute to pollution and resource depletion if not subjected to stringent environmental regulations and oversight. Effective environmental governance and regulatory enforcement are crucial in managing the environmental impact of FDI in Sri Lanka. Strengthening environmental regulations and ensuring their effective implementation can help mitigate potential negative effects while maximizing the positive contributions of FDI to sustainable development. Sri Lanka's unique geographic and ecological characteristics also play a role in shaping the environmental impact of FDI. The island nation's delicate ecosystems, coastal regions, and natural resources require careful consideration in attracting and managing foreign investments. Striking a balance between promoting economic growth through FDI and safeguarding the country's natural environment is vital to ensure a sustainable future.

8.10 Conclusion

This comprehensive review of the impact of FDI on the environment, encompassing CO_2 emissions, air pollution, freshwater withdrawal, and forest depletion, has yielded nuanced conclusions.

Regarding CO_2 emissions, it reveals a multifaceted relationship wherein FDI can both contribute to emissions through industrial activities and stimulate emissions reduction through cleaner technologies and innovation. Stringent environmental regulations are pivotal in curbing emissions associated with FDI. Additionally, the presence of a negative relationship may be attributed to the adoption of cleaner production processes by foreign investors, which can lead to reduced carbon emissions.

In terms of air pollution, FDI exhibits a dual impact—introducing pollution-intensive industries while simultaneously promoting cleaner technologies and environmental best practices. The role of technological transfer and innovation driven by FDI in mitigating air pollution warrants further investigation. The observed negative relationship may be influenced by the adoption of cleaner technologies and pollution control measures by foreign investors.

Concerning freshwater withdrawal, there is a nuanced relationship. While increased FDI may lead to higher water usage in industrial sectors, it can also incentivize efficient resource management and water-saving technologies. Policymakers should focus on the effectiveness of regulations and policies in promoting sustainable freshwater use alongside FDI. The presence of a negative relationship may be due to the simultaneous adoption of water-saving technologies and practices by foreign investors.

With respect to forest depletion, responsible FDI practices, technological advancements, and conservation efforts can help mitigate negative impacts. The chapter emphasizes the importance of government policies in preventing deforestation and promoting sustainable forestry practices. A negative relationship may exist because foreign investors, driven by responsible practices and conservation efforts, contribute to reduced forest depletion.

This chapter underscores the intricate interplay between FDI and environmental indicators, emphasizing the potential for responsible FDI to foster economic growth while concurrently mitigating environmental challenges. It provides valuable insights for policymakers, students, and researchers seeking a balanced approach to economic development and environmental sustainability, considering the potential reasons for a negative relationship between FDI and its environmental impact.

References

Achten, W. M., Verchot, L., Franken, Y. J., Mathijs, E., Singh, V. P., Aerts, R., & Muys, B. (2008). Jatropha bio-diesel production and use. *Biomass and Bioenergy*, *32* (12), 1063–1084.

Adamu, T. M., Haq, I. U., & Shafiq, M. Z. (2019). Analyzing the impact of energy, export variety, and FDI on environmental degradation in the context of Environmental Kuznets Curve Hypothesis: A case study of India. *Energies*, *12*(6), 1076. https://doi.org/10.3390/en12061076

Amadi, C. (2019). *FDI and economic growth in Nigeria: An analysis of the role of financial development on linkages* Doctoral dissertation. Manchester Metropolitan University.

Ambec, S., & Barla, P. (2006). Can environmental regulations be good for business? An assessment of the porter hypothesis. *Energy Studies Review*, *14*(2). https://doi.org/10.15173/esr.v14i2.493

Amendolagine, V., Presbitero, A. F., Rabellotti, R., & Sanfilippo, M. (2019). Local sourcing in developing countries: The role of foreign direct investments and global value chains. *World Development*, *113*, 73–88.

Angelsen, A. (2008). *Moving ahead with REDD: Issues, options, and implications*. CIFOR.

Assamoi, G. R., Wang, S., Liu, Y., & Gnangoin, Y. T. B. (2020). Investigating the pollution haven hypothesis in Cote d'Ivoire: Evidence from autoregressive distributed lag (ARDL) approach with structural breaks. *Environmental Science and Pollution Research*, *27*(14), 16886–16899.

Athukorala, P., & Menon, J. (1996). Foreign investment and industrialization in Malaysia: Exports, employment and spillovers. *Asian Economic Journal*, *10*(1), 29–44.

Belloumi, M. (2014). The relationship between trade, FDI and economic growth in Tunisia: An application of the autoregressive distributed lag model. *Economic Systems*, *38*(2), 269–287.

Blanco, L., Gonzalez, F., & Ruiz, I. (2011). The impact of FDI on CO2 emissions in Latin America. *Pepperdine University, School of Public Policy Working Papers*, *28*.

Brännlund, R., & Lundgren, T. (2009). Environmental policy without costs? A review of the Porter hypothesis. *International Review of Environmental and Resource Economics*, *3*(2), 75–117.

Bulus, G. C., & Koc, S. (2021). The effects of FDI and government expenditures on environmental pollution in Korea: The pollution haven hypothesis revisited. *Environmental Science and Pollution Research*, *28*(28), 38238–38253.

Cai, X., Lu, Y., Wu, M., & Yu, L. (2016). Does environmental regulation drive away inbound foreign direct investment? Evidence from a quasi-natural experiment in China. *Journal of Development Economics*, *123*, 73–85.

Chirilus, A., & Costea, A. (2023). The effect of FDI on environmental degradation in Romania: Testing the pollution haven hypothesis. *Sustainability*, *15*(13), 10733.

Cole, M. A., Elliott, R. J., & Zhang, L. (2017). Foreign direct investment and the environment. *Annual Review of Environment and Resources*, *42*, 465–487.

Copeland, B. R., & Taylor, M. S. (2004). Trade, growth, and the environment. *Journal of Economic Literature*, *42*(1), 7–71.

Damania, R., Fredriksson, P. G., & List, J. A. (2003). Trade liberalization, corruption, and environmental policy formation: Theory and evidence. *Journal of Environmental Economics and Management*, *46*(3), 490–512.

Dasgupta, S., Laplante, B., Wang, H., & Wheeler, D. (2002). Confronting the environmental Kuznets curve. *The Journal of Economic Perspectives*, *16*(1), 147–168.

Dinda, S. (2018). Foreign direct investment in forest: A critical review. *Forest Policy and Economics*, *86*, 1–8.

Du, L., Wei, C., & Cai, S. (2010). CO2 emissions embodied in China's exports and the structural change. *Ecological Economics*, *69*(9), 2127–2135.

Erdogan, A. M. (2014). Foreign direct investment and environmental regulations: A survey. *Journal of Economic Surveys*, *28*(05), 943–955.

Eskeland, G. S., & Harrison, A. E. (2003). Moving to greener PASTURES multinationals and the pollution Haven hypothesis. *Journal of Development Economics*, *70*(1), 1–23.

Franckx, L. (2015). Regulatory emission limits for cars and the Porter hypothesis: A survey of the literature. *Transport Reviews*, *35*(6), 749–766.

Gill, F. L., Viswanathan, K. K., & Karim, M. Z. A. (2018). The critical review of the pollution haven hypothesis. *International Journal of Energy Economics and Policy*, *8*(1), 167–174.

Gui-Diby, S. L., & Renard, M. F. (2015). Foreign direct investment inflows and the industrialization of African countries. *World Development*, *74*, 43–57.

Hao, Y., Ba, N., Ren, S., & Wu, H. (2021). How does international technology spillover affect China's carbon emissions? A new perspective through intellectual property protection. *Sustainable Production and Consumption*, *25*, 577–590.

Havranek, T., & Irsova, Z. (2011). Estimating vertical spillovers from FDI: Why results vary and what the true effect is. *Journal of International Economics*, *85*(2), 234–244.

He, X., & Yao, X. (2016). Foreign direct investments and the environmental kuznets curve: New evidence from Chinese provinces. *Emerging Markets Finance and Trade*, *53*(1), 12–25. https://doi.org/10.1080/1540496x.2016.1138813

Huwart, J.-Y., & Verdier, L. (2013). *OECD insights economic globalisation origins and consequences*. s.l.:OECD Publishing.

Javorcik, B. S. (2004). Does foreign direct investment increase the productivity of domestic firms? In search of spillovers through backward linkages. *The American Economic Review*, *94*(3), 605–627.

Kamal, M., Usman, M., Jahanger, A., & Balsalobre-Lorente, D. (2021). Revisiting the role of fiscal policy, financial development, and foreign direct investment in reducing environmental pollution during globalization mode: Evidence from linear and nonlinear panel data approaches. *Energies*, *14*(21), 6968.

Kang, S. J., & Lee, H. (2011). Foreign direct investment and De-industrialisation. *The World Economy*, *34*(2), 313–329.

Kawai, M., & Naknoi, K. (2016). ASEAN's TRADE AND FOREIGN DIRECT INVESTMENT: LONG-TERM challenges for economic integration. *Singapore Economic Review*, *62*(03), 643–680.

Kobrin, S. J. (1976). Foreign direct investment, industrialization, and social change. *Journal of Conflict Resolution*, *20*(3), 497–522.

Koop, S., & Tole, L. (2018). Foreign direct investment in agricultural land and water: Adapting international law to address environmental and social impacts. *Review of European, Comparative & International Environmental Law*, *27*(3), 285–297.

Lau, L.-S., Choong, C.-K., & Eng, Y.-K. (2014). Investigation of the environmental Kuznets curve for carbon emissions in Malaysia: Do foreign direct investment and trade matter? *Energy Policy*, *68*, 490–497. https://doi.org/10.1016/j.enpol.2014.01.002

Mahmood, H., Furqan, M., Alkhateeb, T. T. Y., & Fawaz, M. M. (2019). Testing the environmental Kuznets curve in Egypt: Role of foreign investment and trade. *International Journal of Energy Economics and Policy*, *9*(2), 225–228.

Marques, A. C., & Caetano, R. (2020). The impact of foreign direct investment on emission reduction targets: Evidence from high- and middle-income countries. *Structural Change and Economic Dynamics*, *55*, 107–118.

Mottaleb, K. A., Rahut, D. B., Ali, A., Gérard, B., & Erenstein, O. (2017). Enhancing smallholder access to agricultural machinery services: Lessons from Bangladesh. *Journal of Development Studies*, *53*(9), 1502–1517.

Opoku, E. E. O., & Boachie, M. K. (2020). The environmental impact of industrialization and foreign direct investment. *Energy Policy*, *137*, 111178.

Porter, M. E., & Linde, C. V. D. (1995). Toward a new conception of the environment-competitiveness relationship. *The Journal of Economic Perspectives*, *9*(4), 97–118.

Potterie, B. v. P. d. l., & Lichtenberg, F. (2001). Does foreign direct investment transfer technology across borders? *The Review of Economics and Statistics*, *83*(3), 490–497. Ratner, B., 2009.

Ravinthirakumaran, K., Selvanathan, E., Singh, T., & Selvanathan, E. (2015). Determinants of foreign direct investment in Sri Lanka. *South Asia Economic Journal*, *16*(2), 233–256.

Raymond, P. A., Hartmann, J., Lauerwald, R., Sobek, S., McDonald, C., Hoover, M., Butman, D., Striegl, R., Mayorga, E., Humborg, C., & Kortelainen, P. (2013). Global carbon dioxide emissions from inland waters. *Nature*, *503*(7476), 355–359.

Ridzuan, A. R., Kumaran, V. V., Fianto, B. A., Shaari, M. S., Padilla, M. A. E., & Albani, A. (2022). Reinvestigating the presence of environmental Kuznets curve in Malaysia: The role of foreign direct investment. *International Journal of Energy Economics and Policy*, *12*(5), 217–225. https://doi.org/10.32479/ijeep.13461

Sabir, S., Qayyum, U., & Majeed, T. (2020). FDI and environmental degradation: The role of political institutions in South Asian countries. *Environmental Science and Pollution Research*, 32544–32553.

Sadoff, C. W., Hall, J. W., Grey, D., & Aerts, J. C. (2015). Will the nexus approach unlock sustainable development goals or will it remain a buzzword? *Water International*, *40*(5–6), 613–624.

Santos, A., & Forte, R. (2021). Environmental regulation and FDI attraction: A bibliometric analysis of the literature. *Environmental Science and Pollution Research*, *28*, 8873–8888.

Shaffer, R., & Zhang, X. (2004). Paradoxes in China's water policy. *Pacific Affairs*, *77*(2), 175–203.

Shahbaz, M., Nasir, M., & Roubaud, D. (2018). Environmental degradation in France: The effects of FDI, financial development, and energy innovations. *Energy Economics*, *74*, 843–857.

Singhania, M., & Saini, N. (2021). Demystifying pollution haven hypothesis: Role of FDI. *Journal of Business Research*, *123*, 516–528

Terzi, H., & Pata, U. K. (2020). Is the pollution Haven hypothesis (PHH) valid for Turkey? *Panoeconomicus*, *67*(1), 93–109.

Voumik, L. C., & Ridwan, M. (2023). Impact of FDI, industrialization, and education on the environment in Argentina: ARDL approach. *Heliyon*, *9*(1), e12872.

Wagner, M. (2003). *The Porter hypothesis revisited: a literature review of theoretical models and empirical tests* (pp. 22–24). CSM.

Wang, L., Liu, G., Alkhatib, S., Wang, X., Dai, J., Abbas, S. Z., & Khan, Y. A. (2022). The impact of foreign direct investment on environment: Evidence from newly industrialized countries. *Environmental Science and Pollution Research*, *29*, 70950–70961.

Wang, Q., Yang, T., & Li, R. (2023). Does income inequality reshape the environmental Kuznets curve (EKC) hypothesis? A nonlinear panel data analysis. *Environmental Research*, *2016*(1), 114575.

Waqih, M. A. U., Bhutto, N. A., Ghumro, N. H., Kumar, S., & Salam, M. A. (2019). Rising environmental degradation and impact of foreign direct investment: An empirical evidence from SAARC region. *Journal of Environmental Management*, *243*, 472–480.

Wheeler, D., & Mody, A. (1992). International investment location decisions: The case of US firms. *Journal of International Economics*, *33*(1–2), 57–76.

Yang, J., Guo, H., Liu, B., Shi, R., Zhang, B., & Ye, W. (2018). Environmental regulation and the pollution Haven hypothesis: Do environmental regulation measures matter? *Journal of Cleaner Production*, *202*, 993–1000.

Zhang, W., Li, G., Uddin, M. K., & Guo, S. (2020). Environmental regulation, foreign investment behavior, and carbon emissions for 30 provinces in China. *Journal of Cleaner Production*, *248*, 119208.

Zugravu-Soilita, N. (2017). How does foreign direct investment affect pollution? Toward a better understanding of the direct and conditional effects. *Environmental and Resource Economics*, *66*, 293–338.

Chapter 9

Foreign Direct Investment: West Africa Case Study on Sustainable Development

Abstract

This chapter examines the impact of foreign direct investment (FDI) on sustainable development in West Africa. Despite the growing body of research on FDI and sustainable development in the region, there remains a noticeable gap in the literature, particularly in terms of comprehensive reviews covering specific regions of Africa. While there has been a notable increase in African literature on the subject, there persists a bias toward the economic aspect of the phenomenon. This highlights the need for a more balanced approach that considers the broader implications of sustainable development beyond purely economic factors, given that the relationship between FDI and sustainable development has significant implications for academic research and practice. It underscores the importance of exploring diverse dimensions of sustainable development beyond economic growth alone. Governments are encouraged to direct FDI inflows toward developing human capital and protecting the environment, alongside infrastructure development.

Keywords: FDI; West Africa; sustainable development; SDGs; carbon emission

9.1 Introduction

The United Nations has established 17 sustainable development goals (SDGs) to be achieved by 2030 for the economies it targets. These goals encompass ending poverty, safeguarding the environment, and fostering equitable and peace-oriented societies that ensure well-being for all, among others. Examining the economic dimension of sustainable development reveals its aim to maintain the current level of welfare for future generations by enhancing the prosperity of nations while ensuring sustainability. Economic sustainability is defined as ensuring the

Foreign Direct Investment, 133–149

Published under exclusive licence by Emerald Publishing Limited
doi:10.1108/978-1-83662-900-920261009

continuity of income and consumption. Simultaneously, the environmental and social dimensions of sustainability delineate the boundaries of economic growth. Within the framework of sustainable development, foreign direct investment (FDI) has been observed to yield both positive and negative effects across social, environmental, and economic factors. The 17 SDGs generate significant investment requirements, posing various challenges for the international community. While the public sector plays a crucial role in mobilizing capital to attain these goals, FDI and private sector investments serve as vital external financing sources, particularly for developing countries.

In today's global landscape, FDI stands as an essential component from both national and international perspectives, exerting a significant influence on sustainability. Elevated levels of FDI correlate with growth, productivity, competitiveness, and sustainable development. Particularly, prioritizing sustainable industrial development becomes crucial, especially in nations embracing an FDI-centered integration strategy. This approach, aimed at bolstering internal production capacity while enhancing environmental performance and employment, underscores sustainability goals (Gallagher, 2005).

FDI is often perceived as a means for the investing country to address investment deficits stemming from savings shortages in the host country. The effects of innovation, renewable energy, employment generation, production expansion, and economic growth within invested sectors are instrumental in achieving objectives in the economic dimension of sustainable development, aligning with Neo-classical theory. According to this theory, FDI contributes to economic development in host countries by injecting capital, enlarging the labor force, and fostering technological advancement (Aust et al., 2020).

Considering the economic impacts of FDI on sustainable development, these effects can be categorized into macro- and microdimensions. Macroeconomic effects encompass elements such as stimulating economic growth, investment, and employment; assisting in addressing capital shortages; assisting in narrowing current account deficits; and potentially exacerbating balance of payments issues through increased imports. On the other hand, microeconomic effects include enhancing labor productivity, fostering managerial skills, influencing export and import levels, introducing new products and technologies, and potentially impacting the production dynamics of national firms (Awodumi, 2021).

Over the past three decades, the influx of FDI into the Economic Community of West African States (ECOWAS) has steadily increased. According to UNCTAD statistics, there has been a notable increase in FDI inflows over the years, with figures surging from around $195.96 million in 1986 to a peak of approximately $35.88 billion in 2011. This upward trajectory underscores the escalating importance of foreign investment in bridging the widening technology and finance gaps essential for fostering growth within the region. Indeed, the inflow of FDI into these economies catalyzes direct capital financing, facilitates the transfer of cutting-edge technologies, and introduces innovative processes and managerial expertise, thereby conferring significant advantages to domestic firms (Voica et al., 2015).

Conversely, data from the World Bank development indicators (WDI) reveal a notable increase in real output (real gross domestic product [GDP] at market prices) within ECOWAS, which soared by over 250% between 1980 and 2015. This growth has been accompanied by a significant rise in carbon emissions, increasing by 70% over the same period. However, while carbon intensity experienced a marginal increase from 7.11 kg (per kg of oil equivalent energy use) in 1980 to 8.12 kg in 2015, carbon emissions per unit of output are lower in recent years compared to over two decades ago (Awodumi, 2021).

Many nations worldwide have initiated measures, such as entering into international agreements, aimed at addressing pressing issues like carbon emissions through mechanisms such as trading certificates or investing in low-emission technologies. However, the financial burden associated with transitioning to a low-carbon economy is substantial, often exceeding the capacity of governments alone to bear. This necessity underscores the importance of involving the private sector in adopting sustainable business practices. While developed countries typically boast more advanced financing mechanisms, developing nations often possess competitive advantages that attract FDI (Voica et al., 2015).

Nevertheless, the question of whether FDI genuinely contributes to sustainable development remains a subject of significant debate and concern, particularly within the context of West African economies. Despite the substantial influx of FDI into the region in recent decades, there persists uncertainty regarding its actual impact on key sustainable development indicators such as economic growth, environmental preservation, social equity, and technological advancement. This ambiguity presents a critical challenge for policymakers, investors, and stakeholders striving to devise effective strategies to promote sustainable development in West Africa.

Therefore, conducting a comprehensive examination of the relationship between FDI and sustainable development from a West African perspective becomes imperative. Such an analysis is essential to inform evidence-based policy decisions and facilitate the implementation of initiatives aimed at fostering lasting socio-economic and environmental progress in the region. By understanding the nuanced dynamics at play between FDI and sustainable development, policymakers and stakeholders can better formulate strategies that leverage FDI to drive positive socio-economic and environmental outcomes in West Africa.

9.2 Case Study Questions

9.2.1 How Does FDI Contribute to Economic Growth in West African Countries?

There is a growing consensus among scholars that FDI has an impact on economic growth (Aitken & Harrison, 1999; Amadi, 2019; Balasubramanyam et al., 1996; De Mello, 1997). However, the actual effect of FDI on economic growth presents mixed results. While De Gregorio (2005) and Borensztein et al. (1998) discovered a positive correlation between FDI and economic growth, others such as Görg and Greenaway (2004) found either no evidence or no significant effect on growth. These discrepancies suggest that the impact of FDI on the economic growth of the receiving country depends on the presence and effectiveness of certain characteristics within that country.

9.2.2 What Is the Impact of FDI on Carbon Emission in West Africa?

Fossil fuels, comprising approximately 80% of global fuel consumption, pose dual challenges of energy security and environmental degradation due to their high carbon content and finite nature. This has sparked widespread debate among scientists, policymakers, and governments, with the International Energy Agency (IEA) warning of a potential doubling of global carbon dioxide (CO_2) emissions from energy-related activities by 2050 without decisive action. In addressing this urgent issue, FDI emerges as a crucial driver for technological advancement, playing a pivotal role in fostering innovation, research and development (R&D) capacities globally. By leveraging FDI, countries can accelerate the transition toward sustainable energy solutions and mitigate the adverse impacts of fossil fuel dependence on both the environment and global development goals.

9.2.3 What Is the Influence of FDI on Poverty Levels in West Africa?

A plethora of studies have endeavored to examine the impact of FDI on poverty levels, yet a diversity of findings characterizes the discourse on this matter. While some investigations support the assertion that FDI contributes to poverty alleviation, others argue the contrary. For example, Lazreg and Zouari (2018) explored the relationship between FDI and poverty reduction in Tunisia over the period 1985 to 2015, employing fully modified ordinary least squares (FMOLS). Their study reveals a significant positive effect of FDI on poverty alleviation. Similarly, Bharadwaj (2014) analyzed the impact of FDI on poverty across 35 developing countries from 1990 to 2004, affirming the beneficial role of FDI in reducing poverty levels.

However, contrasting viewpoints also exist in the literature, with some studies suggesting that FDI has little to no influence on poverty levels. For instance, Rye (2016) conducted a comprehensive analysis of FDI's impact on poverty across 134 countries worldwide, utilizing instrumental regression. The study found that FDI does not exert a significant effect on poverty. Likewise, Arabyat (2017) investigated the relationship between FDI and poverty reduction in developing nations using a panel error correction model, concluding that FDI has minimal impact on poverty levels. Furthermore, Gohou and Soumare (2012) employed two-stage least squares regressions to assess FDI's impact on poverty across 52 African countries from 1990 to 2007, revealing negligible influence on poverty.

9.3 Foreign Direct Investment in West Africa

FDI stands as a cornerstone of global economic interaction, involving an investor gaining significant control and interest in a foreign enterprise or establishing a subsidiary abroad. The landscape of FDI has seen remarkable growth across various regions worldwide, solidifying its position as the largest and most reliable source of external finance. It outstrips other forms of capital flows, including official development assistance (ODA), portfolio investments, bank loans, and international remittances. Importantly, FDI exhibits lower volatility compared to alternative capital flows (Noorbakhsh et al., 2001). Acknowledged as a fundamental catalyst for economic development and sustainable growth, FDI transcends mere financial infusion and job creation. It generates positive spillover effects from global trade integration, such as technology diffusion, productivity gains, and the introduction of innovative production methods and managerial expertise. These factors collectively drive economic expansion and contribute to poverty alleviation.

The evolution of FDI in the late 20th and early 21st centuries introduced new actors into the arena. Sovereign wealth funds (SWFs), government-controlled entities empowered to acquire significant equity stakes in foreign firms, emerged as major players. Similarly, private equity (PE) firms expanded their cross-border activities, while emerging-market multinational enterprises (EMNEs) intensified their overseas investments and acquisitions. Moving forward, further research is needed to explore the nuanced dynamics of FDI and its impact on host economies. This entails delving into the mechanisms through which FDI spurs economic growth and poverty reduction, as well as identifying potential barriers and challenges hindering its effectiveness. Additionally, investigations into the role of emerging players like SWFs, PE firms, and EMNEs in shaping the FDI landscape are warranted. Such endeavors will enrich our understanding of FDI's multifaceted implications and inform policymakers on strategies to optimize its benefits for sustainable development.

Recognizing FDI's pivotal role, particularly in Africa where high poverty levels and low domestic savings and income persist, underscores the importance of attracting various forms of FDI inflows. Given the unpredictable nature of foreign aid flows, Africa's limited share in global trade, and the volatility of short-term capital inflows, West African countries must prioritize strategies aimed at attracting larger volumes of this crucial potential resource. Doing so is essential for economic development and stability in the region. To this effect, Anyanwu and Yameogo (2015) conducted a study to explore the determinants of FDI in West Africa. Their findings revealed positive and significant effects for various factors, including the quadratic element of real per capita GDP, domestic investment, trade openness, the first-year lag of FDI, natural resources endowment (specifically oil and metals), exports, and monetary integration on FDI inflows to the region. Conversely, they identified a negative relationship between FDI inflows and the loan component of ODA, economic growth, level of economic development (real GDP per capita), life expectancy, and domestic credit to the private sector within West Africa.

Contributing to the discourse on renewable energy consumption and economic growth, Appiah-Otoo et al. (2023) investigated the moderating role of FDI in this relationship across a panel of 15 West African countries spanning from 1990 to 2021. Employing the panel-corrected standard errors and the feasible generalized least squares (FGLS) techniques, the study revealed that renewable energy consumption hinders economic growth in the region. However, it also uncovered a positive influence of FDI on economic growth. Notably, the interaction between renewable energy consumption and FDI was found to have a positive effect on economic growth. Thus, FDI plays a pivotal role in facilitating renewable energy consumption, thereby fostering a positive impact on economic growth in West Africa.

Lamine and Yang (2010) aimed to explore the impact of FDI on economic growth in the Republic of Guinea. The study employed the Granger causality test to analyze the relationship between FDI and proxies for economic growth. The findings revealed that the current level of FDI remains insufficient to foster economic growth in Guinea. Specifically, the Granger Causality Test indicates that an increase in GDP could stimulate higher levels of FDI, suggesting a positive correlation between GDP and FDI. Moreover, factors such as employment are identified as potential drivers of FDI, emphasizing the crucial role of the Guinean government in promoting employment to attract foreign investments. Additionally, the study suggests that improvements in school enrollment can lead to GDP growth, indirectly influencing FDI. The economic landscape of Guinea could be enhanced through the implementation of policies and regulations aimed at attracting and safeguarding investors, including efforts to encourage investment from the Guinean diaspora.

9.4 Sustainable Development in West Africa

Research focusing on sustainable development in West Africa remains limited. De Soysa and Neumayer (2005) suggest that higher levels of FDI correlate with increased growth rates in genuine savings. However, factors such as income inequality, poor institutional quality, conflicts, and excessive reliance on natural resource exports like oil negatively impact genuine savings growth in West Africa (Bissoon, 2017). Leadership plays a pivotal role in sustainable development, with effective leadership deemed crucial for achieving SDGs in West Africa (Dartey-Baah, 2014). Transformational leadership, characterized by long-term vision, stakeholder engagement, and ethical governance, can address governance weaknesses and promote sustainable development. Sustainable development in West Africa hinges on economic efficiency, social cohesion, and environmental responsibility (Dartey-Baah, 2014).

Since 2016, the West Africa SDG Index and Dashboards report has aimed to assist countries in the region in identifying priorities, understanding implementation challenges, and closing gaps to achieve SDGs by 2030. National and regional dialogues and planning are essential for SDG attainment in West Africa. However, data availability remains a challenge, with only 37.8% of official SDG indicators data accessible to countries in the region. This underscores the need for a West Africa-specific report to address data gaps. In 2018, West African countries scored between 0 and 100 on 97 indicators across 17 SDGs, with Ghana achieving a score of 62, indicating its progress toward SDGs. The West Africa SDG dashboard and report highlight key challenges, including inadequate data quality, lack of political support, and insufficient financial resources.

Sustainable development in West Africa transcends mere economic growth; it encompasses inclusive growth strategies aimed at reducing poverty and fostering shared prosperity for both present and future generations (World Bank). Successful implementation of sustainable development requires meticulous planning, sufficient financial resources, and a well-structured approach that delivers immediate and long-term benefits for people, the planet, and overall prosperity. Agyekum et al. (2020) aim at the global imperative for clean and sustainable energy that has prompted nations to seek alternatives to fossil fuels, given their detrimental environmental impact. Ghana, recognizing this need, aims to incorporate nuclear power into its energy mix by 2029. This study employs the SWOT analysis tool to evaluate the internal strengths and weaknesses, as well as the external opportunities and threats, of Ghana's nuclear power program. The findings reveal that despite Ghana's concerted efforts to fulfil requirements for licensing, contracting, construction, and operation of a nuclear facility, significant gaps still exist that could potentially impede progress. The research underscores Ghana's numerous strengths and opportunities, which render nuclear power investment economically feasible. However, challenges such as porous security systems, corruption, weak borders, and policy discontinuity resulting from changes in political leadership pose threats to the seamless implementation and operation of a nuclear power plant in the country.

9.5 Foreign Direct Investment and Economic Growth in West Africa

Previous research examining the connections between FDI and economic growth has yielded varied outcomes. Moreover, ongoing debates persist regarding the specific types of FDI that exert the greatest influence on economic growth. Despite these divergent findings, there seems to be a consistent consensus that FDI contributes positively to economic growth. The research findings indicate a favorable correlation between globalization and political governance concerning economic growth. Despite some ambiguity surrounding the relationship between FDI and growth, the study reveals that FDI indeed fosters growth within the sub-region, with political governance amplifying its positive effects on economic development. Additionally, other contributing factors to growth, namely labor, capital, and government size, exhibit distinct impacts: labor and capital are associated with negative effects on growth, while government size demonstrates a positive influence.

Over the years, the significance of FDI inflows to Africa has been widely acknowledged as a key driver of economic growth (Ozturk, 2007). This perception stems from the belief that FDI fosters output expansion, technology dissemination, knowledge exchange, and innovation, facilitated by governmental policies and initiatives (Anyanwu, 2012). Consequently, government strategies regarding FDI influence both the nature and quality of national comparative advantages and knowledge transfers. As a result, numerous African nations have actively sought FDI, anticipating its beneficial impact on output, income, and the transfer of knowledge and technology (Anyanwu, 2012). FDI typically enters through various modes such as joint ventures, greenfield investments, mergers, and acquisitions, while the assets transferred encompass management expertise and technology from one country to another.

In their extensive analysis, Shittu et al. (2020) delved into the complex interplay among FDI, globalization, and political governance in driving economic growth across West Africa. By employing the autoregressive distributed lag technique and harnessing data from reputable sources like the World Bank and the KOF Institute, their study shed light on the nuanced dynamics at play. They uncovered a positive correlation between globalization, political governance, and economic growth within the region, emphasizing the multifaceted nature of factors influencing growth trajectories. Furthermore, their findings provided valuable insights into the specific roles of factors such as labor, capital, and government size in shaping economic outcomes, underscoring the importance of comprehensive policy frameworks in fostering sustainable development.

Meanwhile, Pelinescu and Radulescu (2009) contributed significantly to our understanding of the pivotal role played by FDI in driving economic growth. Their research highlighted a direct correlation between FDI inflows and GDP growth per capita, illuminating the transformative impact of foreign investments on macroeconomic indicators. By tracing the historical patterns of foreign investment activities, they underscored the fundamental role of FDI in catalyzing economic growth and facilitating the diversification of economies away from traditional sectors.

Moreover, Seyoum et al. (2015) research on the Granger causal relationship between FDI and economic growth across 23 African countries enriched our understanding of the dynamics driving economic expansion on the continent. By employing advanced panel econometric techniques, they uncovered bidirectional causality between FDI and economic growth, highlighting the mutually reinforcing nature of these factors. Their findings underscored the critical role of FDI in driving economic progress across diverse African contexts, emphasizing the need for targeted policies to attract and leverage foreign investments effectively. Anyanwu and Yameogo (2015) contributed valuable insights into the drivers of FDI to West Africa, revealing a nuanced relationship between economic development and FDI inflows. Through their rigorous analysis, they identified key factors influencing FDI inflows, providing policymakers with valuable guidance on fostering an enabling environment for foreign investments in the region.

9.6 Foreign Direct Investment and Carbon Emission in West Africa

Environmental degradation has become a paramount contemporary concern, posing a significant threat to the sustainable development and well-being of economies worldwide. Over recent decades, the escalation of global warming, primarily driven by the rising concentration of greenhouse gases in the atmosphere, notably CO_2, has garnered considerable attention from policymakers and societies alike. Moreover, Grossman and Krueger (1991) posited that FDI could impact the environment of host countries through three primary mechanisms: alterations in the scale of the economy, shifts in industrial structure, and changes in production techniques. In contrast, Adu and Denkyirah (2019) were unable to establish the presence of the Kuznets environmental curve in seven West African nations. However, Halliru et al. (2020), employing a quantile panel regression method, identified a U-shaped relationship between economic growth and CO_2 emissions across all quantiles in examining this hypothesis spanning from 1970 to 2017 for six West African countries.

Countries with lenient environmental regulations may possess a comparative advantage in attracting greater FDI, thereby potentially compromising environmental sustainability. This phenomenon was examined in the context of West African countries by Keho (2015). Through time series data analysis, Keho observed that FDI led to an increase in CO_2 emissions in some countries, while in others, it either reduced emissions or had no discernible effect. Furthermore, numerous studies conducted in both developed and developing countries have demonstrated a positive association between high levels of pollution and increased FDI inflows, thus affirming the validity of the pollution haven hypothesis (Gyamfi et al., 2021; Ohajionu et al., 2022).

The notion that FDI might reduce pollution intensity finds support in Shabir et al. (2022). Similarly, Opoku et al. (2022) discovered a positive correlation between FDI and CO_2 emissions in 22 Sub-Saharan African countries from 1995 to 2014. Conversely, Raza et al. (2021), in their assessment of the environmental performance of South and East Asian countries, found no significant relationship between FDI and environmental performance. Furthermore, they observed that trade liberalization had a detrimental effect on environmental performance, while GDP had a positive impact. Using a vector error correction model (VECM) and data from China spanning from 1990 to 2012, Si et al. (2021) determined that agricultural land and other uses significantly contributed to greenhouse gas emissions in the long run. To elaborate on the diverse perspectives concerning financial development and carbon emissions in prior research, proponents of the positive linkage argue that financial development tends to bolster economic growth, thereby prompting ecological and environmental implications through increased energy consumption and depletion of environmental quality (Boutabba, 2014). Furthermore, the financial development of a country can act as a catalyst for FDI, which flows into productive sectors and spurs growth. Essentially, the development of the financial sector elevates the living standards of a country's populace by enhancing access to finances and stimulating economic activities, consequently leading to heightened energy consumption and a subsequent increase in carbon emissions (Vitenu-Sackey, 2020).

Tamazian et al. (2009) examined the impact of financial development on carbon emissions in China and concluded that the relationship between the two is inverse. Therefore, during the period from 1992 to 2004, financial development had a negative effect on carbon emissions in China. Supporting these findings, Jalil and Feridun (2011) investigated the relationship between environmental quality and financial development, concluding that an increase in financial development in emerging economies leads to a decrease in carbon emissions.

9.7 Foreign Direct Investment and Poverty Levels in West Africa

Alongside studies supporting the FDI–poverty reduction hypothesis, several have found that FDI has an insignificant influence on poverty. For example, Rye (2016) explored the effect of FDI on poverty across 134 countries worldwide, employing instrumental regression and finding that FDI does not significantly impact poverty. Similarly, Arabyat (2017) assessed the impact of FDI on poverty reduction in developing countries using a panel error correction model, concluding that FDI has no significant influence on poverty. Gohou and Soumare (2012) analyzed the impact of FDI on poverty using two-stage least squares regressions across 52 African countries from 1990 to 2007, revealing an insignificant effect of FDI on poverty. Correspondingly, Quinonez et al. (2018) examined the impact of FDI on poverty incidence in Latin America for a panel of 13 economies, concluding that FDI does not significantly reduce poverty in the region. Moreover, Anetor et al. (2020) employed the FGLS technique to explore the impact of FDI, trade, and foreign aid on poverty in SSA, revealing that FDI and foreign aids increase poverty and suggesting that the requisite level of FDI to alleviate poverty has not been attained.

Akinlo and Dada (2021) investigated the interplay between FDI, environmental degradation, and poverty reduction across 39 Sub-Saharan African countries. Utilizing panel data spanning from 1986 to 2018, dynamic Generalized Method of Moments (GMM) techniques were employed for estimations. The findings revealed nuanced relationships between these variables based on different measures of poverty reduction. Initially, when poverty reduction was assessed through household final consumption expenditure, the interaction between FDI and environmental degradation did not significantly contribute to poverty reduction. However, when measured by the human development index, the interaction between FDI and environmental degradation was found to enhance poverty reduction efforts. Interestingly, when poverty reduction was evaluated using life expectancy, the interaction term of FDI and CO_2 emissions proved detrimental to poverty reduction. Conversely, the interaction terms of FDI with other measures of environmental degradation showed no significant effect on poverty reduction.

These findings underscore the complexity of the relationship between FDI, environmental degradation, and poverty reduction in sub-Saharan Africa. They highlight the importance of considering multiple dimensions of poverty and environmental impact when assessing the effectiveness of FDI in promoting sustainable development. Additionally, the study suggests the need for targeted policy interventions aimed at mitigating the adverse effects of environmental degradation on poverty reduction, particularly in contexts where FDI interacts unfavorably with environmental factors. Further research in this area could explore specific mechanisms and policy interventions to harness the potential benefits of FDI while minimizing its negative environmental and social impacts, ultimately contributing to more sustainable and inclusive development outcomes in the region.

Furthermore, some studies have attempted to elucidate the causal relationship between FDI and poverty. For instance, Magombeyi and Odhiambo (2017) explored the causal relationship between FDI and poverty in South Africa using time series analysis, revealing a unidirectional causality from poverty reduction to FDI. Conversely, Dhrifi et al. (2020) identified a bidirectional causality between poverty and FDI for a sample of developing countries. The conflicting findings regarding the impact of FDI may arise due to differences in geographical context, the type and nature of FDI, and the estimation techniques utilized. Additionally, FDI's impact may be contingent upon the absorptive capacity of the host country.

9.8 Conclusion

FDI plays a vital role in bolstering economic growth across West African nations by catalyzing investment, driving technological progress, and boosting productivity within critical sectors. Nevertheless, the efficacy of FDI as a driver of economic expansion is contingent upon a myriad of factors, encompassing the caliber of institutions, the coherence of policy frameworks, and the intricacies of sector-specific dynamics. Therefore, policymakers and stakeholders are urged to accord paramount importance to initiatives aimed at fortifying the investment climate, enhancing institutional capabilities, and fostering diversification across sectors. By doing so, they can effectively harness the transformative potential of FDI, thereby maximizing its beneficial impact on economic growth and sustainable development in West Africa. Moreover, fostering collaboration between public and private entities, promoting innovation and entrepreneurship, and fostering inclusive growth strategies are additional avenues through which the positive effects of FDI can be magnified. Ultimately, a concerted effort to address these multifaceted challenges and capitalize on the opportunities presented by FDI holds the key to unlocking West Africa's full economic potential and ensuring long-term prosperity for its populace.

The impact of FDI on carbon emissions in West Africa demands scrutiny to assess environmental sustainability and devise effective mitigation strategies. While FDI fuels economic growth, its influence on carbon emissions depends on factors like industry types and technology adoption. To mitigate emissions, policymakers can promote sustainable investment, incentivize clean technologies, enhance energy efficiency, and strengthen environmental regulations. International cooperation can facilitate knowledge sharing and technology transfer, fostering inclusive and sustainable development. By proactively addressing environmental concerns, West African countries can achieve sustainable growth while mitigating carbon emissions, ensuring a greener future for generations to come.

While FDI holds promise for poverty alleviation in West Africa through fostering economic growth and creating employment opportunities, its effectiveness hinges on a multitude of socio-economic factors and mechanisms. Policymakers must prioritize initiatives that enhance the investment climate, bolster institutional capacity, and promote inclusive growth strategies to fully harness the poverty-reducing potential of FDI in the region. Moreover, fostering international cooperation and knowledge sharing is imperative to adopt best practices and strategies for effectively addressing poverty. By addressing these challenges and leveraging the opportunities presented by FDI, West African nations can move closer to achieving SDGs and ensuring prosperity for all segments of society.

9.9 Practical Implication

a. Policymakers and institutions to prioritize the formulation of laws and regulations that foster sustainable development across all facets of the economy. This entails going beyond traditional economic metrics and considering the social and environmental implications of investment activities.
b. The interconnectedness of economic, social, and environmental factors in shaping sustainable development outcomes. For instance, while FDI may stimulate economic growth, its impact on social welfare and environmental sustainability depends on various factors such as the quality of governance, the enforcement of regulations, and the adoption of environmentally friendly practices.
c. Governments and institutions are urged to adopt a balanced approach to policymaking that promotes sustainable development across all sectors of the economy. This includes enacting laws and regulations that promote environmental conservation, social equity, and economic prosperity simultaneously. Additionally, fostering partnerships with stakeholders, including the private sector, civil society, and international organizations, can facilitate the implementation of sustainable development initiatives and ensure their long-term success.
d. Embracing a comprehensive approach to policymaking that considers economic, social, and environmental objectives, West African countries can achieve sustainable and inclusive development that benefits present and future generations. This requires a concerted effort to create an enabling

environment for responsible investment, foster innovation, and address the root causes of poverty and inequality while safeguarding the environment for future generations.

9.10 Recommendations

a. One of the key factors influencing the impact of FDI on sustainable development is the investment climate. To attract more investment and ensure its positive contribution to development, West African countries should prioritize efforts to enhance the investment climate. This includes streamlining administrative procedures, reducing bureaucratic hurdles, and ensuring legal certainty for foreign investors. By creating a conducive environment for investment, countries can stimulate economic growth, create job opportunities, and promote technology transfer.
b. Effective governance and institutional capacity are essential for ensuring that FDI contributes to sustainable development in West Africa. Governments should invest in institutions responsible for monitoring and regulating FDI, as well as enhance their capacity to enforce environmental and labor standards. This includes training and capacity-building programs for government officials, as well as strengthening regulatory frameworks to ensure compliance with international standards. By strengthening institutional capacity, countries can better manage the social and environmental impacts of FDI and ensure that its benefits are equitably distributed across society.
c. Inclusive growth strategies are essential for addressing poverty and inequality in West Africa and ensuring that the benefits of FDI reach all segments of society. Governments should prioritize investments in education, healthcare, and social protection programs to enhance human capital development and provide vulnerable populations with the tools and resources needed to lift themselves out of poverty. Additionally, fostering entrepreneurship and supporting small and medium-sized enterprises (SMEs) can create opportunities for economic empowerment and livelihood improvement, particularly in rural areas.
d. International cooperation and knowledge sharing play a crucial role in maximizing the benefits of FDI for sustainable development in West Africa. Countries should engage with international organizations, development partners, and neighboring countries to exchange insights and collaborate on initiatives aimed at addressing development challenges effectively. By learning from successful strategies implemented elsewhere and leveraging global best practices, West African nations can accelerate progress toward SDGs and ensure prosperity for all.
e. While FDI can stimulate economic growth, its environmental impact must be carefully managed to ensure long-term sustainability. Governments should enact laws and regulations that promote environmental conservation and sustainable resource management. This includes implementing measures to

mitigate pollution, protect biodiversity, and promote renewable energy sources. Additionally, fostering green investments and incentivizing environmentally friendly practices can help attract responsible investors and promote sustainable development in West Africa.

f. Promoting sustainable development through FDI requires a concerted effort from policymakers, stakeholders, and the international community. By enhancing the investment climate, strengthening institutional capacity, promoting inclusive growth strategies, fostering international cooperation, and addressing environmental concerns, West African countries can harness the full potential of FDI to drive economic growth and improve the well-being of their citizens. With strategic planning, effective governance, and collaboration, SDGs can be achieved, ensuring a brighter future for generations to come.

References

Adu, D. T., & Denkyirah, E. K. (2019). Economic growth and environmental pollution in West Africa: Testing the Environmental Kuznets Curve hypothesis. *Kasetsart Journal of Social Sciences*, *40*(2), 281–288.

Agyekum, E. B., Ansah, M. N. S., & Afornu, K. B. (2020). Nuclear energy for sustainable development: SWOT analysis on Ghana's nuclear agenda. *Energy Reports*, *6*, 107–115.

Aitken, B. J., & Harrison, A. E. (1999). Do domestic firms benefit from direct foreign investment? Evidence from Venezuela. *The American Economic Review*, *89*(3), 605–618.

Akinlo, T., & Dada, J. T. (2021). The moderating effect of foreign direct investment on environmental degradation-poverty reduction nexus: Evidence from sub-Saharan African countries. *Environment, Development and Sustainability*, *23*(11), 15764–15784.

Amadi, C. (2019). *FDI and economic growth in Nigeria: An analysis of the role of financial development on linkages* Doctoral dissertation. Manchester Metropolitan University.

Anetor, F. O., Esho, E., & Verhoef, G. (2020). The impact of foreign direct investment, foreign aid and trade on poverty reduction: Evidence from Sub-Saharan African countries. *Cogent Economics & Finance*, *8*(1), 1737347.

Anyanwu, J. C. (2012). Why does foreign direct investment go where it goes?: New evidence from African countries. *Annals of Economics and Finance*, *13*(2), 425–462.

Anyanwu, J. C., & Yameogo, N. D. (2015). What drives foreign direct investments into West Africa? An empirical investigation. *African Development Review*, *27*(3), 199–215. https://doi.org/10.1111/1467-8268.12141

Appiah-Otoo, I., Chen, X., & Ampah, J. D. (2023). Exploring the moderating role of foreign direct investment in the renewable energy and economic growth nexus: Evidence from West Africa. *Energy*, *281*, 128346.

Arabyat, Y. A. (2017). The impact of foreign direct investment on poverty reduction in the developing countries. *International Finance and Banking*, *4*(2), 92–111.

Aust, V., Morais, A. I., & Pinto, I. (2020). How does foreign direct investment contribute to sustainable development goals? Evidence from African countries. *Journal of Cleaner Production*, *245*, 118823.

Awodumi, O. B. (2021). Does foreign direct investment promote environmental efficiency in developing economies? Evidence from Economic Community of West African states. *Business Strategy & Development*, *4*(2), 170–186.

Balasubramanyam, V. N., Salisu, M., & Sapsford, D. (1996). Foreign direct investment and growth in EP and IS countries. *The Economic Journal*, *106*(434), 92–105.

Bharadwaj, A. (2014). Reviving the globalisation and poverty debate: Effects of real and financial integration on the developing world. *Advances in Economics and Business*, *2*(1), 42–57.

Bissoon, O. (2017). Is sub-Saharan Africa on a genuinely sustainable development path? Evidence using panel data. *Margin: The Journal of Applied Economic Research*, *11*(4), 449–464.

Borensztein, E., De Gregorio, J., & Lee, J. W. (1998). How does foreign direct investment affect economic growth? *Journal of International Economics*, *45*(1), 115–135.

Boutabba, M. A. (2014). The impact of financial development, income, energy and trade on carbon emissions: Evidence from the Indian economy. *Economic Modelling*, *40*, 33–41.

Dartey-Baah, K. (2014). Effective leadership and sustainable development in Africa: Is there "really" a link? *Journal of Global Responsibility*, *5*(2), 203–218.

De Gregorio, J. (2005). The role of foreign direct investment and natural resources in economic development. In *Multinationals and foreign investment in economic development* (pp. 179–197). Palgrave Macmillan UK.

De Mello Jr., L. R. (1997). Foreign direct investment in developing countries and growth: A selective survey. *Journal of Development Studies*, *34*(1), 1–34.

De Soysa, I., & Neumayer, E. (2005). False prophet, or genuine savior? Assessing the effects of economic openness on sustainable development, 1980–99. *International Organization*, *59*(3), 731–772.

Dhrifi, A., Jaziri, R., & Alnahdi, S. (2020). Does foreign direct investment and environmental degradation matter for poverty? Evidence from developing countries. *Structural Change and Economic Dynamics*, *52*, 13–21.

Gallagher, K. P., (2005). FDI as a sustainable development strategy: Evidence from Mexican manufacturing. In *Working Papers Series Center for Latin American Studies University of California, Berkeley*. https://escholarship.org/uc/item/57f1q95v

Gohou, G., & Soumare, I. (2012). Does foreign direct investment reduces poverty in Africa and are there regional differences. *World Development*, *40*(1), 75–95.

Görg, H., & Greenaway, D. (2004). Much ado about nothing? Do domestic firms really benefit from foreign direct investment? *The World Bank Research Observer*, *19*(2), 171–197.

Grossman, G. M. and Krueger, A. B., (1991). *Environmental impacts of a North American free trade agreement.*

Gyamfi, B. A., Adedoyin, F. F., Bein, M. A., & Bekun, F. V. (2021). Environmental implications of N-shaped environmental Kuznets curve for E7 countries. *Environmental Science and Pollution Research*, *28*, 33072–33082.

Halliru, A. M., Loganathan, N., Hassan, A. A. G., Mardani, A., & Kamyab, H. (2020). Re-examining the environmental Kuznets curve hypothesis in the Economic Community of West African states: A panel quantile regression approach. *Journal of Cleaner Production*, *276*, 124247.

Jalil, A., & Feridun, M. (2011). The impact of growth, energy and financial development on the environment in China: A cointegration analysis. *Energy Economics*, *33*(2), 284–291.

Keho, Y. (2015). Foreign direct investment, exports and economic growth: Some African evidence. *Journal of Applied Economics and Business Research*, *5*(4).

Lamine, K. M., & Yang, D. (2010). Foreign direct investment effect on economic growth: Evidence from Guinea Republic in West Africa. *International Journal of Financial Research*, *1*(1), 49–54.

Lazreg, M., & Zouari, E. (2018). The relationship between FDI, poverty reduction and environmental sustainability in Tunisia. *Journal of Economics and Management Sciences*, *1*(1), 114.

Magombeyi, M. T., & Odhiambo, N. M. (2017). Causal relationship between FDI and poverty reduction in South Africa. *Cogent Economics & Finance*, *5*(1), 1357901.

Noorbakhsh, F., Paloni, A., & Youssef, A. (2001). Human capital and FDI inflows to developing countries: New empirical evidence. *World Development*, *29*(9), 1593–1610.

Ohajionu, U. C., Gyamfi, B. A., Haseki, M. I., & Bekun, F. V. (2022). Assessing the linkage between energy consumption, financial development, tourism and environment: Evidence from method of moments quantile regression. *Environmental Science and Pollution Research*, *29*(20), 30004–30018.

Opoku, E. E. O., Acheampong, A. O., Dzator, J., & Kufuor, N. K. (2022). Does environmental sustainability attract foreign investment? Evidence from developing countries. *Business Strategy and the Environment*, *31*(7), 3542–3573.

Ozturk, I. (2007). Foreign direct investment-growth nexus: A review of the recent literature. *International Journal of Applied Econometrics and Quantitative Studies*, *4*(2).

Pelinescu, E., & Radulescu, M. (2009). The impact of foreign direct investment on the economic growth and countries' export potential. *Romanian Journal of Economic Forecasting*, *4*(1), 153–169.

Quinonez, P., Saenz, J., & Solorzano, J. (2018). Does foreign direct investment reduce poverty? The case of Latin America in the twenty-first century. *Business and Economic Horizons*, *14*(3), 488–500.

Raza, M. A. A., Yan, C., Abbas, H. S. M., & Ullah, A. (2021). Impact of institutional governance and state determinants on foreign direct investment in Asian economies. *Growth and Change*, *52*(4), 2596–2613.

Rye, S.-Z. (2016). *Foreign direct investment and its effects on income inequality*. Master's thesis at the Economics Institute. University of Oslo.

Seyoum, M., Wu, R., & Lin, J. (2015). Foreign direct investment and economic growth: The case of developing African economies. *Social Indicators Research*, *122*(1), 45–64.

Shabir, M., Ali, M., Hashmi, S. H., & Bakhsh, S. (2022). Heterogeneous effects of economic policy uncertainty and foreign direct investment on environmental quality: Cross-country evidence. *Environmental Science and Pollution Research*, *29* (2), 2737–2752.

Shittu, W. O., Yusuf, H. A., El Moctar El Houssein, A., & Hassan, S. (2020). The impacts of foreign direct investment and globalisation on economic growth in West Africa: Examining the role of political governance. *Journal of Economic Studies*, *47*(7), 1733–1755.

Si, R., Aziz, N., & Raza, A. (2021). Short and long-run causal effects of agriculture, forestry, and other land use on greenhouse gas emissions: Evidence from China using VECM approach. *Environmental Science and Pollution Research*, *28*, 64419–64430.

Tamazian, A., Chousa, J. P., & Vadlamannati, K. C. (2009). Does higher economic and financial development lead to environmental degradation: Evidence from BRIC countries. *Energy Policy*, *37*(1), 246–253.

Vitenu-Sackey, P. A. (2020). Financial development, foreign direct investment and carbon emissions: A comparative study of West Africa and Southern Africa regions. *International Review of Research in Emerging Markets and the Global Economy (IRREM) An Online International (Double-Blind) Refereed Research Journal*, *6*(1), 1550–1569. https://www.nugschina.org/portal/member_academics/academics_uploads/30abdbb2e479679f4bca3e16c54d6e9e.pdf.

Voica, M. C., Panait, M., & Haralambie, G. A. (2015). The impact of foreign direct investment on sustainable development. *Petroleum-Gas University of Ploiesti Bulletin, Technical Series*, *67*(3). https://upg-bulletin-se.ro/old_site/archive/2015-3/10.Voica_Panait_Haralambie.pdf.

Chapter 10

Foreign Direct Investment: Developing Countries' Group Case Study

Abstract

Foreign direct investment (FDI) has become an important macroeconomic instrument with which developing countries continuously rely on to catalyze their economic potential and capabilities, subject to their absorptive capacities. This chapter examines the case of a group of developing countries (Sri Lanka, Philippines, Vietnam, and India) and concludes with recommendations on how individual governments can leverage on FDI for economic growth and development.

Keywords: FDI; Developing countries; Sri Lanka; Philippines; Vietnam; India

10.1 Introduction

Foreign direct investment (FDI) and economic growth in developing nations have a complex and nuanced relationship. There are statistically significant trends when it comes to developing nations. Research conducted in Bangladesh demonstrates a weak positive link between FDI and gross domestic product (GDP) growth, a positive correlation between FDI and inflation, and a negative correlation between FDI and the balance of trade (BOT) (Vasa & Angeloska, 2020). These numbers demonstrate that FDI has little bearing on GDP expansion. In fact, it has been connected to inflation and a widening trade gap.

Since rising inflation makes it difficult for individuals to buy products and can slow down the economy (Antony, 2009), a large positive correlation between FDI and the inflation rate may be cause for concern. When imports are higher than exports, a negative trade balance occurs, making it difficult for poor countries to acquire the resources they require. However, it is important to remember that the study found FDI to have a positive but insignificant influence

Foreign Direct Investment, 151–161

Published under exclusive licence by Emerald Publishing Limited
doi:10.1108/978-1-83662-900-920261010

on GDP growth. These results are concerning for the governments of developing countries because FDI is a key part of a country's long-term growth.

Evidence shows that the effect of FDI on economic growth depends on the receiving country's absorptive abilities, which include things like trained human resources, technology, infrastructure, trade policy, institutional change, and political conditions (Amadi, 2019). Several things get in the way of foreign investment in developing countries. This includes a lack of skilled workers, bad infrastructure, a slow privatization process, inefficient bureaucracy, political volatility, and frequent natural disasters. Corruption and a lack of openness make the business situation even worse. Even though developing countries have a comparative edge in low-cost labor, the country needs to educate and train its labor force to make its labor market more efficient and effective. Skilled work is important for development and economic growth because it is a complex part of production.

In addition, the governments of developing nations must implement the reforms and policies required to improve the functionality of foreign investment. Improving the country's absorptive capacity through measures such as an educated labor force, solid infrastructure, uninterrupted utility supply, investment-friendly policies, advanced technology, and political stability is essential for maximizing the benefits of FDI (Har et al., 2008). It is essential to recognize that the benefits of FDI are not automatic and that the government must take proactive measures to create a conducive environment for foreign investors. There can be several negative effects of FDI as well. The dependency school contends that FDI predominantly benefits industrial core economies at the expense of developing nations.

Frequently, the wealth generated in the host country is transferred to the central countries, resulting in an increase in global inequality and limited accumulation of wealth in the host economy. Increased competition from multinational corporations resulting from FDI can result in the displacement of local businesses that are unable to compete. This can lead to employment losses rather than job creation, especially in sectors where local businesses lack the efficacy and resources to compete with foreign investors. In some instances, the interests of foreign investors and the recipient economy may diverge. There is a risk of exploitation, such as low wages, poor working conditions, and environmental degradation, if investors prioritize their own profits over the well-being of the host nation.

FDI frequently entails the acquisition of control over domestic companies by foreign-owned companies (Antras et al., 2009). This can result in a loss of control over critical industries and economic decision-making, potentially undermining the host country's sovereignty and autonomy. Although there are theoretical considerations supporting the positive impact of FDI on economic growth, the results of empirical research vary. One important observation is that the benefits of FDI, such as technology transfers, management expertise, and employee training, are frequently more prevalent in the manufacturing sector than in the agriculture and mining sectors. This suggests that potential FDI benefits may be sector specific (Danmola, 2013). Moreover, for FDI to have a significant impact on economic growth, local economic ties are essential. In some instances, foreign investments can function as isolated enclaves, with primary products extracted from mines, wells, or plantations departing the country without contributing significantly to the rest of the economy.

This phenomenon has been criticized because it limits the residual effects and broader developmental influence of FDI (referred to as "enclave" development). The relationship between FDI and economic growth in developing nations is one that is both intricate and complicated. When it comes to developing nations, there are tendencies that are noteworthy according to the statistics. According to research carried out in Bangladesh (Vasa & Angeloska, 2020), there is some evidence to suggest that FDI contributes to a weakly positive association between GDP growth and FDI, that there is a positive correlation between FDI and inflation, and that there is a negative correlation between FDI and the BOT. This shows that FDI has very little impact on the growth of GDP. In fact, it has been linked to both rising prices and a widening imbalance in trade. A negative trade balance happens when imports are larger than exports. This makes it harder for developing nations to get the resources they require since it creates a negative trade balance. It is essential, however, to keep in mind that the research showed that FDI had a favorable but minor influence on the expansion of the GDP.

10.2 Sri Lanka

FDI in Sri Lanka has responded positively during periods of relative economic and political stability. During specific time periods, including 1979–1982, 1990–1993, and 2002, FDI inflows to Sri Lanka reached a maximum of US$ 242 million. In 2003, FDI inflows increased by US$ 30 million, including proceeds from privatizations (Balamurali & Bogahawatte, 2004). Power and energy, port-related developments, telecommunications, and manufacturing are among the Sri Lankan industries that have attracted substantial foreign investment. These sectors have benefitted from foreign investments, which have contributed to the economic growth of the nation. Notably, the net FDI in Sri Lanka was marginally lower in 2003 than in 2002 due to a larger outflow of US$ 27 million compared to US$ 11 million. This indicates that there were obstacles or factors that impacted the net FDI flow during that year (Samantha & Haiyun, 2017).

FDI in developing nations across the globe increased significantly from approximately US$ 9 billion in 1995 to US$ 250 billion in 2000. The relationship between foreign multinational corporations and their host countries, including Sri Lanka, can vary significantly based on variables such as the characteristics of the host country and the policy climate. According to the World Bank, FDI has the potential to promote economic development by enhancing productivity growth and facilitating technological advancement. The precise nature of this relationship varies across nations and industries (Sultanuzzaman et al., 2018). Maintaining a stable economic and political climate is essential for Sri Lanka to attract and maximize FDI. In addition, policies that support capital formation, technology transfer, productivity improvement, and export promotion can play a crucial role in maximizing the benefits of FDI for sustainable economic growth. Prior research has highlighted the importance of FDI inflows to a nation's development. Additionally, neoclassical growth theory supports the notion that FDI promotes economic development by fostering capital accumulation. Prior to the 2008 global economic crisis, FDI and exports in the South Asian region grew substantially.

However, the post-crisis period witnessed varying development rates among regional economies, and Sri Lanka was unable to completely insulate its economy. Nevertheless, Sri Lanka experienced adjustments in terms of GDP growth, FDI inflows, and trade between 2008 and 2016 (Ranasinghe & Sugandhika, 2018). Sri Lanka's textiles and garments exports in 2009 were negatively impacted by the economic crisis in the United States and the Eurozone, which were significant export markets for Sri Lanka. However, after 2009, Sri Lanka's textile and apparel exports increased significantly (Jahfer & Inoue, 2014). The country's economy has shifted from one dominated by agriculture to one dominated by the service sector. The service sector has contributed to increased exports, and Sri Lanka's economic development has been driven by its overall export performance, which includes both products and services. Sri Lanka's export-driven growth has been stimulated by economic growth, innovation, technological advancement, and advancements in the trade sector correlated with FDI (Roy & Mandal, 2012). FDI is regarded as the primary generator of export growth and economic expansion. FDI inflows, primarily from multinational corporations, increase the recipient country's production and export capacity. In developing countries such as Sri Lanka, where domestic businesses are hampered by economic constraints, FDI can be a crucial support. FDI typically entails venture capital, technology transfer, productivity growth, capital transfer, the production of qualified labor, and the alleviation of poverty in the host nation (Chaudhury et al., 2020). Numerous empirical studies have demonstrated that FDI has a direct positive impact on economic development in recipient nations.

FDI contributes to capital accumulation, total factor productivity, resource utilization, technology diffusion, and export expansion. The Organisation for Economic Cooperation and Development (OECD) emphasizes the positive effects of FDI on poverty reduction, employment opportunities, and economic growth in developing economies (Jahfer & Inoue, 2014). This favorable environment depends on elements such as low corruption, infrastructure development, technological progress, and political stability. Sri Lanka has instituted attractive strategies to attract FDI from abroad. Nonetheless, FDI has fluctuated over the past few decades, in part due to the cancellation of Generalized System of Preferences (GSP) quotas by importing nations such as the European Union and the United States, where Sri Lanka was designated as an exporter.

Moreover, Sri Lanka confronted terrorism-related obstacles, which impeded the implementation of FDI and export-led growth. Despite these obstacles, FDI remains a key indicator of economic growth in Sri Lanka (Sultanuzzaman et al., 2018). Even though the numbers on FDI, exports, and economic growth in Sri Lanka change all the time, there are plenty of chances for foreign investors to look for business opportunities and help export-led growth. In Sri Lanka, buyers need to think about how long it will take to make a profit. Indochina, Vietnam, and Bangladesh are other countries that have been able to attract FDI and grow their exports quickly. Bangladesh is now one of the fastest-growing economies and a major producer of readymade garments (RMGs) (Chaudhury et al., 2020).

10.3 Philippines

FDI has been a big part of the economic growth of the Philippines. The country's economy has gone up and down, and FDI has been seen as a possible way to boost output, economic growth, and progress. At the start of the 1980s, the Philippines had a lot of economic problems, which made the average GDP growth slow down. To solve these problems, the government came up with a plan to open the economy, with a focus on trade and business. According to Damooei and Tavakoli (2006), the privatization of government-owned companies and the creation of free trade agreements (FTAs) with several other governments were important moves made to draw FDI. Throughout the 1990s, the government kept trying to open the economy by putting in place sector-wide changes, especially in the banking, transportation, and communications sectors.

The private sector was very important to keeping the economy growing, as it made up more than 90% of GDP and jobs (Agbola, 2014). Infrastructure projects, like making power and building trains, were started by private organizations. The government also fixed problems that made it hard for the private sector to spend, such as a lack of infrastructure, a weak banking sector, and the need for better contract enforcement. Even though the world economy was hard to predict at the start of the 21st century, the Philippine economy was strong, thanks in part to rising private spending and money sent home by Filipinos who worked abroad. Recovery in the services and manufacturing sectors also contributed to economic expansion. In contrast to other Association of Southeast Asian Nations (ASEAN) countries' economies, however, domestic investment remained modest.

The government launched campaigns to increase tax revenue and improve public expenditure management in response to rising budget deficits. Strategies for prudent monetary management helped reduce inflation rates and achieve fiscal consolidation (Roy & Mandal, 2012). Trade has been an integral part of the Philippine economy, and the nation is highly reliant on exports. The United States, Japan, and other nations have been significant sources of foreign investment and trading partners (Moudatsou & Kyrkilis, 2011). The Philippines weathered the 2008-2009 global financial crisis thanks to its limited exposure to international securities and robust domestic consumption.

Going forward, the challenge for policymakers in the Philippines will be to sustain annual GDP growth above the government's target range of 5–6% to provide productive employment for the expanding population (Agbola, 2014). Sustaining economic growth and development will require continued efforts to attract FDI, improve infrastructure, strengthen the business climate, and resolve economic challenges.

10.4 Vietnam

The rapid development of Vietnam's economy can be attributed in large part to FDI. The beginning of Vietnam's economic transition may be traced back to 1986, when the Doi Moi reform agenda was first implemented. FDI inflows have expanded dramatically since the liberalization of FDI legislation in 1987, from $0.32 billion in 1988 to around $4.0 billion in 2005 (Anwar & Nguyen, 2013). There are many ways in which FDI has helped the Vietnamese economy expand. First, FDI widens access to finance, which in turn encourages investment and drives economic expansion. Second, FDI can help spread new technologies, which in turn can boost productivity and the creation of new jobs (Quoc & Thi, 2018). Increases in both the supply and demand for skilled workers are fostered by this sharing of technological know-how. FDI's impact in Vietnam has been notable. Initially, FDI was mostly responsible for the expansion of industrial output, while it had a comparatively small effect on the expansion of the labor force.

However, FDI has been more important in recent years, not only as a source of investment money but also as a driver of export expansion (Bon, 2019). The manufacturing sector's contribution to GDP has continuously surpassed the agriculture sectors since 2001. The presence of foreign companies in Vietnam has also benefited the government's tax revenue and the growth of the private sector. FDI has provided much-needed capital, diversified the economy, and increased competition (Anwar & Nguyen, 2011). However, it is important to note that FDI has been concentrated regions, namely the Red River Delta and the Southeast. With limited success, efforts have been made to attain a more even distribution of FDI across all regions.

The 1997-1998 Asian financial crisis had a significant impact on Vietnam's FDI inflows. FDI activity remained subdued until 2001, despite advancements in FDI-related laws and investor confidence. From 2001 to 2003, changes to foreign investment laws, the signing of an FTA with the United States, and other government policies led to an increase in FDI. Vietnam's accession to the World Trade Organisation (WTO) in 2006 increased its appeal to foreign investors, resulting in a sharp increase in FDI. FDI has contributed significantly to Vietnam's economic growth by attracting capital, technology, and stimulating export-oriented industries. Vietnam's success in attracting FDI and integrating into the global economy has been aided by the government's efforts to improve the investment climate and advance economic reforms.

The 1997-2000 Asian financial crisis led to a decline in FDI as investor confidence declined. During this period, FDI fell annually. Vietnam's accession to the WTO in 2006 created new opportunities for foreign investors. From 2007 to 2010, Vietnam experienced an unprecedented FDI growth, attracting a total of $123 billion, surpassing the period of success from 2001 to 2005 (Anwar & Nguyen, 2013). In 2008, registered capital attained an all-time high of $64 billion during this period of accelerated FDI growth. Vietnam was able to maintain relatively consistent development and continue to attract significant FDI inflows despite the 2008–2009 global recession.

However, beginning in 2011, foreign investment in Vietnam declined as the market became over bought due to excessive capital inflows. In 2014–2015, the situation began to stabilize (Anwar & Nguyen, 2013). The influx of FDI has been closely linked to Vietnam's economic growth. Following the implementation of economic reforms in 1986, the country progressively opened its markets and implemented a market-oriented strategy. Vietnam experienced substantial economic development from the early 1990s to 1997, with the growth rate increasing from 6% in 1991 to a zenith of 10% in 1997. This time frame coincided with substantial FDI inflows. The 1998–1999 Asian financial crisis had a negative impact on Vietnam's economy, resulting in a decline in growth to 4% in 1999.

However, the nation regained its footing in 2000 and experienced a second development cycle from 2000 to 2007. In 2007, the GDP growth rate reached 8%, representing a period of accelerated expansion. The effective accession of Vietnam to the WTO in 2007 strengthened the country's position as an emergent open economy (Bon, 2019). There are suggestions that Vietnam's economic development strategy should be revised as the nation continues to pursue sustained growth. Current classification of Vietnam as a middle-income country necessitates ongoing efforts to attract FDI and promote economic growth. The government's emphasis on enhancing the investment climate, instituting structural reforms, and fostering innovation can assist Vietnam in maintaining its growth trajectory and consolidating its position in the global economy (Bon, 2019).

10.5 India

The relationship between FDI and economic growth in India has been a topic of discussion and research in the field of development economics. Even though endogenous growth theory predicts a favorable association between FDI and economic growth, actual evidence has been mixed. The impact of FDI on economic growth varies per country due to differences in institutional, policy, and regulatory settings (Verma, 2020).

Economists have recently recognized the importance of the sectoral makeup of FDI in explaining varied findings. According to research, the sectoral distribution of FDI has a significant impact on its effect on economic growth. Different industries have different investment capacities, technological underpinnings, and regulatory frameworks. Not all sectors are equally capable of absorbing foreign money and technology or of establishing links with the rest of the economy (Jayachandran & Seilan, 2010). Human capital, technological base, and FDI dynamics all interact to influence the economic growth connection (Samantha & Haiyun, 2017).

FDI has a good effect on economic growth in developing countries when it is accompanied with human capital. However, FDI with a technology gap might have a large detrimental impact. The sectoral contribution to India's economy is substantial. Only 17.32% of the country's gross value added (GVA) is produced by the primary sector, which includes agriculture and related activities. The secondary sector, which represents manufacturing, accounts for 29.02% of total

GVA, while the service sector accounts for 53.66 % (Kumari & Sharma, 2018). In India, the potential for producing spillover effects and intra-and-inter sectoral linkages varies between sectors. The service sector has the most potential for linkages, followed by the manufacturing and primary sectors. Due to its weak infrastructure, subpar technology basis, and limited output commercialization, the primary sector has the lowest linkage and spill over potential. Due to natural dependencies, its growth is likewise highly unstable (Choi & Baek, 2017).

In contrast, FDI in the manufacturing and service sectors is more likely to have a positive impact on their respective industries. There are clearer ties and opportunities for transfer between manufacturing and services. Although manufactured products can be exported, services require proximity between producers and consumers and are therefore only limitedly tradable. However, India's service sector has significant potential to generate positive effects from FDI. Given the high cross-sectoral versatility, diverse contributions to growth, and heterogeneity of individual characteristics, it is necessary to conduct a sector-specific analysis when examining the FDI-growth relationship in India. The Indian economy has more pronounced sectoral differences in terms of economic contribution, linkages, spill over potential, and external dependence than many other emergent economies (Jayachandran & Seilan, 2010).

Thus, it is necessary to conduct a sector-specific analysis of the FDI-growth relationship in India to comprehend how FDI inflows affect the development of specific industries as opposed to the economy. While previous research has examined the relationship between FDI and economic growth in India, sector-specific analyses have been scarce. Considering the distinct characteristics and impact-generating potential of each sector, such analysis is valuable. Using a production function analysis, Pradhan, 2002 determined that FDI did not significantly contribute to India's economic development. This conclusion was supported by Agrawal & Khan, 2011, who suggested that FDI had a limited relationship with economic development in the country. Chand et al. (2017) used a panel cointegration method and discovered that FDI inflows contributed to India's economic growth. Dash & Parida, 2013 utilized a vector error-correction model and reported a positive impact of FDI on economic growth after accounting for international trade. The key question investigated in these reports was whether FDI inflows into India influenced GDP growth and/or GDP per capita.

Despite this, it is desirable to examine a growth variable that integrates the spillover effects caused by FDI (Pradhan, 2002) because of the relevance of technological spillovers through FDI in enhancing productivity and overall development in developing nations. The key benefits of FDI for the economic development of the host country have been shown to be the transmission of ideas, technological knowledge, organizational expertise, and business knowledge (Choi & Baek, 2017). A growth variable that accounts for these spillover effects is necessary for accurate estimation of the FDI-growth nexus in India. But this point was largely overlooked in the earliest studies of the topic.

10.6 Conclusion and Recommendations

The creation of a favorable business environment that can attract FDI is something that developing countries need to consider seriously. To accomplish this goal, laws should be enacted that make it simple to start a firm, create a solid regulatory environment, give incentives for investors, and decrease other hurdles that discourage investors from participating.

Because it facilitates the exchange of both information and technology, the formation of joint ventures and partnerships between local and international businesses ought to be encouraged by means of the adoption of rules and regulations that are favorable to such endeavors. Additionally, the government can invest in educational and training programs to enhance the attitudes and capabilities of the local workforce.

Infrastructure facilities such as energy, transportation, telecommunication, and logistics need to be expanded to attract foreign investors. This is because having sufficient infrastructure is required to obtain the benefits of FDI and economic growth.

Developing countries' governments should make investments in educational and vocational training programs to enhance the capabilities of the labor force, and FDI should be utilized as a tool to generate employment opportunities. In addition, business owners should be financially supported when they take on additional hiring responsibilities to encourage the creation of additional employment possibilities.

For developing countries to reap the benefits of FDI, it is imperative that the macroeconomic environment is stable. Inflation rates need to be effectively handled, and a robust monetary policy must also be implemented, to accomplish this mission successfully.

Priority should be given by developing countries to innovations, research, and development to enhance their technological capabilities. Government possesses the power to incentivize and promote this endeavor inside academic institutions, research organizations, and other businesses and organizations in the private sector.

The development of new policies is recommended to accomplish the goal of ensuring that the advantages of FDI are distributed fairly. As a result, not only will there be less inequality in terms of wealth, but there will also be less disparity in terms of the distribution of resources across different fields, such as education and healthcare, for example.

References

Agbola, F. W. (2014). Modelling the impact of foreign direct investment and human capital on economic growth: Empirical evidence from the Philippines. *Journal of the Asia Pacific Economy*, *19*(2), 272–289.

Agrawal, G., & Khan, M. A. (2011). Impact of FDI on GDP: A comparative study of China and India. *International Journal of Business and Management*, *6*(10), 71.

Amadi, C. (2019). *FDI and economic growth in Nigeria: An analysis of the role of financial development on linkages* Doctoral dissertation. Manchester Metropolitan University.

Antony, J. (2009). Capital/labor substitution, capital deepening, and FDI. *Journal of Macroeconomics*, *31*(4), 699–707.

Antras, P., Desai, M. A., & Foley, C. F. (2009). Multinational firms, FDI flows, and imperfect capital markets. *The Quarterly Journal of Economics*, *124*(3), 1171–1219.

Anwar, S., & Nguyen, L. (2011). Financial development and economic growth in Vietnam. *Journal of Economics and Finance*, *35*(3), 348–360.

Anwar, S., & Nguyen, L. P. (2013). Foreign direct investment and economic growth in Vietnam. *In Whither South East Asian management*? (pp. 177–196). Routledge.

Balamurali, N., & Bogahawatte, C. (2004). Foreign direct investment and economic growth in Sri Lanka. *Sri Lankan Journal of Agricultural Economics*, 38–50.

Bon, N. (2019). The role of institutional quality in the relationship between FDI and economic growth in Vietnam: Empirical evidence from provincial data. *The Singapore Economic Review*.

Chand, K., Tiwari, R., & Phuyal, M. (2017). Economic growth and unemployment rate: An empirical study of the Indian economy. *Journal of Indian Economy*, 130–137.

Chaudhury, S., Nanda, N., & Tyagi, B. (2020). Impact of FDI on economic growth in south Asia: Does the nature of FDI matters? *Review of Market Integration*, *12* (1–2), 51–69.

Choi, Y. J., & Baek, J. (2017). Does FDI really matter to economic growth in India? *Economies*, *5*(2), 20.

Damooei, J., & Tavakoli, A. (2006). The effects of foreign direct investment and imports on economic growth: A comparative analysis of Thailand and the Philippines (1970-1998). *The Journal of Developing Areas*, *39*(2), 79–100.

Danmola, R. A. (2013). The impact of exchange rate volatility on the macro-economic variables in Nigeria. *European Scientific Journal*, *9*(7).

Dash, R. K., & Parida, P. C. (2013). FDI, services trade and economic growth in India: Empirical evidence on causal links. *Empirical Economics*, *45*(1), 217–238.

Har, W. M., Teo, K. L., & Yee, K. M. (2008). FDI and economic growth relationship: An empirical study on Malaysia. *International Business Research*, *1*(2), 11–18.

Jahfer, A., & Inoue, T. (2014). Financial development, foreign direct investment and economic growth in Sri Lanka. *International Journal of Economic Policy in Emerging Economies*, *7*(1), 77–93.

Jayachandran, G., & Seilan, A. (2010). A causal relationship between trade, foreign direct investment, and economic growth for India. *International Research Journal of Finance and Economics*, *42*(2010), 74–88.

Kumari, A., & Sharma, A. K. (2018). Causal relationships among electricity consumption, foreign direct investment, and economic growth in India. *The Electricity Journal*, *31*(7), 33–38.

Moudatsou, A., & Kyrkilis, D. (2011). FDI and economic growth: Causality for the EU and ASEAN. *Journal of Economic Integration*, 554–577.

Pradhan, J. P. (2002). FDI spillovers and local productivity growth: Evidence from Indian pharmaceutical industry. *Artha Vijnana*, *44*(3–4), 317–332.

Quoc, C. H., & Thi, C. D. (2018). Analysis of foreign direct investment and economic growth in Vietnam. *International Journal of Business, Economics and Law*, *15*(5), 19–27.

Ranasinghe, R., & Sugandhika, M. G. P. (2018). The contribution of tourism income for the economic growth of Sri Lanka. *Journal of Management and Tourism Research*, *1*, 67–84.

Roy, S., & Mandal, K. K. (2012). Foreign direct investment and economic growth: An analysis for selected Asian countries. *Journal of Business Studies Quarterly*, *4* (1), 15.

Samantha, N., & Haiyun, L. (2017). The impact of FDI on the economic growth of Sri Lanka: An ARDL approach to cointegration. *International Journal of Innovation and Economic Development*, 70–82.

Sultanuzzaman, M. R., Fan, H., Akash, M., Wang, B., & Shakij, U. S. M. (2018). The role of FDI inflows and export on economic growth in Sri Lanka: An ARDL approach. *Cogent Economics & Finance*, *6*(1), 1518116.

Van Bon, N. (2019). The role of institutional quality in the relationship between FDI and economic growth in vietnam: Empirical evidence from provincial data. *The Singapore Economic Review*, *64*(3), 601–623.

Vasa, L., & Angeloska, A. (2020). Foreign direct investment in the Republic of Serbia: Correlation between foreign direct investments and the selected economic variables. *Journal of International Studies* (2071-8330), *13*(1).

Verma, D. (2020). Impact of FDI on GDP per capita, trade and inflation: Evidence from four emerging economies. *International Journal for Research in Applied Science and Engineering Technology*, *8*(11), 956–961.

Chapter 11

Foreign Direct Investment: Theoretical Frameworks

Abstract

Foreign direct investment (FDI) is an important phenomenon for students, academics, researchers, practitioners, policymakers, and indeed all social and economic stakeholders. It is therefore pertinent to understand its theoretical foundations and underpinnings for a compressive appreciation of its practical aspects. This chapter has set out to review and bring to fore a very broad range of theories within FDI literature. Within this chapter, readers will read and learn about FDI theories such as production life cycle theory, caves theory, endogenous theory, neo-classical theory, eclectic paradigm theory, internalization theory, new growth theory, mercantilist models trade theory, absolute advantage trade theory, institutional theory, resources-based theory, monopolistic advantageous theory, market implication theory, capital market theory, and institutional FDI fitness theory.

Keywords: FDI; theories; concepts; frameworks; underpinnings

11.1 Introduction

11.2 Concept of Foreign Direct Investment

Foreign direct investment (FDI) is a cross-border initiative undertaken by a person or organization in one nation to pursue economic interests in another, such as establishing operations or acquiring business resources in another country (Eze et al., 2019). Idoko and Taiga (2018) state that it includes intra-organization credits, building new offices, reinvesting gains from overseas operations, and mergers and acquisitions. FDI is the process by which individuals in one nation have influence over the founding, expansion, and day-to-day

Foreign Direct Investment, 163–178

Published under exclusive licence by Emerald Publishing Limited
doi:10.1108/978-1-83662-900-920261011

operations of a business in another nation. It is a company's interest in securing a significant controlling position in an outside firm (more than 10% offer) or establishing an auxiliary in a foreign country (Amadi, 2019).

Human resources, products and businesses, innovation, ideas, and the transfer of administrative norms from one country to another – especially developing countries – are all included in FDI. The most important source of external asset streams for developing countries, according to Mounde (2017), is FDI, which plays a big role in these countries' capital structures. According to Osabohien et al. (2020), FDI can be directed toward the country that provides the capital as an auxiliary of a remote firm, or it can be facilitated by methods for setting up an organization in which a firm in the contributing organization holds value, or by the nationals of the contributing nation producing fixed resources in the other country. In essence, FDI occurs when a foreign corporation or firm controls certain offices or derives money from a local firm over which it effectively exercises control. In essence, FDI occurs when a foreign corporation or firm controls certain offices or derives money from a local firm over which it effectively exercises control.

FDI has been more significant over the past 20 years due to its ability to create chances for economic expansion (Seyoum, 2024). FDI delivers critical assets to developing countries, including finance, innovation, administrative skills, entrepreneurial ability, brand, and access to commercial sectors. Güngör and Ringim (2017) define FDI as long-term speculation that reflects the objective of an enduring premium and control by a resident substance of one economy (the immediate speculator) in a venture in another economy. FDI is essential to a nation's economic growth. It brings in new financial, technological, and intellectual resources that might boost production and create jobs. FDI facilitates the transfer of information, skills, and technology from developed to developing nations, hence aiding in closing the technological divide and fostering economic expansion (Emako et al., 2022). According to Guseva and Mechik (2020), FDI helps the host country expand its market, diversify its risks, acquire new expertise, and improve its balance of payments.

Studies, however, have identified several factors that might prevent FDI, including political uncertainty, the state of the economy, market size, laws, incentives, infrastructure, and employment opportunities (Emako et al., 2022; Sahu, 2021). Seyoum (2024) found that governments may influence FDI by enacting advantageous regulations and legislation. However, overuse of natural resources, harm to the environment, and the eviction of natives are some potential drawbacks of FDI (Sarkodie & Strezov, 2019).

11.3 Theoretical Frameworks of Foreign Direct Investments

11.3.1 Production Life Cycle Theory

"The decision to locate manufacturing is not made by standard factor-cost or labor-cost analysis, but by a more intricate process," Vernon (1966). The product cycle model was developed in the 1960s by Vernon to help us understand

market-driven industrial production by businesses with a specific ownership or nationality (Dunning & Lundan, 2008). The product cycle theory was the first to provide a realistic understanding of the forces influencing international commerce and how they connect (Dunning, 1996). It included numerous distinct market trigger points, technological gaps, and presumptions about information-based and communication expenditures, the majority of which have since proven useful in foreign investment and trade analysis (Dunning, 1996). Vernon divides a product's life cycle into three parts. These steps are critical because they have various effects on a product's global positioning.

The product development process is the first stage. To put it another way, the nature of the firm's product is not standardized (Kogut, 1983).

The maturing of the product is the second stage. This minimizes the need for the product to be close to its intended market, which saves money. These variables influence the firm's locational decision, especially when the product's demand is predicted to grow into other regions, and the corporation must consider whether it is viable to establish production there. This could also mean that the international firm exports to the host country.

Standardizing the product is the third stage. It is an elongation of the mature product stage, in which the product's standardization has gotten to its "apex" and a definitive structure for the product has been established (Kogut, 1983).

The theory suggests a firm should assess its current and potential production curve positions. If a company cannot tell where it is on its production curve, it may try past successes to find out. It suggests that firms will invest more in foreign markets than in domestic markets. It argues that companies can adapt and compete better with new technology (Ebrahimi & Koh, 2021). The production life cycle theory explains and predicts a firms' long-term FDI behavior. This theory assumes that firms will invest to gain access to markets and technologies at certain stages of an industry's development. It has three stages: economic environment, resource scarcity, and product demand. The economic environment includes factors like access to technology, labor costs, and regulations (what products customers want).

11.3.2 Caves Theory

Caves theory argues that government barriers are needed to limit market shares and let other firms enter. Caves suggests that countries should only allow FDI when it is profitable for them, not just because they like foreign companies (Caves, 1996). This theory says companies do not always copy competitors' innovations and new products. Instead, they cut costs or increase production quotas for lower-skilled workers to boost profits. According to this theory, FDI is aimed at gaining a market advantage in a trade partner, not just short-term gains. This notion is also supported by Borensztein et al. (1998). The caves theory says that it is difficult, if not impossible, to move all assets abroad because the government must control capital flows. For FDI to work effectively, it requires economic freedom and currency control.

11.3.3 Endogenous Theory

In the 1980s, endogenous growth theory arose as an alternative to neoclassical growth theory. It challenged how wealth disparities between industrialized and developing countries could exist if physical capital such as infrastructure yields diminishing returns. The endogenous growth theory is a macroeconomic theory that focuses on a country's economic growth as a function of its enterprises' investment decisions (Romer, 1994). It claims that economic growth is the outcome of a build-up of technological knowledge, or an "enabling environment," which then leads to additional growth (Borensztein et al., 1998).

The endogenous theory states that domestic firms or industries decide whether to invest in foreign industries. It assumes foreign operations are undertaken by existing domestic firms (e.g., a subsidiary) to avoid external costs and efficiency losses. Endogenous theory is a neoclassical approach because it states that value for money is not influenced by economic factors like cost effectiveness or market instability in foreign markets. It also ignores local conditions like government policies (Borensztein et al., 1998).

The endogenous theory says there are only two ways to explain FDI: either it is a response to host country demand, or it is a way for a firm to overcome domestic obstacles. If FDI is explained as national self-interest, it becomes another example of economics being a political argument. FDI is exogenous because it has no direct relationship between two countries or within one, but it affects a country's economy.

Endogenous growth model emphasizes on the important role of human capital in economic progress, as well as externalities and science and technology (Romer, 1994; Yao & Wei, 2007). According to the model, economic growth is driven mostly by internal rather than external influences. The model asserts that increased productivity is strongly linked to more human resource expenditure and increased innovation via organizations and governments (Mahembe & Odhiambo, 2014). Borensztein et al. (1998) stated that endogenous growth model is Romer's paradigm, whereby technical development is defined as the production of new types of commodities. They identified two groups of enterprises in the economy's intermediate segment, one being generating commodities resulting from higher level of technological innovation (extension effect) and the other, to prove that the economy's development rate is partly determined by the relative weight of each type (external effect). As stated by Nair-Reichert and Weinhold (2001), the theory considers long-run development because of technical development, and seeks to provide a foundation within which FDI may constantly boost the economic growth rate of the receiving nation through spillover effects, knowledge transfer, and diffusion.

Berthélemy and Demurger (2000) asserted that FDI is frequently emphasized as a source of technology dissemination. If multinational investors introduce more sophisticated technology into the receiving nation, the difference between "low-tech" and "high-tech" enterprises might be viewed as in respect of domestic against foreign enterprises. To investigate how FDI affects economic growth, they postulated that the commodities with greater technological degree of innovation are produced and distributed by foreign-owned enterprises based in the local market, whereas commodities with a lower technology level are produced and distributed by locally owned enterprises. FDI has the potential to be a source of long-term growth and development, provided its presumed capabilities to: aid in the creation of human capital and growth,; help the receiving nation in integrating into international economic trade, create technological spillovers, support the formation of highly competitive market setting, and strengthen business growth and development (Mahembe & Odhiambo, 2014).

11.3.4 Neoclassical Growth Theory

The neoclassical growth model was introduced by Solow (1956); the theory is also known as the Solow–Swan growth theory. The model holds that economic growth of a nation is produced by the accumulation of external elements of production including labor and capital stock. This approach has been demonstrated that capital accumulation contributes positively to economic growth in relation to capital's contribution to national production. Consequently, economic growth is dependent on labor market expansion and technology advancement. As per the model, FDI enhances the receiving nation's capital stock, which has an impact on economic growth (Mahembe & Odhiambo, 2014). According to the theory, low economies will expand quicker than affluent economies. If all economies are supposed to be in a similar steady state, the differences between nations is their beginning stock of capital, with impoverished economies growing quicker since they are farther away from their state and the process is referred to as absolute convergence (Cole & Neumayer, 2003).

The neoclassical growth theory does not account for long-term growth and development, rather, it explains the potential of avoiding production per capita stagnation due to technological development caused by positive external externalities. According to Mahembe and Odhiambo (2014), neoclassical growth theory has demonstrated that FDI may have a direct influence on economic growth via capital accumulation and the incorporation of foreign technology and new inputs into the receiving nation's labor and capital. Consequently, based on the theory, FDI stimulates a nation's economy by boosting the volume and effectiveness of investment.

In summary, the Solow–Swan growth theory aims to explain the long-run economic growth by examining wealth accumulation, human capital or population increase, and productivity advances, sometimes known as technical advancement (Solow, 1956). Based on this theory, FDI's possible positive impact on economic growth is limited to the short to medium term. Due to the law of diminishing returns on capital investment, the beneficiary economy may behave similarly to the rate of growth assuming as if FDI had never occurred, providing no lasting influence on the economic growth of a country (De Mello & Fukasaku, 2000). This demonstrates that the potential benefits of FDI are limited to the short run. According to Mankiw (2003), when using the Solow growth model, private corporations invest in both conventional capital such as heavy machinery and industrial facilities and emerging capital such as processors and robotics. The government, on the contrary, spends on infrastructure such as railroads, roads, and bridges. It also contends that policymakers seeking to encourage growth must address the requirements of the economy and aims to identify the type of capital that produces the highest marginal goods.

11.3.5 Eclectic Paradigm Theory

The OLI framework (ownership, location, and internalization), also known as Dunning's eclectic paradigm theory, offers a thorough framework for comprehending the causes of FDI. This theory, which was developed by John Dunning, emphasizes how internalization of operations within multinational enterprises interacts with firm specific advantages, location-specific advantages, and both (Sharmiladevi, 2017).

According to Dunnig's eclectic paradigm hypothesis, firms engage in FDI when they have ownership-specific advantages that can help them succeed in global markets (Dunning, 2015). The term "ownership-specific advantages" refers to the distinctive resources, skills, or assets that businesses have, such as superior technology, a strong brand name, or managerial know-how. To take these advantages and gain a competitive advantage in the international market, firms with significant ownership benefits are more likely to engage in FDI (Dunning, 2015). An organization will directly invest in a different country if and only if these three conditions were met. These conditions include: the advantages of ownership, location, and internalization (OLI).

First, the organization must have an ownership-specific asset that gives it a competitive advantage over other companies and is unique to the organization. The term "ownership advantages" refers to firm-specific characteristics that are sometimes referred to as "competitive" or "monopolistic" advantages. These advantages must be adequate to cover the costs of establishing and running a foreign value-adding operation in addition to the costs faced by domestic producers. These attributes include things like a strong brand, research and development, market access, patents, and advanced technology, which the host nation might lack. When foreign companies use such qualities to take advantage of opportunities in the host country, they use adverse selection in an unfavorable market environment to support their activities. Thus, competition with multinationals becomes challenging due to knowledge asymmetry and the lack of characteristics that host country enterprises may offer. This might lead to foreign investors displacing domestic investments because they have ownership advantages over domestic companies (Miberg, 1996).

Second, there must be a benefit to establishing production in a specific foreign country rather than relying on exports (Blomstrom, 2000). These include features unique to the host nation that may persuade multinationals to base an economic operation there. They include economic elements like affordable communication and transportation costs, government subsidies, the availability of relatively inexpensive production inputs, and regulatory elements like tariff barriers, tax structures, and market access, among others (Buckley & Casson, 1976). Location-specific advantages are just as important to FDI decisions as ownership advantages. The qualities and features of a specific nation or area that make it a desirable location for investment are included in location-specific advantages. Businesses are looking to set up shop in nations that provide hospitable conditions and can increase their competitiveness in the global market.

Third, it must acknowledge these assets instead of outsourcing or licensing them. Internalization-specific benefits result in the production process becoming internal to the firm. Internalization is also motivated by the desire to avoid transaction costs, protect the market, and finance, avoid tariffs, and capture economies of scale from production (Dunning & Lundan, 2008). Despite criticism for just stating the prerequisites for FDI without elucidating its phenomena, Yarbrough and Yarbrough (2002) note that this theory has significantly influenced the theory of international production. The concept of internalization – integrating and coordinating of operations within multinational corporations (MNCs) – is emphasized. Companies engage in FDI to internalize specific activities that would be more advantageous to carry out within their own organizational structure than to rely on transactions on the open market (Dunning, 2015). By internalizing, businesses can safeguard their confidential information, keep control of important assets, and cut down on the costs of market transactions.

In summary, the eclectic theory, also known as the OLI framework, integrates various factors that influence FDI decisions. According to this theory, firms invest in foreign countries when they possess ownership advantages (e.g., proprietary technology, brand reputation), the location offers specific advantages (e.g., access to resources, market size), and internalization benefits outweigh the costs of transacting in the external market. Additionally, firms may choose to internalize certain activities, such as project development and marketing, to capture value and mitigate transaction costs. Thus, the OLI framework provides a comprehensive perspective on the factors driving FDI.

This theory provides a thorough framework for comprehending the causes of FDI. Policymakers and businesses can assess the variables that affect FDI decisions and make well-informed decisions regarding international investments by taking ownership-specific advantages, location-specific advantages, and the internalization of activities into consideration.

11.3.6 Internalization Theory

The internalization theory was founded by Coase in 1937, and it is believed that transaction costs on foreign activities moderate the firm to the position where it becomes more profitable to internalize the market rather than to enter a foreign market (Buckley & Casson, 2020). Buckley and Casson expanded the argument in 1976, warning that MNE growth via FDI can be realizable if the enterprise has a competitive edge in the competition with other enterprises (Benito et al., 2019). This implies horizontal interactions by working out upward coordination through the act of the company incorporating new activities and operations instead of middle-level enterprises doing them.

The initial theory identified two significant determinants of FDI: removing competition and increasing positive attention to be paid to some duopolistic firms in a particular activity (Buckley et al., 2017). Buckley and Casson (1976) advocate that value-based companies intentionally use regulations to gain private benefits, such as wrongfully monopolizing and hurting public interests. As demonstrated in the work of Banalieva and Dhanaraj (2019), internalization proposes to explain why firms go in the way of FDI instead of relying on contracts with subcontractors and foreign companies. The concept also elaborates on the driving forces behind the investment of value-driven companies from different monetary tactics used by various governments.

The internalization theory, also known as the eclectic paradigm, developed by John Dunning, a leading economist during the 1970s, describes factors behind the firms' decision to venture abroad and the approaches they use for undertaking FDI. The theory consists of three components: the owning advantages of the trademark, location-specific advantages of the customer market, and the internalization advantages obtained as the activities are conducted inside the firm. The utilization of internalization theory is therefore vital in understanding how firms internalize specific advantages via FDI, which in turn gives insight into their strategic decisions and domestic investment impact.

11.3.7 New Growth Theory

The new growth theory states that the economy can always improve and grow, unlike the old theory of decreasing returns to learning and innovation. It notes that the process is self-procreation, stemming from fiscal action and ideal investment in human capital (Cvetanović et al., 2019). This results in higher efficiency and a shift of focus from routine tasks to creative endeavors. McCann and Van Oort (2019) indicate that the transfer of cutting-edge innovation strengthens work-life preparation skills, skill learning, option presentation drills, and decision-making hierarchies that receive or implement such technologies. FDI can be witnessed in that it complements efficiency in the recipient economy and stimulates households to target speculation and innovation. It is expected to reduce the gap between the huge catchment areas and families with a small amount of savings. Palley (2017) noted that FDI should be included in the country's monetary process via diversifying funds and lowering additional housing demand. Eventually, through such a linkage, the potential will be created for additional firm businesses and investment-making activity.

11.3.8 Mercantilist Models Trade Theory

Mercantilism is the economic theory whereby a country wants to attain self-sufficiency through a surplus trade balance (Lind & Press, 2018). The essence of mercantilist policies is grounded in retaining value and economic expansion and maintaining an advantageous trade balance with foreign countries. As

Shanlin (2019) put it, mercantilism thought trade was like a zero-sum-game in which the other's trade deficit could offset a country's trade surplus. Globalism has aimed to focus on the accumulation of national resources and utilization of those assets with one-sided terms of trade. Chijioke et al. (2021) contended that mercantilism is the principal way in which nations conduct inter-country exchange, considering wealth and political sway in export over import. The way to wealth is to get masters in metal commodities like gold, and this can be done by controlling exports, which must be more than imports. It supports a monetary system that the government controls and imposes certain restrictions like royalties, which lay stress on the exchange policy (Cvetanović et al., 2019). Nevertheless, it does not invite rebellion against governance to keep society in order and is also supported by financial principles (McCann & Van Oort, 2019). According to the mercantilist's view, the wealth of a nation is a zero-sum game, which means what is gained by one trading partner could be the loss to another, and those partners may include aliens.

The mercantilist period was originally based in the 16th to 18th centuries. Like precious metals, the domestic industry was encouraged by trade barriers and tariffs. It considered exports to be a national treasure and used them to support the economy while largely banning imports. The historical perspective of mercantilism could give a picture of how the traditional views harbor a difference from the present economic practices and give a perfect understanding of the drivers of FDI and domestic investments.

11.3.9 Absolute Advantage Trade Theory

The conceptualized cost advantage theory by Adam Smith in his book The Wealth of Nations in 1776 was believed to be the best solution for countries (Burstein & Vogel, 2017). As Osagie and Ukwuoma (2022) highlight, they argued that a nation can enjoy the benefit of comparative advantage in production by concentrating its efforts on producing goods it is relatively more productive in and importing from other nations that it is relatively less capable of producing. In the alternative to this view, absolute advantage is considered a single person, business, or country's ability to turn out more of the special good or service with the same amount of input at a lower cost. This specialization of production from the entire globe will raise world output, which the exchange countries will share. This would be playing a role of noncompetition that would enable all countries to achieve simultaneous gain of benefits.

The absolute advantage theory gives a deeper understanding of how FDI affects local investment. Absolute advantage is the basis for global product specialization, with FDI being capable of influencing it. Technological transfer, managerial skills, and capital inflows that can improve productivity could be achieved because of this. The granting of resources can directly contribute to the formation of perhaps a country's comparative advantage in one industry and makes it possible to achieve high rates of domestic production.

11.3.10 Institutional Theory

Institutional theory suggests that the institutional environment of a country significantly influences FDI decisions. Institutions encompass formal rules (e.g., laws, regulations) and informal norms (e.g., cultural practices, social conventions). Institutional factors such as political stability, legal framework, property rights protection, and regulatory transparency are crucial determinants of the business environment for FDI. Investors are more likely to commit capital to countries with stable political systems and transparent legal frameworks that protect property rights and ensure contract enforceability. Conversely, political instability, corruption, and regulatory uncertainties can deter FDI inflows (Amadi, 2019).

11.3.11 Resource-Based Theory

According to the resource-based theory, firms invest in countries that offer valuable, rare, and nonsubstitutable resources. A country's geographic location can increase its appeal as an investment location (for example, if it offers access to both local and international markets). However, essential components including infrastructure, skilled workforce, and enabling government policies are required to fully utilize the benefits of FDI.

11.3.12 The Monopolistic Advantageous Theory

The Linder hypothesis, also known as the monopolistic advantageous theory, provides insight into the drivers of FDI based on market demand and product differentiation. Monopolistic advantage theory, presented by Stefan Linder in 1961, argues that firms participate in FDI to exploit their monopoly advantages in specific markets or industries and to meet the needs of foreign customers (Luo & Bu, 2018). Some of the unique characteristics of multinational companies and their unique advantages, such as trademarks, state-of-the-art technologies, brand names, marketing economies of scale, and managerial capabilities, had begun to be studied. This argues that firms engage in FDI when their products are distinctive, differentiated, and consumers in foreign markets find them more attractive than consumers in home markets. This hypothesis highlights the importance of demand variables for FDI. Businesses make international investments to reach consumers who share income levels with the preferences and tastes and lifestyles of their home markets (Makino et al., 2002).

According to the theory, businesses that have a competitive advantage in terms of brand recognition, product quality, or innovation are more likely to participate in FDI. These businesses try to take advantage of their distinctive advantages by entering foreign markets and gaining market share. Businesses can overcome trade restrictions like tariffs and quotas and gain a competitive advantage in international markets by providing differentiated products (Makino et al., 2002).

A 2005 study by Blonigen and Wang also looked at the connection between FDI and export similarity. According to their research, businesses are more likely to invest in countries with comparable export structures, highlighting the importance of commodity differentiation in FDI decisions (Blonigen & Wang, 2005).

The theory explains how consumer demand and product differentiation influence FDI. Policymakers and companies can decide wisely about market entry strategies and investment opportunities by being aware of the distinct advantages that firms possess and the preferences of foreign consumers.

11.3.13 Market Implication Theory

The market implication theory also known as market power theory offers perceptions into the drivers of FDI, which are based on the desire to take advantage of market flaws and gain a competitive edge. The theory developed by Stephen Hymer in 1960s contends that companies engage in FDI to establish a presence in foreign markets and take advantage of their market power.

According to market implication theory, companies should invest in international markets to solve problems with global markets. These market defects include things like barriers to entry, misinformation, high transaction costs, and lack of perfect competition. Firms using FDI are likely to have significant market power because of things like unique technology, high brand awareness, or economies of scale (Zahra, 2005). Firms hope to control distribution networks, gain access to resources, and use their market dominance to gain a competitive advantage in international markets. Businesses can avoid trade restrictions, lower transaction costs, and increase operational control by investing directly in foreign markets. As a result, they can increase their profitability, expand their market share, and solidify their current position (Zahra, 2005).

Empirical research has validated market implication theory. For example, Caves (1971) analysis of the relationship between FDI and market power found that enterprises with greater market power were more likely to adopt FDI. Similar research was done by Zayed et al. (2021) on financial goals and market influence in MNCs. These findings indicated that MNCs with strong market power are more likely to engage in FDI to benefit from market imperfections and improve their competitiveness.

The theory influences FDI decisions. Policymakers and businesses can analyze market structure, evaluate potential entry barriers, and make strategic decisions regarding international investments by comprehending these dynamics.

11.3.14 Capital Market Theory

The capital asset pricing model (CAPM), also referred to as capital market theory, explains how risk and return interact in the financial markets. This theory, established in the 1960s by William Sharpe, John Lintner, and Jan

Mossin, contends that investors choose their investments based on the trade-off between risk and anticipated return (Perold, 2004).

The expected return of an investment is based on its systematic risk, also known as beta, according to the capital market theory (Sharpe, 1964). Risk that is connected to market-wide factors and cannot be eliminated by diversification is referred to as systemic risk. Diversification can eliminate specific risk, also known as unsystematic risk. According to the theory, what investors are most concerned about is the systematic risk of an investment.

The theory supported by empirical studies (Jylhä et al., 2018) investigated the relationship between beta and predicted stock returns. According to their findings, stocks with higher betas tended to have higher expected returns, consistent with the predictions of capital market theory. Differences in the currencies of the source and host countries led to FDI (Nayak & Choudhury, 2014). More FDI can flow into countries with weaker currencies than those with stronger currencies, and they can gain more from variations in market capitalization rates. Furthermore, since portfolio investors do not consider the foreign components of source country MNCs, MNCs based in hard currency areas can borrow money at lower interest rates than host country firms. The possession of cheap sources of capital by foreign subsidiaries and affiliates provides home country enterprises with the advantage of borrowing (Makoni, 2015).

This capital market theory was supported by data from developed nations like the United Kingdom, the United States, and Canada, but it has since been refuted by later scholars on the grounds that it ignores fundamental concepts in financial risk management. Furthermore, Nayak and Choudhury (2014) pointed out that this theory is unable to explain investment between developed nations with comparable currency strengths.

11.3.15 Institutional FDI Fitness Theory

The theory provides an explanation for the uneven distribution of FDI among the nations. The four main pillars of this theory are the government, education, socio-cultural, and market fitness. Primarily in an African context, the institutional FDI fitness theory has been empirically supported. A country's ability to attract foreign investors depends on its economic openness, level of domestic investment, GDP growth rate, availability of credit, rate of return, and economic policies. This model was evaluated, with a conclusion that more than one risk factor was involved in determining FDI inflows (Amadi, 2019).

11.4 Conclusion

The notion that FDI has a positive correlation with economic growth is positioned within growth theories that accentuates the role of improved technology, efficiency, and productivity in facilitating growth. FDI's potential contribution to growth is dependent mainly and strictly on the circumstances of individual recipient countries. Some basic conditions in a host country are needed to facilitate the spillover effects. The effect FDI has on economic growth is mostly analyzed in the standard growth accounting framework/theory, in which the basic assumption is that capital stock consists of two capital components, which are domestic capital stock and foreign owned capital stock.

References

Amadi, C. (2019). *FDI and economic growth in Nigeria: An analysis of the role of financial development on linkages* Diss. Manchester Metropolitan University.

Banalieva, E. R., & Dhanaraj, C. (2019). Internalization theory for the digital economy. *Journal of International Business Studies, 50*, 1372–1387.

Benito, G. R., Petersen, B., & Welch, L. S. (2019). The global value chain and internalisation theory. *Journal of International Business Studies, 50*, 1414–1423.

Berthélemy, J. C., & Demurger, S. (2000). Foreign direct investment and economic growth: Theory and application to China. *Review of Development Economics, 4*(2), 140–155.

Blomstrom, M. (2000). Internationalisation and growth: Evidence from Sweden. *Swedish Economic Policy Review, 7*(1), 185–201.

Blonigen, B., & Wang, M. (2005). Inappropriate pooling of wealthy and poor countries in empirical FDI studies. *Applied Economics Letters, 12*(13), 825–828.

Borensztein, E., De Gregorio, J., & Lee, J.-W. (1998). How does foreign direct investment affect economic growth? *Journal of International Economics, 45*(1), 115–135. https://doi.org/10.1016/s0022-1996(97)00033-0

Buckley, P. J., & Casson, M. (1976). *Future of the multinational enterprise*. Palgrave Macmillan.

Buckley, P. J., & Casson, M. (2020). The internalisation theory of the multinational enterprise: Past, present and future. *British Journal of Management, 31*(2), 239–252.

Buckley, P. J., Doh, J. P., & Benischke, M. H. (2017). Towards a renaissance in international business research? Big questions, grand challenges, and the future of IB scholarship. *Journal of International Business Studies, 48*(9), 1045–1064.

Burstein, A., & Vogel, J. (2017). International trade, technology, and the skill premium. *Journal of Political Economy, 125*(5), 1356–1412.

Caves, R. E. (1971). International corporations: The industrial economics of foreign investment. *Economica, 38*(149), 1–27.

Caves, R. E. (1996). *Multinational enterprise and economic analysis*. Cambridge university press.

Chijioke, O. C., Aloysius, A., & Obi, D. O. (2021). Mercantilism in perspective: A historic review. *Global Economy Journal, 21*(01), 2150001.

Cole, M. A., & Neumayer, E. (2003). The pitfalls of convergence analysis: Is the income gap really widening? *Applied Economics Letters, 10*(6), 355–357.

Cvetanović, S., Mitrović, U., & Jurakić, M. (2019). Institutions as the driver of economic growth in classic, neoclasic and endogenous theory. *Economic Themes, 57*(1), 111–125.

De Mello Jr, L. R., & Fukasaku, K. (2000). Trade and foreign direct investment in Latin America and Southeast Asia: Temporal causality analysis. *Journal of International Development: The Journal of the Development Studies Association*, *12*(7), 903–924.

Dunning, J. H. (1996). *The geographical sources of the competitiveness of firms: Some results of a new survey*. University of Reading, Department of Economics.

Dunning, J. H. (2015). The eclectic paradigm of international production: A restatement and some possible extensions. In *The eclectic paradigm: A framework for synthesizing and comparing theories of international business from different disciplines or perspectives* (pp. 50–84). Palgrave Macmillan.

Dunning, J. H., & Lundan, S. M. (2008). Institutions and the OLI paradigm of the multinational enterprise. *Asia Pacific Journal of Management*, *25*(4), 573–593. https://doi.org/10.1007/s10490-007-9074-z

Ebrahimi, S. M., & Koh, L. (2021). Manufacturing sustainability: Institutional theory and life cycle thinking. *Journal of Cleaner Production*, *298*, 126787.

Emako, E., Nuru, S., & Menza, M. (2022). The effect of foreign direct investment on economic growth in developing countries. *Transnational Corporations Review*, *14*(4), 382–401.

Eze, A. A., Nnaji, M., & Nkalu, N. C. (2019). Impact of foreign direct investment on manufacturing sector output growth in Nigeria. *International Journal of Applied Economics, Finance and Accounting*, *5*.

Güngör, H., & Ringim, S. H. (2017). Linkage between foreign direct investment, domestic investment and economic growth: Evidence from Nigeria. *International Journal of Economics and Financial Issues*, *7*(3), 97–104.

Guseva, V. E., & Mechik, S. V. (2020). Econometric study of the dynamics of foreign direct investment in Russia. *Amazonia Investiga*, *9*(27), 92–103.

Idoko, C. U., & Taiga, U. U. (2018). Effect of foreign direct investment (FDI) on manufacturing output in Nigeria (1981–2016). *Advances in Social Sciences Research Journal*, *5*(5).

Jylhä, P., Suominen, M., & Tomunen, T. (2018). Beta bubbles. *The Review of Asset Pricing Studies*, *8*(1), 1–35.

Kogut, B. (1983). Foreign direct investment as a sequential process. *The multinational corporation in the 1980s*, 38–56.

Lind, J., & Press, D. G. (2018). Markets or mercantilism? How China secures its energy supplies. *International Security*, *42*(4), 170–204.

Luo, Y., & Bu, J. (2018). Contextualizing international strategy by emerging market firms: A composition-based approach. *Journal of World Business*.

Mahembe, E., & Odhiambo, N. M. (2014). Foreign direct investment and economic growth: A theoretical framework. *Journal of Governance and Regulation*, *3*(2).

Makino, S., Lau, C. M., & Yeh, R. S. (2002). Asset-exploitation versus asset-seeking: Implications for location choice of foreign direct investment from newly industrialized economies. *Journal of International Business Studies*, *33*, 403–421.

Makoni, P. L. (2015). An extensive exploration of theories of foreign direct investment. *Risk Governance and Control: Financial Markets & Institutions*, *5*(2), 77–83.

Mankiw, G. (2003). *Macroeconomics* (5th ed.). Worth Publishes. Measurement Systems, *Business Process Management Journal*, 11(2) 109–122.

McCann, P., & Van Oort, F. (2019). Theories of agglomeration and regional economic growth: A historical review. In *Handbook of regional growth and development theories* (pp. 6–23). https://doi.org/10.4337/9781788970020.00007

Miberg, W. (1996). The rhetoric of policy relevance in international economics. *Journal of Economic Methodology*, *3*(2), 237–259.

Mounde, W. L. (2017). Causal relationship between foreign direct investment and manufacturing output in Nigeria. *International Journal of Advanced Studies in Business Strategies and Management*, *5*(2), 233–267.

Nair-Reichert, U., & Weinhold, D. (2001). Causality tests for cross-country panels: A new look at FDI and economic growth in developing countries. *Oxford Bulletin of Economics & Statistics*, *63*(2), 153–171.

Nayak, D., & Choudhury, R. N. (2014). *A selective review of foreign direct investment theories*. https://www.unescap.org/sites/default/files/AWP%2520No.%2520143.pdf

Osabohien, R., Awolola, O. D., Matthew, O., Itua, O. Q., & Elomien, E. (2020). Foreign direct investment inflow and employment in Nigeria. *Investment Management and Financial Innovations*, *17*(1), 77–84.

Osagie, O. E., & Ukwuoma, A. C. (2022). Absolute advantage theory. *BW Academic Journal*, 5.

Palley, T. I. (2017). Inequality and growth in neo-Kaleckian and Cambridge growth theory. *Review of Keynesian Economics*, *5*(2), 146–169.

Perold, A. F. (2004). The capital asset pricing model. *The Journal of Economic Perspectives*, *18*(3), 3–24.

Romer, P. M. (1994). The origins of endogenous growth. *The Journal of Economic Perspectives*, *8*(1), 3–22. https://doi.org/10.1257/jep.8.1.3

Sahu, J. P. (2021). Does inflow of foreign direct investment stimulate economic growth? Evidence from developing countries. *Transnational Corporations Review*, *13*(4), 376–393.

Sarkodie, S. A., & Strezov, V. (2019). Effect of foreign direct investments, economic development and energy consumption on greenhouse gas emissions in developing countries. *Science of the Total Environment*, *646*, 862–871.

Seyoum, B. (2024). Industrialisation and the role of foreign direct investment. In *State fragility, business, and economic performance: An Ethiopian perspective* (pp. 179–224). Springer International Publishing.

Shanlin, W. (2019). Mercantilist origin of United States' trade protectionism. *China Economist*, *14*(5), 31–40.

Sharmiladevi, J. C. (2017). Understanding Dunning's OLI paradigm. *Indian Journal of Commerce & Management Studies*, *8*(3), 47–52.

Sharpe, W. F. (1964). Capital asset prices: A theory of market equilibrium under conditions of risk. *The Journal of Finance*, *19*(3), 425–442.

Solow, R. M. (1956). A contribution to the theory of economic growth. *The Quarterly Journal of Economics*, *70*(1), 65–94.

Vernon, R. (1966). International investment and international trade in the product cycle. *International Executive*, *8*(4), 16. https://doi.org/10.1002/tie.5060080409

Yao, S., & Wei, K. (2007). Economic growth in the presence of FDI: The perspective of newly industrialising economies. *Journal of Comparative Economics*, *35*(1), 211–234.

Yarbrough, B. V., & Yarbrough, R. M. (2002). *The world economy: Trade and finance*. SouthWestern College Publishers.

Zahra, S. (2005). A theory of international new ventures: A decade of research. *Journal of International Business Studies*. https://doi.org/10.1057/palgrave.jibs.8400118

Zayed, N., Anwarul Islam, K. M., Shahi, S. K., Rahman, Md. S., & Raisa, T. S. (2021). *An analysis on the effects of coronavirus (COVID-19) on the financial management of multinational corporations*. Australian Finance & Banking Review. https://doi.org/10.46281/afbr.v5i1.1015

Printed and bound by CPI Group (UK) Ltd, Croydon, CR0 4YY
29/07/2026
14931731-0001